2 Anita Salazar

└─Patricia

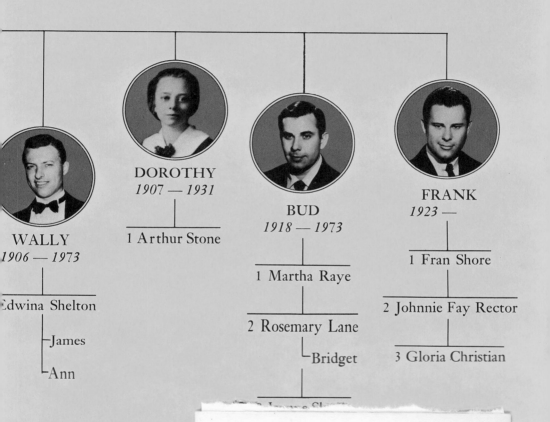

DOROTHY
1907 — 1931

1 Arthur Stone

WALLY
1906 — 1973

Edwina Shelton

├─James

└─Ann

BUD
1918 — 1973

1 Martha Raye

2 Rosemary Lane

└─Bridget

FRANK
1923 —

1 Fran Shore

2 Johnnie Fay Rector

3 Gloria Christian

**THE WESTMORE
FAMILY TREE**

THE
WESTMORES
OF
HOLLYWOOD

THE
WESTMORES
OF
HOLLYWOOD

*by Frank Westmore
and
Muriel Davidson*

J. B. LIPPINCOTT COMPANY
PHILADELPHIA AND NEW YORK

791.43027
W52w
100407
Mar. 1977

Photograph on page 92: Copyright 1938, Harold Lloyd
   Corporation, courtesy of Rich Correll
Photographs on page 98: Scotty Welbourne
Photographs on pages 210–11: John Launois
Photograph on page 241, bottom: Larry Barbier

U.S. Library of Congress Cataloging in Publication Data

Westmore, Frank, birth date
   The Westmores of Hollywood.

   Includes index.
   1. Westmore family.   2. Moving-picture industry—
California—Hollywood.   3. Film make-up.   I. David-
son, Muriel, joint author.   II. Title.
PN1998.A2W43   791.43′027′0922 [B]   75–33210
ISBN–0–397–01102–4

To all Westmores,
past, present, and future

FRANK WESTMORE

For Bill

MURIEL DAVIDSON

LIST OF ILLUSTRATIONS

Dorothy Lamour with Muck the chimp — 14
Fredric March as "Mr. Hyde" — 21
Frank Westmore, age six — 28
George and Anita Westmore with their daughter, Patricia — 29
Handbill advertising George Westmore's first shop — 38
George Westmore in front of his Hollywood shop — 39
A 1922 portrait of the Westmore family — 50
Nita Naldi and Rudolph Valentino — 57
Bette Davis as Queen Elizabeth — 87
Harold Lloyd — 92
Ruby Keeler — 98
James Stewart — 99
The lobby of The House of Westmore — 106
The Westmore brothers at the opening of
      The House of Westmore — 107
Perc at the opening with Kay Francis, Una Merkel,
      and Claudette Colbert — 107
The Westmore brothers at a Christmas party — 120
Ola Carroll — 121
Frank Westmore and Cecil B. DeMille — 160
Frank Westmore in front of a pyramid in Egypt — 161
Frank Westmore transforming Shirley MacLaine
      into a Japanese geisha — 210–11
Frank Westmore at work — 240–41

ACKNOWLEDGMENTS

The authors acknowledge with gratitude the contributions of Julie Adams, Fred Astaire, Dani Bianca, Dorothy Blair, Ann Blyth, Harry Brand, Justin Buehrlen, Mel Burns, Sr., Leonard Byrd, Allan Cahan, Teet Carle, Richard Carlson, John Carradine, Kenny Carter, Tom Case, John Chambers, Rich Correll, Bing Crosby, Bette Davis, Sol Dolgin, Nat Dytch, Hank Edds, Will Fowler, Reva Fredrick, Dottie Gagliano, Larry Germain, Gail Gifford, Alexander Golitzen, Ben Halpern, Clara Halpern, Susan Hayward, William Holden, Shelly Hull, Ross Hunter, Dorothy Joy, Harry Kaplan, Jack Kevan.

Also Dorothy Lamour, Rollie Lane, Jack Lemmon, Melba Lingriner, A. C. Lyles, Shirley MacLaine, Nellie Manley, Dean Martin, Bob Matz, Lorraine McDermott, Jim Merrick, Robert Mitchum, Berenice Mosk, Ben Nye, Dr. Charles Pincus, Harry Ray, Ronald Reagan, Gilbert Roland, Don Siegel, Allen (Whitey) Snyder, Herb Steinberg, Joyce Sterling, Carol Stevens, James Stewart, Jack Stone, William Tuttle, Grace Varco, Robert Wagner, Murray Weissman, Robert Wise, Jane Wyman, Bob Yeager, Gene Young, and Max Youngstein.

A special thanks to all the Westmores who helped so much: Michael, Marvin, Mont, Jr., Pat, Marian, Wati, Lassie, Norma, Molly, Bobby, and Jim.

And our *very* special appreciation to three beautiful women, Gloria, Edith, and Ola Westmore, without whose memories and memorabilia this book might well not have been.

Beverly Hills, California
1976

I

I was sixty feet above the ground on a sound stage at Paramount Pictures, straddling a girder, eyeball to eyeball with an enraged chimpanzee named Muck. After what I'd done to that chimp, he had every reason in the world to be enraged.

The year was 1942 and I was only nineteen and still trying to learn the craft of screen makeup. My position wouldn't have been so disgraceful had my last name been anything other than Westmore. As it was, I could simply be grateful that those makeup geniuses, my father and my five older brothers, weren't around to witness my humiliation.

I had been hired to do a picture called *Beyond the Blue Horizon,* which starred Dorothy Lamour, Jack Haley, and a bunch of animals. My particular charge was Muck. Lamour was terrified of chimpanzees and had refused to work with them ever since she had made *Jungle Princess* and had seen a woman spectator badly mauled by a chimp named Jiggs. (The woman later sued Paramount for $100,000 for letting the chimp wander around loose, and she won the suit.)

The director of our film, Alfred Santell, had tried to accommodate Dorothy by hiring a midget named Billy to portray a chimpanzee. I made a chimp suit for Billy to wear, and Trader Horn, the great animal trainer, was to teach him the creature's peculiar lurching gait. Billy was to work with Lamour in the long shots in which they'd be walking together, holding hands. That meant the only time Dorothy actually would have to be near the real chimp was in a scene where he was above her in a tree and had to hand her a banana. The trouble was that poor Billy just couldn't learn to walk like a chimpanzee. So Dorothy, good sport that she is, finally agreed to emote with the real McCoy.

Muck, a male, had the damnedest set of privates I've ever seen. Obviously he was very proud of his manhood, because he would constantly examine himself, causing a huge erection. Also, he had a large, hairless, and pale-pink behind. The behind was easy enough to cover; I just slapped on some black pancake and saw to it that he didn't sit down before his scenes. The front was a bigger problem. I puzzled about it for some time and then came up with what I thought was a splendid idea. I bought a child's-size pair of jockey shorts and ventilated black hair all over the shorts. ("Ventilating" in our business means sewing hair onto something, such as on the "lace" for a wig or toupee.) Then I put the shorts on Muck. He looked very respectable.

When it was time for the banana-handing scene, I put Muck up into the tree on the set, director Santell called, "Action," and the camera started rolling. All of a sudden I heard Santell yelling, "Cut, cut!" Muck was standing on the branch of his tree, wildly yanking down his ventilated pants; apparently they were tickling him like crazy.

"Frank, this chimp is not going to wear those pants," Santell said. "Now come up with another idea and fast, because you're holding up the whole company." Dorothy didn't say anything. She just stood there, looking apprehensive.

I didn't know what to do, but I didn't dare tell the director that, so I said, "I'll take off those pants and lay a little hair. I'll put some spirit gum on his—uh, anyway, don't you worry about it, Al, because I'll lay some black hair in front of all those privates."

I did that to Muck, put him back in his tree, and again Santell called "Action!" But instead of handing Dorothy the banana, Muck started pulling out the hair I had stuck on him and throwing it down by the handful. Lamour had been looking up at him, waiting for him to give her the banana. The gluey black hair came floating down onto her face and stuck to her neck and chin. She looked like Abe Lincoln in Illinois.

At this point, Dorothy's nerve cracked. She shrieked at Muck to stop and then ran crying to her dressing room.

Santell was furious. He didn't yell, but he said in a very threatening voice, "Okay, Frank, you're two down and none to go. Come up with something else—*or* else."

I said to one of the set painters, "Get me some lampblack. I'll mix it with oil and rub it on those privates and it won't bother him and they'll be blacked out for sure." Unfortunately the painter was so rattled he grabbed the wrong can. It was glue instead of oil. And I was so rattled that I didn't check. I just mixed the lampblack with the glue and plastered the mixture all over Muck's privates and legs.

Muck began to screech and jump up and down, picking wildly at the rapidly hardening glue on his crotch.

Trader Horn, who owned Muck, got very excited. "You moron! You dummy!" he yelled. "That's my prize chimp! Unglue him, you dumb little bastard!"

I made the mistake of taking acetone and trying to get the glue off with it. Acetone stings a whole lot—which is why Muck climbed up a sixty-foot girder and I had to go up after him.

When I finally cornered him on that girder, he just beat the hell out of me. He pummeled my face and body with his powerful arms, he sank his teeth into my neck, and then he swung himself under me and started chewing away on my legs. (They were so badly bruised I walked a little like Muck for about a week.) Actually, I never did solve the problem. Trader Horn did. The next morning he brought in a gentle old female chimpanzee. Her private parts didn't show.

For the rest of the shooting I was relegated to painting Mabel the elephant a darker shade of gray for Technicolor. Each day as I mounted my ladder with a can of paint in one hand and a huge house-painting brush in the other, I'd start slathering away at the pachyderm (who'd roll in the dust, removing most of the dye overnight) and wonder if I would ever be able to uphold the illustrious and powerful name of Westmore.

13

Dorothy Lamour with Muck, after I blacked out his private parts.

The doubts persisted until the day in 1972, thirty years later, when I heard my name called out at the Television Academy Awards function at the Century Plaza Hotel in Los Angeles. I ran to the stage and was presented with an Emmy: Best Makeup of the Year for the TV movie *Kung Fu*, which became the pilot for the Warner Brothers-ABC series. In my acceptance speech, I tried my best to keep my emotions under control as I said, "I accept this award in the name of my father and my brothers."

Today the others are all dead. I'm the only one left, although a third generation of Westmore makeup artists is carrying on. And I no longer have any uncertainties about my contribution to the reputation of a fifty-eight-year dynasty of lusty, brawling, powerful men, as important and as colorful in the history of Hollywood as the Warners, the Cohns, the Selznicks, Louis B. Mayer, and Irving Thalberg.

My father, George, founded the first movie makeup department in history in 1917 and was one of the recognized giants of the early days of silent films. At one time or another, a Westmore headed up the makeup departments at Paramount, Universal, Warner Brothers, RKO, 20th Century-Fox, Selznick, Eagle-Lion, First National, and a dozen other movie lots that once flourished in the industry. The Westmores' artistry in creating ingenious horror and aging makeups helped change the movies from a make-believe to a realistic medium. For thirty years the private family-run House of Westmore on Sunset Boulevard was the most famous beauty salon in the world. Various Westmores were intimates of such stars as Clara Bow, Douglas Fairbanks, Bette Davis, Robert Mitchum, Spencer Tracy, Ray Milland, Bing Crosby, James Stewart, Shirley MacLaine, John Barrymore, Elizabeth Taylor, Fred Astaire, William Holden, Harold Lloyd, Rudolph Valentino, and the Carradines, John through David. Many of these stars would not make important career decisions without first consulting the appropriate Westmore. Clark Gable paid us the supreme accolade of removing his false teeth in our presence. Cecil B. DeMille wouldn't make a film without a Westmore by his side.

Perhaps we were even more colorful than DeMille, the Selznicks, and Mayer because we came into far more personal contact with the stars than the moguls did. These close relationships frequently led to situations in which Westmores helped to prevent stars from defecting from a studio. Thus, my family helped preserve the face of Hollywood as well as alter it. Westmores also literally changed the face of the world through their changes in their stars' faces. For five years, for instance, the Rudolph Valentino look—slicked-down hair, long sideburns, Latin sultriness—was the standard for men on five continents, wherever movies were shown, and to a great extent that look was created by my oldest brother, Mont Westmore, not Valentino.

Even more does this apply to women. Most women may not realize what an influence the Westmores had on their appearance —the shaping of mouths and eyebrows, the way they do their hair—but chances are they're following a style once designed by a Westmore for a Bette Davis, a Katharine Hepburn, or a Shirley MacLaine on the screen. A prime example of Westmore influence is the Shirley Temple period, when an entire generation of little girls had their hair twisted around fingers, pulled into curlers, or permanent waved as their mothers vainly tried to duplicate the famous Temple ringlets. Somehow their hair never came out looking like Shirley's—and for a good reason. Those weren't Shirley's curls, they were my father's. He had invented them a generation before, for Mary Pickford.

Pickford commissioned George Westmore to make dozens of long twisted sausage curls to supplement her own long but baby-fine hair. (America's Sweetheart never knew that my dad obtained most of the hair he used from the heads of the prostitutes in Big Suzy's French Whorehouse.) Mary would be chauffeur-driven to Father's tiny one-chair beauty shop on Hollywood Boulevard, where she would sit for hours, watching in fascination, while he fashioned her hairpieces. He painstakingly wrapped the golden hair around a smooth round stick to the exact length of the curl he wanted to fabricate. Around that, he applied damp toilet paper. Then the curl would be set aside to dry. When the curl was taken off the stick, not one hair was out of place. Then, with just one hairpin, George would strategically place the false curl among the strands of Mary's own hair. He even made a leather carrying case to house his creations when she traveled. She really needed the fake curls then, because all too often a zealous fan would come at her with a pair of scissors and snip off a hunk of her hair for a souvenir. Dad couldn't have been happier about that. He soaked Miss Pickford fifty bucks a lock.

The importance of my oldest brother, Mont, to Cecil B. DeMille is shown by the fact that in 1926, when DeMille was starting production on *The King of Kings*, he offered Mont $250 a week, then an absolutely unprecedented fee for a makeup artist. Mont and my father were to do the makeup on H. B. Warner, who portrayed Christ. In addition, Mont was responsible for co-star Dorothy Cummings as the Virgin Mary and had to supervise the hair and makeup of more than three thousand extras. He balked at C.B.'s request that he also oversee the grooming of fifteen hundred assorted animals.

The task was monumental. Also, from the beginning Mont had a problem with H. B. Warner; the actor had become so overwhelmed by the very idea of being Jesus Christ that he had resumed the heavy drinking of his early years. Mont knew that if DeMille had any idea that Warner was so much as sniffing a cork, he would be fired at once, no matter what it cost C.B. or how much reshooting would be needed. Mont himself was horrified at the idea of a drunken Christ and decided to do something about it. So whenever Warner showed up in the morning smashed, Mont made him drink half a glass of cod-liver oil. Warner would promptly throw up. For several weeks the battle between the bottle, Warner, and Mont continued, but Mont's primitive form of therapy worked: Warner finally stopped boozing altogether rather than face Mont's cod-liver oil. And DeMille never did suspect that there had been a problem.

However, throughout the shooting, DeMille's own company was in dire financial trouble, aggravated by the lavish production's cost, which was soaring to over two million dollars. C.B. was desperately fighting an imminent merger with the Pathé Film Company. His temper, which was anything but even at best, was always at breaking point. Almost everyone except Mont was tongue-lashed hourly by the harassed director; in fact, he fired my father. But Mont continued to do his thorough, superbly researched makeup job and managed to stay out of DeMille's way.

One morning, as Mont approached an extra to adjust the man's false nose, DeMille suddenly and for no reason zeroed in on him and screamed through his megaphone, "Westmore, I just hope that child you're expecting has more brains and ability than you're displaying!"

At that, Mont's own control snapped. He snatched the false nose off the startled extra, strode over to DeMille, and said, "Take this nose and shove it up your ass!"

Everyone waited for DeMille to fire Mont. Instead, the director threw back his head and burst out laughing.

DeMille was a good actor himself. I've often wondered if he really felt like laughing. He probably wanted to fire Mont, but although he could have replaced H. B. Warner, the old man must have realized he couldn't replace his makeup man. Three thousand new noses was too much to contemplate.

Only five years later, in 1931, still another studio production head, Jesse Lasky of Paramount Pictures, became dependent upon another of my brothers, Wally, for the performance of Fredric March in *Dr. Jekyll and Mr. Hyde*. Robert Louis Stevenson had described a dual personality. How, asked Lasky, could it be shown on the screen?

March himself was apprehensive, and he and Lasky conferred with Wally for days about the makeup involved in the transformation of Jekyll into Hyde. March was leery of Russian-born director Rouben Mamoulian, who was a fervent disciple of Stanislavsky. Freddie was from the New York stage, and his acting technique was instinctive and spontaneous. He knew little about Stanislavsky (and what was later to become known as "The Method") and listened with growing horror to the hours-long lectures Mamoulian spouted in his heavy Russian-Armenian accent. In fact, after March's first session with the director, he insisted that Wally sit in on the rest—and there were many.

18

When Mamoulian got started on topics such as "subjective photography," neither March nor Wally knew what he was talking about. March asked Jesse Lasky, a frequent but silent observer at these meetings, just what subjective photography was, but Lasky just threw up his hands and said, "My God, if you don't know what subjective photography is, what are you doing in this business?"

"Well, what *is* it?" persisted March.

"How the hell do I know?" said Lasky. And he never attended another meeting, nor did he appear on the set at any time during the shooting.

In designing a horror makeup that would transform gentle Dr. Jekyll into murderous Mr. Hyde, Wally had to keep in mind March's almost pathological fear of appearing ridiculous. Mamoulian suggested that the Hyde makeup be copied after Neanderthal man. Wally agreed, did some anthropological research, and came up with a fairly faithful reproduction of the bestial, prehistoric cave dweller. He made hundreds of sketches, consulting with March all the while, before he was satisfied. Then he made a plaster-of-Paris mold of March's face so that he could experiment on the mold instead of forcing March to sit in the makeup chair for hours.

Wally started by patting soft clay onto the cheeks, nose, jawline, mouth, and ears of the face mold. The most difficult task lay in creating the fangs and a set of protuberant teeth. The device had to be comfortable enough for March to wear for prolonged periods of time, during which he had to be able to speak his lines clearly despite a mouth full of dental work not his own.

Wally packed up March's face mold and took it to his own dentist, Dr. Charles Pincus. Together they studied the problem, and then March went to Dr. Pincus to have a wax mold made of his teeth.

Meanwhile, Wally made another plaster-of-Paris mold of March's face so that he could prepare the Mr. Hyde wig. Using the hair-lace base invented by my father, he ventilated a wig which fitted far down on the forehead. Then he went back to Dr. Pincus. The dentist had exceeded Wally's wildest expectations.

There, in porcelain, were the perfect fangs. There was only one thing wrong. Although they fit the face mold perfectly, they didn't fit correctly into March's own mouth. This time the actor himself had to sit in a chair for hours as the dentist altered this fang and changed that tooth. But when the final full horror makeup (a four-hour job) was placed on Fredric March, it was perfect; it combined the Neanderthal with the Satanic without seeming ludicrous.

Since the application of the makeup was so complicated, Wally had to do it in his own department on the Paramount lot, even when the picture was shooting on location. And since Lasky would not entrust his precious star to a studio driver, Wally was enlisted to drive March to and from those locations. One morning Wally put on March's makeup, and the two men left the lot and headed toward a day's shooting at Busch Gardens in Pasadena. They stopped to pick up the movie's publicity man, who climbed into the back seat, and the three drove on, talking.

It never occurred to any of them that the man in the front passenger seat looked unusual—never, that is, until Wally wheeled into a gasoline station to ask how to find the location site. The attendant, who came up smiling, took one look, gasped, and screamed. Wally often wondered whether that poor man ever tried to tell anyone about what he had seen in an auto at seven thirty one sober morning in 1931.

My brother Ern, perhaps the most talented makeup artist of all the Westmores, used to love to tell the story of a calamity which befell W. C. Fields, one of the most notorious drinkers of his time. (Ern was no slouch in that department either.) One evening of gloriously sodden proportions, when Ern was a houseguest in the home of another crony, John Barrymore, the telephone rang. It was Fields. "Jack," he screamed, "my nose just exploded!" Then he hung up.

Barrymore and Ern, each carrying a full glass of the actor's Scotch, leaped into Ern's car and drove to Fields's house. There they found the comedian clutching his huge veined proboscis with one hand, blood trickling through the fingers, while delicately bal-

Fredric March as "Mr. Hyde," made up by Wally.

ancing a martini with the other. He had, it seemed, blown his nose and several blood vessels had burst.

Ern flung his entire glass of Scotch into Fields's face, literally cauterizing the nose with alcohol. The bleeding stopped. Ern then soothed the hypochondriacal comedian, and work on the movie *If I Had a Million*, which Fields was filming at the time, resumed without interruption the following morning.

Maybe the best example of the kind of influence the Westmores could have on the making of a movie was provided by my brother Perc (pronounced "Purse"). Perc had more clout in the industry than any other Westmore; sometimes he was called the fifth Warner brother.

One night early in 1945, Perc's boss, Jack Warner, called him at home. He had just had a terrible fight with his biggest male star, Humphrey Bogart, Warner explained. Bogart had flatly refused to show up in the morning to start his next picture, *Conflict*. "Bogie says," Warner told Perc, "that he won't do the movie because his co-star, Alexis Smith, is too tall. Now you *know* that isn't why he doesn't want to do the film."

Perc knew. Just the year before Bogart had fallen madly in love with a young New York actress with whom he had co-starred in her first movie, *To Have and Have Not*. Her name, Betty Joan Perske, had been changed to Lauren Bacall. Bogart was determined to change Betty's name once more, to Bogart. The hitch was that he was still married to Mayo Methot, and the wild brawls he was having with Mayo over her attempts to block a divorce were hitting the newspapers almost as often as Bogie and Mayo were hitting each other. During that time, Perc frequently had to apply makeup very skillfully to some of Bogart's bruises.

Warner told Perc that Bogart was going to walk out on his contract, the studio, his entire career. He was a rich man anyway, and he just didn't give a damn. "You're the only one I can count on. Do something," Warner ordered Perc.

Perc hung up and immediately called Bogart at his home. The beleaguered actor answered by saying, "*Now* what?" thinking it was Warner again. Perc plaintively told Bogie it was his birthday (although it was actually seven months away) and that he was alone and depressed. Would Bogie come out and have some drinks with him? Not without some suspicion, Bogart agreed, saying, "But if that son of a bitch Warner thinks you can make me change my mind, he's crazy and so are you."

Next, Perc called the Westmores' favorite dining and watering hole, Don the Beachcomber, then the "in" restaurant in Hollywood. (Special ivory chopsticks with names hand etched on them were made for special customers. Mine and all my brothers' are still there, encased in a glass breakfront.) On the phone Perc ordered a pair of personalized chopsticks for Bogart and instructed the bartender to serve Bogart his usual navy grogs but to make every second drink of Perc's plain fruit punch.

An hour later, Perc and Bogie arrived and were seated, at Perc's instructions, in a booth at the back of the big room where it was so dark they could hardly see each other across the table.

Along about his fourth navy grog (to Perc's two), Bogie abandoned his vilification of Jack Warner and launched into a maudlin rehash of his love problems. He cried. Perc cried too. On Bogie's next potent drink, Perc uncorked his biggie. Few people knew, least of all the movie stars, that Perc had a lifetime contract with Warner Brothers as head of their makeup department, breakable only by Perc himself, so what Perc said sounded believable. "I got you here under false pretenses, I guess," he confessed. "Warner *did* call me tonight. And he fired me. Said if you weren't going to report for work, there's no need for me. But that's all right. I've got a few bucks. 'Course, it's all tied up in our beauty shop, The House of Westmore, and we maybe can't make the next mortgage payment, but that's okay, too. I'll always manage. Wally may be able to find a place for me at Paramount combing wigs or something."

Bogie picked up his brand-new chopsticks and hurled them across the room. "I *told* you that bastard Warner is a son of a bitch," he snarled. "Well, I'll fix *him*. I'll *make* that movie."

The next morning a badly hung-over Bogart reported to the makeup department. Perc, immaculate as always in his white doctor's coat, did his makeup. Only once during the shooting of the film did Bogie complain. "Alexis Smith *is* too tall," he told Perc. "I have to stand on a box to kiss her."

Very early in my brother Bud's career—he was next youngest to me—he became known as the Irving Thalberg of makeup artists. This was because, like Thalberg, he was so handsome that he became a romantic target for nearly every aspiring actress. He did marry two of them, Martha Raye and Rosemary Lane. The marriages did not hurt in solidifying his position as the executive in charge of the huge makeup department at Universal Pictures for almost twenty-four years.

Among us, we Westmore brothers chalked up a possible entry for the *Guinness Book of World Records* in that we had a composite total of eighteen wives. But Bud's marriage to Martha Raye probably still ranks as the most spectacular.

In 1937 when Paramount Pictures brought Martha from New York to Hollywood to star in *Rhythm on the Range,* she took one look at nineteen-year-old Bud—the makeup man assigned to her— and was totally smitten. For the first time in her own tender years, she did not consult her mother, Peggy, the ultimate in stage mothers. On May 31, without Peggy's permission, the couple eloped to Las Vegas. Bud, however, had not reckoned on the power of a protective mother. His bride was so much under Peggy's influence that she slept with a gun under her pillow and an apple pie in the bed between them lest he "try to get at her" during the night— the pie being an ingenious variation on the old New England bundling board.

Under these trying conditions, it was not surprising that the marriage lasted only three months. The divorce action was featured luridly on the front pages of all the tabloid newspapers, with Martha making the classic remark that she had to make the choice "between my mother, who made me what I am today, and Bud, who can make me up better than anyone else." The press had a field day as the case went on in the courts for days.

Nine years later, William Goetz, a Louis B. Mayer son-in-law, remembered the imbroglio when he became production head of what was then called Universal-International Studios. As Bud recalled, Goetz summoned him, saying, "Anyone who could make Martha Raye look that good can't be all bad." And he hired my brother to be his makeup czar at Universal.

The family's importance to the movie industry can probably best be illustrated by an incident that took place on the night of March 4, 1936. It was at the ninth annual Academy Awards presentations, then held at the ballroom of the Biltmore Hotel with George Jessel as master of ceremonies. As everyone expected, Paul Muni won the Best Actor award for his remarkable performance in *The Story of Louis Pasteur*. But in total departure from the practice of nearly every other award winner over the years, Muni did *not* thank everyone from the producer to the cop at the studio gate. He thanked only one man.

Muni said, "Perc Westmore did my makeup for Louis Pasteur. The first morning after he finished, I looked in the mirror and I didn't see myself. I saw Louis Pasteur. In fact, only then did I *become* Louis Pasteur. Yes, I did the lines, but I was a man who no longer was Paul Muni. I was Pasteur. Perc Westmore deserves as much credit as I for this award."

2

FROM the very beginning, it never was easy for me to be a Westmore. I was the last of nineteen children born to Ada and George Westmore, making an unheralded entrance into this world in Maywood, California, on April 13, 1923, in a house built by my father and his sons. (They all were great amateur carpenters.) Since my mother had spent most of her life littering two continents with her progeny, either nursing them or burying them —only seven survived—her telephone call to the doctor indicated no urgency regarding the imminence of my birth. By the time the obstetrician arrived, my sixteen-year-old sister, Dorothy, had bitten off the umbilical cord with her teeth, and I was doing well.

Not so my mother, however. Incessant travel and childbearing had aggravated her congenital heart condition. Probably sensing her own mortality, she packed me up soon after my birth and took me to San Antonio, Texas, the one city she loved and where she had made friends. Five months later she died there. She was forty-three.

It isn't difficult to understand why my family then developed a sort of emotional constipation over what to do with me. Of the other six surviving Westmore offspring, four of my brothers were old enough to be my father. Taking them in chronological order, complete with their fanciful names, there was Montague George (Mont), twenty-one years older than the infant Frank and already married; the twins, Percival Harry and Ernest Henry (Perc and

Ern), nineteen years older; and Walter James (Wally), seventeen years older. My brother Hamilton Adolph (Bud), who was five, was nearly as much of a problem as I. Back in Los Angeles, poor Dorothy—the only daughter—was trying to cope with little Bud and my father, while also trying to keep up in high school. But it was obvious that at five months of age I couldn't be left to my own devices in San Antonio, so my father dispatched Mont and Wally to return me to California. All the way home on the train, they tossed my used diapers out the window, not knowing what else to do with them. When they ran out of diapers, they stole the train's towels. My sister-in-law Edith, Mont's wife, swears that the words "Santa Fe" were faintly inked on my bottom when she first saw me.

I made my debut in the movie industry just after my arrival in Los Angeles, when I was six months old. My father was doing the makeup for Norma Talmadge in a silent picture called *Secrets*. For a couple of scenes, Miss Talmadge was required to hold a baby. My old man prevailed on director Frank Borzage to use me because he desperately needed money to bring my mother's body back from Texas for a decent burial in Los Angeles at Forest Lawn Cemetery. Despite all the money he made, he never held onto a nickel of it. He was a compulsive spender and never failed to indulge himself in any excesses which took his fancy.

For the first two years of my life, I lived with Mont and Edith and Mont, Jr., who was only two months younger than I. Then my father met his match in a fiery, red-haired hairdresser, Anita. He married her. To this day my stepmother maintains that George fell in love with her knee-length hair, not her. Whatever the reason, they took me in so I could be a brother to half-sister Pat, to whom Anita gave birth in 1926.

Less than a year later, my father had had it with my "brother-ing." When I was not quite four, he entered me in the first of a ghastly succession of military schools which, in those days, really were highly priced orphanages. Bud was popped in and out of them too, but it didn't matter to me whether he was there or not. The five-year disparity in our ages kept us in different dormitories and different classes anyway.

I was a seasoned cadet by the age of six.

My father with Anita and their daughter, Patricia.

By the time I was six, my father's new marriage had turned stormy. Anita was beginning to hate him and was threatening to leave him. He, in his turn, kept threatening to commit suicide. One day Anita *did* temporarily leave, taking their daughter with her. The old man announced to my sister-in-law Edith that he intended to kill himself, but appalled her by saying that he didn't want to go alone. Before Edith could figure out what he meant, he was off—making one of his rare visits to Bud and me at the Golden State Military Academy in Puente, California. This institution was one of the worst to which we had been committed. The place stank of dampness and mold. The building had been a mission and the walls were four feet thick; you could have hollered your head off and no one outside those walls would have heard. I know. I tried it.

I had been out picking persimmons, for which I got ten cents for a burlap sackful, when George arrived. Since I was only a first-grader, I had to be helped into my uniform, forcing my father and eleven-year-old Bud to wait for me in the sitting room. When I arrived, breathless and excited, I found I wasn't going anywhere after all. When one of the instructors asked my father what time he would be bringing us back, George said, "They won't *be* back. We are going to the Santa Monica pier, where we three will hold hands and jump into eternity." So convincing was his bizarre declaration that we kids were hustled out of the sitting room and back to our dorms.

The next year, in one of their fitful periods of peaceful coexistence, my stepmother took us out of that school. Bud went to live with Ern, and I went home with Anita and my father. About a month after I arrived, I was in the kitchen tossing an orange up and down in the air. On one toss I missed the catch, and the orange landed right in the middle of George's homemade still in which he was making gin. The still broke and booze spilled all over the floor. The old man was enraged, screaming at me that I'd ruined his best batch and assuaging his fury by beating me with his ever-handy cat-o'-nine-tails.

The next day, Perc came to get me and put me into Pacific Military Academy in Culver City. This school was the worst of all. We wore Russian Cossack uniforms and had liver every Friday night for dinner. In an early protest demonstration, I stuck my fingers down my throat one night and threw up my liver all over the table. This impelled an instructor to hurl a fork at me, hitting me above my right eye. I still have the scar. Later, a sympathetic group of older cadets helped me ambush that instructor and beat hell out of him with a two-by-four. My learning at Pacific Academy was not exactly of a rah-rah-yea-team kind.

Shortly after my act of revenge, Dorothy came to school to tell me our father was dead. I was too young to be told how he died, and I didn't really know until several years later when I saw his death certificate, a copy of which I still have. It reads, in part: "George Westmore, 52 years and 15 days old. Date of death, July 12, 1931. The Cause of Death was as follows: Bichloride of Mercury Poisoning. Suicide."

The day she gave me the news, Dorothy took me to see a movie called *Trader Horn*. There were all sorts of animals in it, and grass huts, and I loved it. Not until I got into bed that night back at school did I think again about my father's death. I was very relieved.

Only two months after that, Perc arrived with a suitcase, packed my clothes, and drove me to his big house in Beverly Hills. He was twenty-seven then, very rich, very successful—one of the top executives at Warner Brothers—and married to a lovely woman whom everybody called Tommy, though her real name was Virginia. They had a pretty daughter, Norma, six years old and a source of immediate confusion to me, because I was only eight and she was my niece. Perc, Tommy, and Norma helped me unpack in a room which had been so hastily converted into a boy's bedroom that some of the toys and games were still in their boxes. Then Perc told me that our sister, Dorothy, now twenty-four, was dead. As Dorothy herself had done when my father killed himself, he spared me the details, which I learned later. She had entered a hospital for a minor corrective cervical operation, but in one of those monstrous surgical accidents a main artery was severed and she bled to death. I had barely known my only sister, but she had

31

been kind to me in our brief contacts, and this time I genuinely grieved until I fell asleep that night. Grief, however, is hard for a child of eight to sustain, and in the morning the joy of being out of military school, plus the intriguing shape of the still-unpacked toys, was overwhelming. I just couldn't help being happy.

That fall of 1931, I entered Hawthorne Grade School in Beverly Hills. For the first time in my life I was in a public school, wearing corduroy pants and, in true Westmore tradition, already watching the pretty little girls. Up until then I don't think I realized that girls even went to school. I joined the Boy Scouts with a friend, a kid named Jackie Cooper; he was really good at scouting, but I never got past Tenderfoot. Perc's wife, Tommy, tolerated me; she allowed me to play with Norma much as if she were my younger sister. Of course Perc was away all day, at his studio or on location. I wasn't exactly sure what he did, except that the cook told me he put makeup on movie stars, even men. I remember thinking that was a strange thing for a grown man to do for a living. My friends' fathers were lawyers or doctors, things like that.

One night when the cook, Lee, was preparing dinner for me in the kitchen, where I normally ate, she excitedly told me I could stay up a little bit later so I could look through the double doors into the dining room where the great Al Jolson was to be a dinner guest. Even *I* had heard his name because Perc had a collection of his records which I had listened to. When I saw him, I was disappointed. Lee, who was black, had told me that Jolson had been the first to talk and sing in the movies and that he had a black face. He didn't have a black face at all. He just looked like any ordinary old guy, with flat brown hair and long ridges down his cheeks and a whiny speaking voice. (I remember, though, how pretty his wife was. She was, of course, Ruby Keeler.)

Then something happened which made me realize Perc's importance for the first time. Jolson said to my brother, "Perc, I want your opinion on a song I'm supposed to sing in my next movie. If you don't like it, I ain't gonna do it." With that, sitting right there at the dinner table, Jolson started to sing: no piano, nothing, just this pure sound. He sang, "Hallelujah, I'm a Bum."

When he finished, Lee was crying, Perc was clapping, and I burst through the big doors and said, "That was good!"

"Whozis?" asked Jolson.

"My brother," answered Perc.

As I was being ushered back to the kitchen, I heard Jolson say, "You never told me you had such a little brother." Well, that figured.

Another time Carole Lombard, one of the most beautiful ladies I had ever seen, showed up for dinner with her fiancé, singer Russ Columbo. I knew of him, too, because Perc had his most famous record, "I Surrender, Dear," which I had heard over and over again. Lee had cooked spaghetti in honor of Columbo. I was about to eat my usual meal in the kitchen before the grown-ups were served, but Carole caught sight of me and insisted I be allowed to have dinner with her and Perc and Tommy and Russ. Norma was too young and was sent off to bed. It was an evening filled with laughter and joking. The next night Lee told me Russ Columbo was dead. The cook explained that Russ had been examining an antique pistol which belonged to a friend of his when a corroded bullet discharged from the gun and blew his brains out. He was only twenty-six years old. Lee kept wailing, and I was very upset.

Soon it was back to another miserable military school for me, and it wasn't until 1935, when I was twelve, that I had my second glimpse of what the outside world could be like. That summer Perc rented a beach house at Malibu and allowed me to spend my vacation with him and his family. By then I was old enough to be really thrilled by direct contact with Perc's houseguests. Eleanor Holm, for instance, was a frequent visitor, along with her constant companion, Billy Rose. He would sit on the beach, smoking a huge cigar, while Eleanor and I went swimming together. She was wild and funny, and she taught me the backstroke and the Australian crawl. We'd swim for what seemed like hours at a time. Then she'd flop down on the beach and drink champagne out of the bottle, even though she was in training for the 1936 Olympics in Berlin. (It was her taste for champagne that got her kicked off the swimming team; she was caught drinking a glass as she and her teammates sailed for the games and was disqualified.)

Dick Powell and Joan Blondell, who were married the following year, came down nearly every weekend to fish and listen to Perc's gossipy stories. They weren't meant for my ears, but I'd skulk around and listen anyway. A couple of stories particularly appealed to my juvenile sense of humor.

In the mid-thirties, Warren Hymer, the character actor, was under contract to Warner Brothers. He had a distinctively ugly, menacing face and was cast as a subordinate gangster in nearly every underworld picture made by men like James Cagney, Humphrey Bogart, and Edward G. Robinson. After several years, however, he was fired by Harry Warner for his general riotous behavior. He cemented his dismissal, and made Warner's decision irrevocable, by unbuttoning his fly and urinating on Warner's pants leg and his shoe tops.

Then there was Lee Tracy, who was co-starring with Wallace Beery in *Viva Villa!* The movie was on location in Mexico. Every night Lee and Beery would get drunk. One night during a fiesta taking place beneath the balcony of their hotel suite, Tracy passed the point of no return. He stepped out on the balcony and serenely and copiously peed on the crowd below, nearly starting a revolution. This incident precipitated the following famous telegram sent by a *Time* magazine correspondent to his office: TRACY NUDE, LEWD, RUDE, STEWED AND PEED ON PARADE. Tracy was fired from the picture and was replaced by Stuart Erwin.

Edmund Lowe and John Boles were often at the Malibu house that summer, playing heated games of bridge with two of Perc's closest pals, Ann Sheridan and Kay Francis. They were there one Sunday when I saved Norma's life. My little niece had gone into the ocean way beyond her depth. I plunged after her and held her up until a Malibu lifeguard named Gene Roemer swam out and got her safely back to shore. In gratitude Perc apprenticed Roemer to him as a makeup man. He gave me a dollar for my trouble, but the amount of the reward didn't matter. I fervently hoped my act of heroism would impel Perc to let me stay with him.

But between his full-time studio chores and the beauty salon, Perc had no time for another kid. (He and Tommy had adopted an infant girl, Gina, that summer of 1935.) So in the fall he casually informed me that he was sending me back to the Lake Elsinore Naval and Military School. My entire always-tenuous young world was about to collapse again. But this time I was old enough to rebel. Without even packing, I pedaled my bicycle from Perc's house in Beverly Hills more than six miles to my brother Mont's house, which was near the Farmer's Market in Hollywood. I didn't know where else to go. Mont's wife, Edith, was there. She listened to my tale of woe and on the spot decided to provide me with my first really permanent home. From that moment on, I have loved Edith the best of anyone in my large family. She, in fact, became the mother I always needed—and Mont became my substitute father. They both decided that night that there would be no more military schools for me and no more being handed around from brother to brother.

So I moved in with them for good, acquiring, in the process, their three sons, Mont, Jr., Marvin, and Michael, as my brothers. Mont, Jr., was my contemporary, and we registered in the same class in LeConte Junior High School together the very next day. After years of boarding school, I settled into a family routine as if I had always been there.

So, at the age of twelve, with loving people to explain my background to me, I finally began to learn about the Westmores of Hollywood, the dynasty into which I had been born.

3

IT was strange but fascinating sitting around Mont's dining table and discussing events which occurred as far back as a quarter of a century before I entered the world. This prehistory centered, of course, on George—the Westmore founding father. In my fleeting exposures to him, I had formed a child's impression of a distant, cold, tyrannical parent whose unexplained rages and banishments created a constant sense of terror and anxiety that beclouded my preteen years. What I did not know was that George was a dark brooding genius, a man of monstrous appetites and ambitions, whose uncontrollable drives spared no one in my family —neither my mother nor my older brothers—as he pushed relentlessly toward his all-consuming goal of making the name of Westmore famous throughout the world.

One of the first of the startling facts I learned from Mont and Edith was that my father claimed an assist from none other than Winston Churchill in founding the Westmore Dynasty.

My father was born June 27, 1879, on the Isle of Wight in England, the descendant of a centuries-long line of bootmakers, bakers, and barrelmakers. When he was "twenty and five-twelfths years old," George enlisted in the British Army during the Boer War and became a private in the famous 21st Lancers. In February 1900, just before the Battle of Paardeberg in South Africa, George was doubling as a baker-barber for his company (an unusual combination of occupations which is still traditional with military units in the field). One day a handsome and dashing young war correspondent for the London *Morning Post* swaggered into George's tent and said, "Your renown as a barber has reached my ears. My name is Winston Churchill. I have come here not to get an article for my paper but to have you cut my hair." It was only then, according to George, that he truly became aware of his "genius."

This story may have been romanticized by hindsight and my father's constant retelling, but the fact is that something did impel him to take the plunge and open his own "Hair-dressing Saloon" in Newport on the Isle of Wight after he was mustered out of the 21st Lancers in 1901 as "medically unfit" (not otherwise explained).

Shortly before the opening of his establishment, he had courted and married Ada Savage, a pretty Isle of Wight barmaid he had fancied for some years. My mother was attracted to him because of his penetrating steel-gray eyes, thick brown hair, and military bearing, which made him seem taller than his 5 feet 8 inches.

George's plan, of course, was to train Ada to work with him in the shop. He himself foiled the plan almost immediately by making her pregnant with my brother Mont, who was born on the island on July 22, 1902. Nevertheless, George's hairdressing saloon soon prospered to the point where he felt his genius should be exported to more appreciative and important areas. His compulsive wanderlust took him to Canterbury on the British mainland (where Perc, Ern, and Wally were born), and thence to Canada and the United States. He plied his hairdressing trade in such disparate cities as Montreal, Toronto (Dorothy's birthplace), Quebec, Pittsburgh, San Antonio, New Orleans, Buffalo, St. Louis, and Washington, D.C.

A sojourn in Cleveland beginning in 1913 was the turning point for my father; he began to move beyond hairstyling to creative makeup techniques for women's faces. In those days, only two classes of women "painted"—actresses and prostitutes. In Cleveland George was given the opportunity to work and experiment on the latter category.

This came about because my family then lived in an apart-

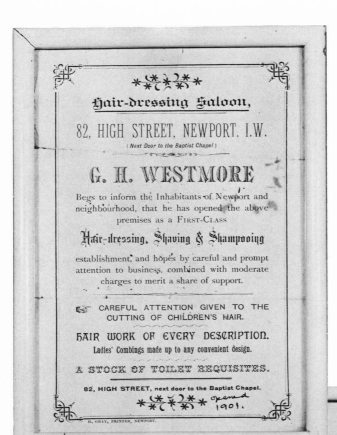

The back and front of a framed handbill advertising George's first shop on the Isle of Wight.

My father in front of his one-chair beauty parlor in Hollywood.

ment building that was largely a bordello, and when the ladies discovered my father's occupation, a mutually profitable alliance developed between them. Every night after he had finished his normal work for the day, he would gather up his rouge pots and other equipment, put them in his black makeup case, and begin his rounds of the apartments, practicing his makeup techniques. Ada, pregnant as always, was partially mollified by his telling her that he was really learning anatomy for the first time. Also, he assured her, it would mean extra money. Little did she dream just how well he was learning anatomy. He used his rouge on nipples, hipbones, ankle bones, the backs of thighs, knees, and other interesting areas. Although the experience undoubtedly was invaluable to a makeup artist, George rarely came home with the extra money he had promised Ada. I suspect he took his fee out in trade. In those days he must have been a completely happy man.

George's cup of euphoria really overflowed when the twins, Perc and Ern, about nine at that time, told him they wanted to learn the art of wigmaking. George was so eager to teach them the craft that he chained his sons by their legs to either end of his long workbench at home, lest their youthful enthusiasm be dimmed by the lure of bicycle riding or other boyish diversions. Hour after hour and day after day they sat at the bench ventilating the hair-lace pieces that their father had invented.

Ern and Perc were so alike the old man never did figure out which one was which. If he wanted one of them, he would call "Percern" and take whichever one arrived first. However, as he watched them at work, and as both grew increasingly more proficient, my resourceful father had a great idea. Business at his beauty shop had not been as brisk as he would have liked. He saw a way of exploiting the twins to give his salon some publicity. Going to the largest department store in Cleveland, he suggested to the owner that he put the twin Westmores in one of the display windows, where they would race each other in the making of an entire wig. The brothers would, he said, stay in the window non-stop until they were finished. The store owner agreed and spiced up the competition with an added starter, the twelve-year-old son of the man who ran the store's own beauty shop. After a sufficient number of ads in the local newspapers, the three boys entered the department-store window and were locked in. The twins were not chained to the worktable, but they might just as well have been. They couldn't get out except to go to the bathroom.

Perc won. He ventilated an entire wig in 23½ hours. Ern was second with a time of 26 hours. The other boy disgraced himself after some 30 hours, first by wetting his pants and then by bursting into tears over his unfinished effort. George was thrilled. His business tripled after the episode.

When George was not occupied either in his salon or with the prostitutes, he loved to go to the movies. It was at various Cleveland picture shows that he conceived his finest notion. The year was 1915. As he watched the big stars of the day, Douglas Fairbanks, Charlie Chaplin, Mary Pickford, Lillian Gish, Anita Stewart, and others, he realized their wigs were so badly made and matlike that, as he put it, only the word "Welcome" was missing from them. The makeup worn by the actresses also was ludicrous. Since all actors and actresses did their own makeup (as they still do on the stage), they never put it on the same way twice, and so in nearly every scene they looked somewhat different. Besides, George noted, the stars were applying their makeup as if they were still projecting their faces to live audiences in the last row in the balcony. Their makeup looked grotesque when recorded by a movie camera standing just a few feet away. George's whores looked a lot better. He had spent years teaching them that, no matter where they wanted to use rouge and powder and lipstick and eye makeup, they should do so with a light hand. My father knew then that the fledgling motion-picture field needed him: George Westmore.

In those days most of the actual filming was done in and around New York City. Vitagraph, Famous Players, Metro, and Essanay, to name a few, all had studios and sound stages in New York and New Jersey. In 1915, though, several production companies had moved their facilities to Southern California, for a simple reason: the weather there was nearly perfect for filming. In New York, they had gone so far as to build sound stages entirely of glass so that natural sunlight could provide the lighting. All

41

too often, though, production would be held up for days because of rain or snow or cloud cover. The only question in George's mind was which direction to move himself and his clan in order to cash in on what he unblushingly considered to be his tremendous talents, New York or California.

As he continued to ponder, he was awakened one night by a chorus of coughs and sneezes from his family, flu-bound during the long Cleveland winter. As he later told Mont, that made up his mind. He chose California.

The Westmore trek to the Promised Land took two years, shaving thirty-eight years off Moses' travel time. It took that long because George was forced to work his way across country. It irked him to be slowed down by his burgeoning family, none of whom were able to provide food and clothing for themselves. Ever-pregnant Ada was never able to help her husband, and troublesome new child-labor laws in many of the cities he tarried in prevented him from exploiting the twins and their expertise in hair and makeup. So he found employment in beauty shops, staying only as long as it took him to fill his poke and start west again. He did pick up one valuable piece of information: The place to work in Los Angeles was a posh salon called Maison Cesare. There, he was told, the rich and famous were customers. So were movie stars. He took it as a good omen that the shop was located on a street named Hope.

The ultimate destiny of the Westmores finally began to take form as George pulled into Los Angeles one warm March day in 1917. He had replaced the axle on his battered old Ford seven times, and the doors were held together with screen-door hooks. Nonetheless, he was immediately and irrevocably fascinated by the place.

Driving into town, he and the family gaped at what they saw. There were still hundreds of orange and lemon groves surrounding the sprawling city. A few brick houses were scattered about, but most were made of adobe. Huge oleander trees provided some shade from the constant sunlight. Near the dirty railroad station was an old Spanish mission on a plaza which boasted the "Pelanconi House," built by a wealthy Italian family in 1850. George saw a plaque marking the spot where Kit Carson had stood when he helped turn the California Republic over to the United States. Doves wandered freely in the streets. There was a ridiculous miniature cable car which climbed a miniature hill about half a block long, but the natives were very proud of it and called it "Angel's Flight." (Mack Sennett's Keystone Kops used it as a location site in any number of movies.)

Before he could explore properly, however, George had to get himself to Maison Cesare, where he was sure he would be hired, and he had to find a place for his family to live. He accomplished both tasks in that order the very day he reached Los Angeles.

Leaving his exhausted family in the hot and filthy car, George spent several hours demonstrating his prowess for Mr. Cesare. He so impressed the small and elegantly dressed salon owner that he was told to report to work the next morning. Then he drove up one street and down another, looking for an apartment to rent. He was appalled by signs stating, "No Jews, actors, or dogs allowed," but, since his entourage included none of these categories, he was able to rent an apartment in one of the buildings for a month. However, he was determined to find a place to lease without restrictions as soon as he had more time. I don't think George had any strong emotions about Jews or dogs, but he certainly didn't want to be shut into a place where he couldn't meet the very people who needed him—actors.

On George's first day of work at Maison Cesare, the little proprietor burst into his booth with a customer. Excitedly he introduced the lady as "the great actress, Laurette Taylor." Of course she was famous on the New York stage, but George had never heard of her. Where were the Gish sisters, Lillian and Dorothy? Or Mary Pickford? Or Billie Burke? He complained to his family at dinner that night that he hadn't met any *real* stars. Ada laughed at him. So did his children. George flew into a rage. In what was only the first of dozens of similar outbursts, he grabbed the edge of the tablecloth and yanked it off the table, shattering almost every piece of crockery Ada had bought at a dry-goods store that day.

By the following Sunday, George had rented a permanent apartment in the very heart of Hollywood. It was on Cahuenga Boulevard within walking distance of Hollywood Boulevard. On the corner of Cahuenga and Hollywood Boulevard stood Sam Kress's Drugstore. Kress would cash the paychecks of anyone who worked in the movie industry, so his store was popular with actors. Just across the street from Kress's was John's Restaurant, *the* eating place for the stars. On the occasional night that George would have a solitary dinner there, he would see William S. Hart, Charles Ray, the Talmadge sisters, Chester Conklin, Charlie Chaplin, Douglas Fairbanks, Mary Pickford, Willie Collier. He was close enough to reach out and touch them—which he fully intended to do, with his rouge pots, powder, and wigs. Reason told him that the place to do that was in a movie studio. All he had to do was solve the problem of getting into one.

Late one Saturday afternoon, after he had finished his stint at Maison Cesare, George got into his Ford and started driving aimlessly on one of the rutted, unpaved dirt roads east of downtown Los Angeles. He found himself on Mission Road, where he saw signs pointing to "The Selig Zoo." There was a zoo there, all right, but George also saw a high black wrought-iron gate with a wrought-iron bison straddling it. Through the gate he glimpsed a movie camera, a lion, several men moving around, and a man wearing puttees, shouting through a megaphone. A director! They were making a movie. This was a moving-picture studio.

George ground to a stop and somehow talked his way inside. Only a year and a half later the studio was to be bought by Louis B. Mayer. When George first saw it in 1917, however, it was the Selig Studio. Nine years earlier, Colonel William N. Selig, originally from Chicago, had transported a company of actors to Los Angeles, where he produced the first motion picture ever to be completed entirely in California, *In the Sultan's Power*, starring Hobart Bosworth. Selig, a hustler, was himself hustled by my father. George convinced him that, even though Selig now was producing only jungle films mainly featuring animals, he needed a makeup department on the lot.

Two days later, in a cubicle off the main sound stage, George Westmore established the first studio makeup department in history. It was crude, of course, and the fastidious George was offended by the musty, inadequate quarters he was allotted. But he was there. He had begun. Selig paid him $25 a week—for part-time services.

His normal workday at Maison Cesare began at 8 A.M., which meant that each morning when there was shooting he had to arrive at "his" studio at 5 A.M. to make up the actors—and even some of the animals. One of his chores was to comb the mane of Jackie, the lion, a friendly, toothless old creature who one day caused a panic by climbing into an automobile and seating himself beside a visiting driver.

For a while George was exhilarated. His discontent began, though, when he realized that Jackie the Lion was not exactly the kind of star he had in mind. Neither were the actor-cowboys who were really playing second banana to the animals.

One morning at Maison Cesare, as he was pondering his next move, Billie Burke walked into his booth. He had seen her many times at John's Restaurant, but now the tiny, beautiful blond star was standing right there before him. She told him she was making a movie at Triangle Studio, and Thomas Ince (whose company formed one third of the triangle, along with the combine of Mack Sennett and D. W. Griffith) had ordered her to get a new wig. George agreed with Ince. Her hair was terrible—thin, wispy, and badly dyed.

To Miss Burke's astonishment George promised delivery of the wig by the next day. He measured her head, she left, and, as his twin sons had done in the department-store window, George labored all night long to ventilate a hair-lace wig for her. He knew it would be one of the most important wigs he'd ever made in his life. Triangle had some of the biggest stars in the business under its roof: De Wolf Hopper, Sir Herbert Beerbohm Tree, Willie Collier, Douglas Fairbanks, Joe Weber and Lew Fields, Lillian and Dorothy Gish, Norma Talmadge. If he could con his way into Triangle and set up a makeup department, his fortune would be assured. (Of course he couldn't have known that Triangle was in desperate straits and that soon Samuel Goldwyn was to take over its sixteen-acre studio in Culver City, about fifteen miles to the west.)

Driving to the studio to deliver the wig, George had an uncomfortable ride over dusty, unpaved roads, on either side of which were acres of bean fields. He drove past Triangle's high white wall and three-story office building. He circled around the six glassed-in sound stages until he found a parking place far enough away so that no one could look out and see his Ford, whose doors were now tied together with bailing wire to augment the fragile screen-door hooks. A studio guard directed him to Miss Burke's dressing room. As he walked toward it, he saw Doug Fairbanks outside his own dressing room, doing pushups.

The old man didn't have to con his way this time. When Billie Burke saw herself in her new wig, George reported, she burst into tears, she was so thrilled. But, he told her, her makeup was all wrong, and just by chance he happened to have his box of rouge pots and brushes with him. When he had finished the makeup, something still bothered him about her appearance. It was her eyes. He clipped tiny pieces of hair off the back of her wig and pasted them, one at a time, to her own lashes. False eyelashes were born—and so was the second makeup department at a movie studio.

Even if Billie hadn't insisted—which she did—that George do her makeup every day she was shooting, Thomas Ince was shrewd enough to realize the necessity of having a makeup department right there on the lot. Altogether too much time was lost as the actors, sweating under the intense heat of the lights, stopped to redo makeup which wasn't very good to begin with. Ince offered George $150 a week, a fortune in those days. He immediately accepted and began making up all the actors at Triangle, cannily zeroing in on superstar Douglas Fairbanks.

Now George had a triangle of his own. Mr. Cesare offered him all the free time he needed in order not to lose his services;

George still felt a kind of loyalty to the Selig Studio, although he categorically refused to have anything more to do with Jackie the Lion; and now there was the Triangle Studio, where production was of a higher quality. Since his working day still began at 5 A.M. and often lasted through midnight (or sometimes *all* night), he was temporarily forced to abandon his anatomical studies at Big Suzy's French Whorehouse, which was located miles away from Hollywood in a sleepy, semirural area called Beverly Hills. (As was his custom, he had acquainted himself with the delights and experimental possibilities of the establishment soon after his arrival in Los Angeles.)

George's reputation grew as Douglas Fairbanks's did. He became Doug's shadow, always there when Fairbanks was jumping over high walls or otherwise flinging himself around. No matter how Fairbanks perspired under the heat of the Klieg lights or outside in the glare of the California sunshine, no matter how he wrecked his hair or his makeup, George was by his side to make quick corrections. It took him less than five minutes to smooth Fairbanks out and put him back into leaping condition. George also persuaded the star to let him cut his hair into a manageable mane, which he accomplished by another Westmore innovation. He shaped Doug's hair in layers, a technique commonly used today but then unknown. Even after the athletic actor flew over a wall, his hair would lie thick but sleek against his skull. The camera could move in for a closeup with no time lost.

By 1920 George was so busy—not only with Fairbanks but also with Theda Bara, Nita Naldi, Anita Stewart, and others—that he had little time to spend at Maison Cesare. There was, however, a Westmore in the salon at all times. The old man had gotten Perc a job there as a janitor when his fanatically ambitious son was only fifteen. Perc didn't care what he had to do in the shop, just as long as he could be around hair and makeup—even if it was on the floor.

Early one morning in the fall of 1920, Perc was alone at Maison Cesare, pushing his broom around and generally getting the salon ready for the day's customers. Suddenly the door flew open and a man burst into the shop. He was holding his hand over his mouth as if he had a terrible toothache. Through his fingers he mumbled, "Where's George Westmore the wigmaker?" When Perc informed the man that George Westmore the wigmaker would not be in until late that afternoon, his frantic visitor said, "Then get me someone else. I've had an awful accident." Slowly he lowered his hand. Perc struggled not to laugh when he saw what the "accident" was. Above one side of the darkly handsome, well-dressed gentleman's mouth was a luxuriant, lustrous black mustache. The other side of his mouth was crowned with ragged, patchy stubble. "Razor slipped and I'm making a movie and I'm going to be late and Doug will kill me, get me fired, I don't know," said the distraught actor.

With all the dignity he could muster while still clutching his broom, Perc said, "I am a wigmaker, too."

"Are you crazy?" asked the man. "I have to have Westmore, not some kid."

"I am a Westmore," Perc told him. "And I'm as good as my father."

"Oh, God," mumbled the man. "Well, hell, go ahead and make me the other side of my mustache. Just put some hair there. Maybe I can get by until your father gets back. Name's Menjou, by the way. Adolphe Menjou."

Perc led Menjou into his father's booth. With a ruler, he measured the half mustache that was there. Then he measured the other side after shaving it clean. Next he cut a piece of muslin the correct size. It took him some time to sort through dozens of loose hair shanks until he found just the right assortment of blended colors to match Menjou's own. Then Perc began to ventilate the muslin with a tiny hooked needle, one hair at a time, painstakingly knotting each hair separately. Poor Menjou begged him to hurry.

"Can't hurry a thing like this," said Perc complacently. "It must be right. You said Doug? Is that Mr. Fairbanks?"

"Yes, it's *Mr.* Fairbanks, and *Mr.* Fairbanks can be a downright bastard if you're late. We're doing *The Three Musketeers*, and I'm playing Louis the Thirteenth, King of France. At the rate you're going, by the time I get to the studio, the king will be Louis the *Fourteenth*."

Doggedly Perc continued. It took him ninety minutes, but when he had secured the false piece to the other side of Menjou's mouth, the actor couldn't believe his eyes. It was such a flawless match that, for a moment, he forgot which side he had shaved.

"You're right, young Westmore," he said. "You *are* as good as your father."

A portrait of the Westmore family taken in 1922, before I was born.
Left to right, seated: Ada, George (holding Bud), Dorothy.
Standing: Perc, Wally, Mont, Ern.

4

IN all his life, Perc was never once heard to express doubt about his artistry. When in later years Bette Davis said, "I owe my entire career to Perc Westmore," everybody kidded him about the extravagant statement and quite a few laughed. After all, Bette had won two Academy Awards, and Perc's name did not appear on either Oscar. But he firmly believed that she did owe her success to him. He cheerfully agreed with her accolade and did not demur any more than he had when Paul Muni credited *his* Oscar to Perc's Louis Pasteur makeup.

So it figured that, even at sixteen, Perc accepted Menjou's compliment as his just due. He not only thought he was as good as his father, he had already figured out that he was a damned sight better.

Perhaps he was. Because only three years later, in 1923, at the tender age of nineteen, he became the second Westmore to establish and head up a studio makeup department. This was at First National Pictures, eventually absorbed by Warner Brothers—which became and remained his power base for the next twenty-seven years and where, at one point, Perc had sixty-seven makeup men and hair stylists working under him.

My father, in the meantime, had veered away from the idea of being pinned down to one or even two studios. In any event, Selig and Triangle had folded. The financially troubled Triangle

Company had sold its lot to Samuel Goldwyn, and in 1924—the year after I was born—Goldwyn in turn sold it to a new combine, Metro-Goldwyn-Mayer. None of these convulsions in the industry bothered George. He was in demand at nearly all studios by now, plying his trade at MGM, Paramount, United Artists, De-Mille, and a host of independents. Also, having left Maison Cesare, he opened his own shop and continued his private ministrations to Mary Pickford, Norma and Constance Talmadge, and other stars. He even established the practice of making house calls like a doctor, arriving at an actress's house at 5 A.M. to perform a complete makeup before she left for the studio. He was the acknowledged star of his profession—and enjoyed every minute of it.

Of all my older brothers, the hard-driving, ambitious Perc was his favorite, possibly because he was so much like George himself. So the old man didn't mind when nineteen-year-old Perc, working as his assistant on a Norma Talmadge picture called *Smilin' Through* at First National, talked the studio executives into letting him create and administer a new studio makeup department there. George was pleased. It would mean more work for him—a sort of reverse nepotism.

Besides, George thought that Perc's spectacular ascendancy might stimulate his other sons—all so different in personality—among whom he had always maliciously attempted to foster an unfraternal rivalry. There was Perc's twin, Ern, gentle, uninterested in seeking power, fascinated only by the scientific and experimental aspects of George's profession. There was Wally, the cool and calculating one, who was leaning toward the business world and not at all sure he even wanted to be a makeup artist.

And then there was Mont, his firstborn—plodding, independent, determined to get along on his own without the help of his father, whose self-centered zealousness was alien to him. Mont feared and despised George for his tyranny toward our mother, his manipulation of his children, his extramarital appetites, his ungovernable tantrums. So Mont was the first to leave home, working in a lumberyard while he courted and married lovely young Edith McCarrier, whom he had met in her uncle's movie theater on South Broadway in Los Angeles. And when Mont decided that he too wanted to become a makeup artist, he chose his own route, in his own methodical, independent way.

In 1921, at the age of nineteen, Mont went to the studio then called Famous Players-Lasky—whose films were distributed by Paramount (and with which it later merged)—and got himself a job as a busboy in the studio cafeteria. It was in the commissary that Mont first laid eyes on Rudolph Valentino. The smoldering matinee idol ate his lunch there every day during the filming of *The Sheik,* and Mont sensed that here was a way out of the cafeteria. The problem was how to make himself known to Valentino.

Coincidentally, Valentino himself once had been a dishwasher. The Italian-born actor also had worked as a gardener and, after his arrival in this country, as a gigolo, selling his services—on the dance floor and in bed—to unfulfilled wealthy ladies. His talent in that area must have been considerable, because he was doing very well at it when he was "discovered" by screen scenarist June Mathis. Miss Mathis probably was the finest and most influential screenwriter of her day. She had written five successful screenplays in a row for the great stage actress Alla Nazimova. She was short, chunky, and unattractive, and her weakness was handsome men. She was not above buying their services; Valentino was one of her purchases. While she was still under contract to the Metro Company, and after she had fallen madly in love with Valentino, she persuaded director Rex Ingram to let Rudy star as Julio in her screenplay of Blasco-Ibáñez's famous novel, *The Four Horsemen of the Apocalypse.* Ingram was horrified at the notion. He thought of Valentino as a heavy-lidded, greasy-haired bit player who should only be cast as a gangster. But June was so persuasive and so powerful in the industry that he finally agreed.

Valentino's success was stunning and immediate. The picture was a big hit and he became a big star. Metro put him into three more pictures in succession, including June's screenplay of *Camille,* in which he starred with Nazimova. Miss Mathis was earning $5,000 a week, Valentino $350. He asked for a hundred-dollar-a-week raise. Metro countered with an offer of fifty dollars. Valentino quit. So did June. Both were immediately snapped up by

Famous Players-Lasky. Their joint departure marked the beginning of the end of the Metro Company as such.

During one of Mont's lunch breaks, he saw some men digging ditches around a circle of neat picket fencing surrounding a newly built stable on the lot. Inside the fence were several horses which belonged to Valentino. As Mont watched, the star approached, leaped on the back of one of the horses, and rode him around the ring. The friendly ditchdiggers all called the equally friendly Valentino "Rudy" and commented that it was too bad the horses couldn't be exercised more.

That night, as he had dinner with his new wife, Edith, Mont told her that by the next morning he was going to be a ditchdigger. In less than a week he became *head* ditchdigger, even though he was so tired he could hardly lift his shovel; every night after he finished ditchdigging, he went to a stable near his home and took riding lessons to the point of exhaustion. Poor Mont always hated horses, considering them dumb and dirty. But he felt they would provide a way to meet Valentino. And they did.

One day, as Valentino walked into the studio stable, he saw one of his mounts being cantered around the ring. Since he was so nearsighted that he could barely see two feet in front of him, he had to enter the ring before he could recognize the young man who recently had become head ditchdigger. Mont apologized to Rudy but, as he told him, "I love horses so much that I just couldn't stand their not getting enough exercise." From that moment, and until the day he died, Valentino was Mont's mentor and friend.

The actor first asked Mont to be his valet. When he wasn't in costume, Valentino's "uniform" consisted of an immaculate white short-sleeved shirt, white cardigan sweater, white jodhpurs, and shiny black leather boots with high heels. Possibly because of his early days as a male prostitute, he had a cleanliness fetish. The only thing he didn't wash constantly was his hair. The sleek, seal-like, slicked-down hairdo he affected was his trademark. Just keeping Rudy's white clothing white was a full-time job. Mont didn't like doing that any better than he liked riding the horses. But he bided his time.

The time came while Valentino was still shooting *The Sheik*.

One morning Mont arrived in Valentino's dressing room with his own equipment, a black and shiny makeup box. As usual, because of his poor eyesight, Rudy's nose was pressed against his mirror as he applied his own amateurish makeup on his deeply tanned and flawless skin.

"How about letting me put your makeup on this morning, Rudy?" Mont said.

Valentino replied equably, "Why in hell should I?"

"Because," answered Mont, "my father is George Westmore."

It is doubtful that Rudy had even heard of George Westmore. But he had come to like and respect the quiet, self-assured young man who loved horses and did his laundry so well. He said, "All right," and protested only once, when Mont insisted on washing his hair and applying just a thin coating of Vaseline to it. Mont also modified the heavy penciling of Rudy's eyebrows, plucking them and reshaping them to arch higher over his heavy eyelids, thereby making his eyes look larger. He lightly shadowed Valentino's jaw-line, giving it a more defined, ascetic look, and he considerably reduced the amount of black eye makeup Valentino customarily used. He both lightened his lip color and skillfully added fullness. He also put some Vaseline on the lips to make them shine. When he finished, Rudy looked even more sensual than before.

June Mathis was thrilled with Mont's ministrations to her man, and she immediately got the studio to hire him to perform his artistry on a permanent basis. So Mont became a full-fledged makeup man for the biggest star of them all.

In fact, as time went by, Mont became much more to Valentino. Rudy was married to a grasping, ambitious, and thoroughly obnoxious woman named Natacha Rambova. She was disliked by everyone with whom she came into contact, including her own husband. Until Mont came along, however, Valentino seemed unable to escape from her clutches. But for some reason, Rambova liked and trusted my brother. With Mont's help, Valentino was able to carry on his affair with June Mathis, as well as several other amours, without his wife's becoming suspicious. When Rudy explained that he and Mont were sailing to Catalina for a quiet weekend on the Valentino boat, Rambova would let him go.

Once again, Mont had to learn a new skill; he spent his free time going to navigation school to learn how to operate the small yacht. Valentino himself had no desire to waste his precious free time above decks when it could be spent below in happy dalliance with some reigning actress of the day. One of his grand passions was for the exciting silent star Nita Naldi. Often, while Mont stood on the bridge with his eyes peeled for the treacherous reefs off Catalina, he could hear Nita's melodious voice extolling Rudy's capabilities. Mont always was especially amused when she would comment on his soft, sweet-smelling hair.

Only once that he could remember did Mont have a minor falling-out with Valentino. It was during the filming of *Blood and Sand*. Rudy was playing a matador. Even though Mont no longer was Rudy's valet, he still always checked the star's clothing before he faced the camera. This time, after the wardrobe people had put on Valentino's costume, the matador's "suit of lights," Mont looked him over, pronounced him perfect, and sent him into a scene crowded with hundreds of extras.

As Rudy strode into the bullring, a $3-a-day extra let out a roar of anguish, broke from his position in the rear of the bullfight "audience," and raced out to the star. In a heavy Spanish accent, the extra screamed, "You have got the *pantalones* of the revered suit of lights on backwards!" More of the crowd pressed forward. Mont ran to Rudy and shoved the extra in the chest, sending him sprawling in the dirt. "But my father, he is a brave and famous matador in the bullfights in Mexico," persisted the extra, "and you have the *pantalones* wrong. I cannot let the great Valentino do this."

Without waiting any longer, Valentino helped the frightened young man to his feet and together they walked back to the dressing room, where the extra redressed him, explaining that, since there is no fly in the suit of lights, it was hard for non-bullfighters to tell the back from the front. For some reason, Rudy chose to blame Mont for the mistake. When Valentino again left the dressing room, now properly attired, Mont said to the extra, "Say, what's your name, anyway?"

Nita Naldi and Rudolph Valentino in Blood and Sand, *1922.*
Valentino's natural look and clean, shining hair are Mont's work.

"My name," said the man, "is Gilbert Roland." He was soon to become a star in his own right.

After *Blood and Sand*, Mont continued with Valentino, visually enhancing the star's legend through all the rest of his pictures: *Monsieur Beaucaire* (1923), *A Sainted Devil* (1924), *Cobra* and *The Eagle* (1925), and *Son of the Sheik* (1926). Valentino, worn out by his debaucheries, abruptly died of peritonitis at the age of thirty-one, shortly after finishing *Son of the Sheik*. His funeral caused mass hysteria and even suicide among his fans. Mont did the makeup on Valentino for his public wake, but my brother had little time to grieve. Cecil B. DeMille immediately signed him at the then-fantastic $250-a-week salary to do *The King of Kings*, during which Mont not only practiced his dogged artistry in keeping Christ sober and three thousand extras well-groomed, as described, but displayed his slow-fused but fearless temper when the irascible DeMille rebuked him. The picture also marked a reconciliation between Mont and my father, who started on the film as the specialist who devised Christ's beard. George was very impressed with Mont's progress since he had left home in 1921, reminding him that he could say so because he was the best judge of talent in the makeup profession. No one could deny that. Even while he was estranged from Mont, George had taken Mont's unskilled young wife, Edith, under his wing and had trained her to become one of the best hairstylists in the movie industry.

For the next few years, as Hollywood burgeoned with the advent of sound pictures in 1927, Mont took several leaves out of my father's book. Rather than tie himself down to one star or one studio, he successfully free-lanced, moving from film to film at his now-established $250-a-week fee. He was worth it. For example, he helped initiate the flat-chested flapper look worldwide by strapping Clara Bow's breasts in a picture called *It*. His trend-setting was inadvertent, he later told me, when I was old enough to understand. By using gauze on the nipples and adhesive plaster across Miss Bow's breasts, instead of a brassiere, he was really trying to project the effect of nudity beneath a flimsy garment.

Also—like my father—Mont made house calls to those stars

who preferred to be made up at home before leaving for the studio in the morning. One of his principal clients in the house-call category in the late 1920s was Gloria Swanson, who hated being seen anywhere in public without a full makeup. Mont was a little afraid of Gloria because she was capable of changing moods right in the middle of a sentence—and often did. Some mornings she was charming and would offer Mont coffee and breakfast rolls. Other days she was in a fury. As he got to know her better, he began to realize that her disposition seemed to depend largely upon how she had slept the night before.

One morning when he got to her house, the maid told him that Miss Swanson was still sleeping. "Wake her up," ordered Mont. "I've got to do her makeup and she's got to be at the studio on time." But the maid was horrified; she told Mont she didn't *dare* wake her. Mont went storming up the stairs and into her bedroom, fully intending to do the waking himself. But then he, too, got scared. There she was, lying on her back, sound asleep. So resourceful Mont simply kneeled at her side and did her full makeup while she peacefully slumbered on. (I never quite believed that anybody could sleep through being made up until it happened to me when I was doing Dean Martin's makeup on *Mr. Ricco* in 1974. One morning Dean came to MGM, went straight to his dressing room, and fell asleep. Not only did I accomplish what Mont had done so long ago, but in addition to his regular makeup I added a false "wound" on Dean's forehead, squirting phony blood into it with a hypodermic syringe. Through the whole lengthy process, Dean never woke up.)

Mont ran into an entirely different problem with Mae West, who also liked to be made up at home. He was thrilled when Miss West telephoned him one evening and asked him to come to her Hollywood apartment the next morning to do her makeup. To get her as a regular client would be a big coup. He spent hours gathering his supplies together and packing them into his makeup box. It wouldn't do to forget anything. Early the next day, he arrived, nattily attired in one of the light-beige business suits he habitually wore. A houseman in a scarlet coat ushered him into the white and gold living room, where the first thing that caught his eye was a marble statue of Miss West, stark naked. While Mont waited, staring uncomfortably at the statue, the houseman returned to tell him Miss West was getting ready. Then he came back and escorted Mont to the actress's bedroom. He knocked once and heard the familiar sexy voice say, "Come on in." He opened the door and there stood Mae West, as naked as her statue.

My dumbstruck brother mumbled, "Oh, I'm so sorry. I thought your houseman said you were ready."

"I am, big boy," she answered.

"Well, where's your robe?" asked Mont.

"I never wear 'em unless I'm working," said Mae.

"Start working, then," said Mont, "because I'm not going to do your makeup unless you cover yourself."

Mae roared with laughter and said, "You're the first guy who ever told me to get *dressed*," but she refused to do so. At which point Mont achieved some sort of distinction—because he turned on his heel and walked out of the room. He left the house and refused to return, even though she called him again and begged him to come back. Later I asked Mont why he had suddenly become so puritanical.

He said to me, "Kid, in this business it's gotta be like a doctor-patient relationship."

For all his seeming placidity (except for occasional flare-ups in temper), Mont apparently forgot his own credo in 1929 when he developed something more than a doctor-patient relationship with Cora Williams, who was a script girl at Columbia Pictures while Mont was doing the makeup for *Mexicali Rose* with Barbara Stanwyck. Edith found out about the relationship, became outraged, and divorced Mont—temporarily. (That's the only way to describe what happened, even though Edith didn't remarry Mont for some time.)

Mont married Cora in the interim and moved into an apartment with her, decorating it with all the worldly goods Edith had allowed him to carry away. Almost immediately Cora became disenchanted with Mont's methodical nature. He drove her crazy each night by coming home from work and taking a long, leisurely forty-five-minute shower—no more, no less. About six months after they were married, Mont emerged from the shower to discover that Cora had left him while he was luxuriating under the warm water. The forty-five minutes was just sufficient for her to clear out of the apartment with everything they owned that was movable. "Practically the only things left," he later said, "were the telephone and the towel around my waist."

So Mont, now devoid of any worldly goods whatever, returned to Edith. She agreed to take him back—on a long period of probation that lasted until May 27, 1934, when they slipped away to Mexico to be remarried. (Edith insisted on their living together first in order to make sure Mont was rehabilitated.) To protect her interests, Edith even went to work on many of Mont's films as his hairdresser. They did *Scarface,* in which Mont set another trend —for gangster pictures—with his marvelously sinister scar makeup for Paul Muni. And they worked on Sonja Henie films, for which they had to invent the fish-hook hairpin—because ordinary hairpins would have spilled on the ice, and a single pin, in contact with a skate, would have sent Miss Henie sprawling on her Scandinavian bottom.

By the time I arrived at their home on my bike—a scared little twelve-year-old—to live permanently with Mont and Edith in 1935, it was as if they never had been divorced. Mont was rehabilitated and forgiven and even allowed to go to work alone. The picture he was doing then was MGM's original *Mutiny on the Bounty* with Clark Gable, Charles Laughton, and Franchot Tone. Mont, Jr., and I were big Gable fans (we had even stopped wearing undershirts, following Gable's example in *It Happened One Night*), and we could scarcely control our excitement as Mont sat with us at the dinner table each evening, telling us what had gone on at the set. Then the production company moved to Catalina Island for the sea sequences, and we didn't see Mont for about six weeks. So it was Edith, kept advised by phone calls from the island, who told us about the most hair-raising experience of Mont's long career.

It seems that there was very little to do on Catalina after *Mutiny on the Bounty* finished its daily shooting. Charles Laughton usually read or studied his script. Franchot Tone had his new bride, Joan Crawford, with him most of the time. But Gable, who was unhappily married to Ria Langham, was, for the most part, alone and lonely. He was even then deeply involved with Carole Lombard, although the MGM publicity department, always so good at hiding a potential scandal if it concerned one of their big stars, had clamped a tight lid on the affair. Gable preferred being with the crew members anyway. He was a gutsy, hard-drinking, big and friendly man with a tentative smile (because of his false teeth) and few pretensions. So nearly every Saturday night, when the crew rented a water taxi to take them to the small town of Avalon for the evening, he would join them. He liked nothing better than sitting in some tavern, surrounded by the crew, getting drunk and swapping outrageous yarns.

One morning around 4 A.M., Gable and the others, including Mont, staggered into a water taxi and headed back to the isthmus on the other end of the island where they were billeted. Those who were sober enough started a poker game by flashlight. Others, like Gable, went to sleep. The only problem was that the water taxi driver had obviously been on the sauce, too, because as he crossed the choppy channel he steered his boat smack into treacherous Bird Rock. The craft, which had only long wooden benches lining each side, began shipping water, and the poker money went floating out to sea. One of the men, who had been winning heavily, dove overboard to try to retrieve his money. After he was pulled back into the boat, everybody started yelling for help as they grabbed for the life preservers under the seats. The first priority, naturally, was to get one on Gable, who was awake by now—and sober, as everybody else was. In the initial confusion after the crash, no one noticed Mont's activities. But my brother, who *never* got drunk, had been very busy. Sitting hip deep in the bottom of the boat, he had systematically begun making himself a raft out of every life preserver there and was just about to launch himself off the boat and float to safety. It was then that another makeup man, Bill Tuttle, saw what he had done.

62

"We're gonna drown, you bastard," screamed Tuttle, "and you've got all the life preservers tied up!"

"I can't swim!" Mont screamed back at him.

"Christ," said Tuttle, "don't you realize Gable is on this boat, too?"

"He's a *good* swimmer," said Mont.

But Tuttle made a grab for Mont's raft and started untying the life preservers. Fortunately, all the yelling had alerted the occupants of a nearby boat, which hove to and got all hands off the rapidly sinking water taxi.

As Gable and the soaking-wet crew members landed on the isthmus, Mont said, "I'm sorry, Clark. I wasn't trying to drown you. I was only thinking of my kids, see. I didn't want them to be fatherless."

"Yeah, you're a noble man, Westmore," hissed Gable through his false teeth, dislodged because of the chemical reaction of sea-water on his denture adhesive.

That's the sort of story I thrived on through the next few happy years—as I went to school like a normal kid, enjoyed the pleasant family surroundings of a normal kid, and, like a normal kid, began to venture beyond my immediate world into the world of my strange and colorful brothers.

5

ERN was the brother I knew the least, so during the summer vacation of 1937, when I was fourteen years old, I was delighted when he asked me to help out as a sub-subapprentice on a movie he was doing at United Artists. The film was *Elephant Boy*, the first in the United States for the young actor from India, Sabu. Because it was an important debut for a new star, Ern had been borrowed from his regular job as head of the makeup department at 20th Century-Fox on a "loan-out," much as MGM, say, would loan out Gable for a single picture at Columbia. In our family, Ern took me on a loan-out from Mont.

The experience was not a very exhilarating one for me. My principal job was to smear dark makeup on the bodies of Caucasian extras to convert them into natives. By the time the summer was over, I had half decided it might be better if I considered becoming an actor rather than a makeup man when I grew up. On the other hand, I was fascinated with Ern, who was almost identical in appearance to his twin, Perc, but totally different in personality. He was a kind, patient teacher, and even at fourteen I could appreciate his brilliance in converting the Hindu kid, Sabu, into an exotic hero acceptable to American audiences.

I was too young to be aware of the tragedy surrounding Ern, the fragile genius of the Westmore family, though I wondered about the fresh scars on his wrists—the result of his latest suicide attempt, committed in despondency over the breakup of his marriage to ex-starlet Ethelyne Claire, whom he had married in 1930. But gradually I found out more about Ern from Mont and Edith and from my next older brother, Bud. Bud, then nineteen and working as an assistant makeup man at Paramount, had lived with Ern and his family during one of those intermittent periods when we both were yanked out of military school.

Back in 1921, while training with my father along with Perc, Ern already had begun to drink heavily and was on his way to acute alcoholism. He told Bud he originally sought solace in booze because he was unable to bear the bitter competition our father fostered between him and the hard-driving Perc. In 1922, mostly to escape from home as Mont had done the year before, Ern married Venida Snyder (the first of his four wives), and they had a daughter, Muriel, called Molly. In 1924, Ern escaped from my father completely when he got a job as makeup artist at Warner Brothers, then a small studio housed in what is now television station KTLA on Sunset Boulevard in Hollywood. (Coincidentally, Perc's studio, First National, would later be absorbed by Warner Brothers.)

At first, Ern kept his drinking in check and established his lifelong reputation as the most innovative and creative of all the Westmores—when he was sober. In the classic silent film, *The Sea Beast*, for example, he drew accolades from the entire industry by wrapping a slab of flank steak around John Barrymore's leg and covering it with makeup. When in the film a hot branding iron was pressed against this meat-shielded spot on Barrymore's leg, audiences gasped. The effect was so realistic that it looked as if Barrymore's own flesh was being seared.

Unfortunately for Ern, this was the beginning of a long and terribly corrosive personal relationship with John Barrymore. Not only did Ern frequently become a semipermanent houseguest of Barrymore's (contributing to the deterioration of his marriage to Venida), but he copied the star's excesses with women and whiskey as easily and simply as he had learned the makeup business. He was like a self-destructive sponge. He became a member in good standing of the riotous, hard-drinking coterie of pals who surrounded

John Barrymore: the famous artist John Decker, W. C. Fields, and author Gene Fowler.

During one sodden period, Barrymore and Ern were living in a rented house in Malibu. It was at least a two-hour drive from the various studios where Jack made many of his early swashbuckling silent movies. Since it was so far, Ern would stock the back seat of Barrymore's car with plenty of bootleg liquor to tide them over until they reached their destination, plastered. One such morning in 1927, after a particularly hairy night celebrating his impending marriage to Dolores Costello, Barrymore thought back on the miseries of his previous two marriages and decided he was dying. He ordered my brother to buy a coffin for him and have it delivered to his home to receive his body that evening.

"Get Decker and Fowler and Fields to come over and help you dump my earthly remains into my coffin. And, dear boy, I wish a splendid lying-in, or whatever the hell you call it when you're dead, so you'd better include our bootlegger," suggested Barrymore.

"I think lying-in is when you're having a baby," said Ern.

"Don't quibble," said Jack. "Just report to me when you've completed your purchase."

After Barrymore had staggered out of his car and into the studio, my brother told the driver to take him to Forest Lawn Mortuary. He knew, from having been there at Mother's funeral, that they had a wide selection of coffins. Smelling like a brewery, he made his way into the main office, demanded to "see the manager," and with drunken dignity announced that he wished to purchase a coffin for John Barrymore.

"How terrible!" exclaimed the man. "When did he die?"

"He isn't dead yet," said Ern. "He's going to die tonight, so you'll have to deliver it right away."

Sensing that he had a madman in his office, the gentleman from Forest Lawn asked Ern if he was a mortician.

"Certainly not," said my brother. "I am a makeup artist. Perhaps you've heard the name Westmore." Strangely enough, the man had indeed heard the name Westmore; Perc often offered his

66

services at Forest Lawn for nothing so he could practice his makeup techniques on the stiffs. So instead of throwing Ern out, the man patiently explained that it was against the law to sell caskets to anyone without a certificate of death, and Ern left quietly to relay the bad news to Barrymore.

Despite his alcoholic episodes, Ern managed to solidify his reputation as the most instinctively brilliant of the Westmores, and he continued to advance in the industry. In fact, when Warner Brothers bought First National in 1928, it was a toss-up with Jack Warner and Darryl Zanuck as to whether Perc or Ern would head up the combined new makeup department. Ern obligingly settled the issue for them by disappearing on a two-week bender, during which Perc got the job. Even this act of self-destruction did not constitute a major setback. Within months Ern was hired as head of the new makeup department at RKO, a rapidly emerging major studio which wanted him despite his drinking problem. The overriding consideration was that—as Howard Hughes later said—"he worked on an actress's face with the quick, sure, creative strokes of a great painter like Gauguin."

For instance, it was Ern who, with a few swipes of his lipstick brush over the mouth of Bette Davis, literally changed the shape of the mouths of millions of women throughout the civilized world. He worked on her at RKO in 1931 when she was there making a movie called *Way Back Home*. As was the custom, which had begun before World War I, all actresses had "bee-stung" lips, the elaborately drawn cupid's-bow mouth. That heart-shaped mouth suited a Mary Pickford or a Clara Bow but was wrong for women whose features were not small and delicate. According to Bette herself, when Ern had finished her first makeup at RKO, she sat up and looked into his mirror and saw an entirely different and better Bette—all because of her new mouth. Instead of the two exaggerated points on her upper lip, Ern had drawn her mouth almost straight across, and he had extended the length of her lower lip and made it slightly heavier to correspond to the upper lip.

"I never considered myself any great beauty," Bette said, "except for my large eyes, which I knew were my best feature. Somehow the mouth Ern designed for me even made *them* look better. I think it was because I had been having my mouth made up in that silly way that everyone else did, and it just didn't fit my face. With my new lips, my face suddenly seemed to come together and I began to think I was rather beautiful, even if I wasn't."

When Katharine Hepburn came to RKO that same year to star in *A Bill of Divorcement*, Ern gave her the same mouth—and that totally ratified the new look in lips.

When he first saw Claudette Colbert, Ern scrutinized her naturally beautiful face, immediately perceived what could go wrong when the camera photographed it, and set to work rearranging her features with makeup. He did so at the request of our then relatively inexperienced twenty-three-year-old brother Wally, who, solely because his name was Westmore, became head of Paramount's makeup department in 1926. Confronted with the young Claudette's oddly shaped face, Wally panicked and SOS'd for Ern, the family teacher and theorist.

Claudette has what we call a diamond-shaped face—that is, a playing-card diamond. She has a narrow forehead, wide, high, full cheekbones, and a narrow chin. Though it's lovely to look at in the flesh, a face like that can be devastated by a camera's emphasizing the width across the line of the cheekbones. Also, she has a tiny bump in the middle of her nose, which, again, can't even be seen by the naked eye but which the camera eye can expose as a miniature Mount Everest.

In a complete reversal of the usual process of highlighting the cheekbones, Ern used a blended makeup base there at least two shades darker than that which he applied to the rest of Colbert's face. He applied the dark base on the highest point of the broad cheekbone, blending it carefully in a circular field. He avoided carrying this shading into the hollows of the temples and the lower part of the cheek. From her ears to the corners of her mouth, he used a slightly lighter shade of base. Then he plucked her eyebrows into a very gentle arch. On her narrow chin, he applied a makeup base that was two shades lighter, to accentuate it. On her lips he used a natural lip rouge, forming a mouth that was gently curved and not too wide. The mouth treatment lent the appearance of width across the lower part of the face. He eradicated the tiny bump on her nose by drawing a fine white line down the middle of the full length of the nose.

Presto! Claudette was just as gorgeous on camera as she was off screen. She never quite believed it, though. Until her last picture, *Parrish* in 1961, she never once allowed herself to be photographed full-face. With the makeup Ern had devised for her, she was absolutely superb from *any* angle, but she liked her left profile better than the right one, and as she grew in stardom, she became adamant about having only her left side photographed. Even the set dressers were instructed to place couches and chairs at a certain angle so that Claudette could glide into place with her left-side to the camera.

Ern soaked up ideas wherever he could get them. Actually, it was Marlene Dietrich who taught him the line-down-the-nose trick, which she had imported from Germany along with herself. When she first came to this country in 1930, Ern immediately noticed the unusual technique she was using, even though she was making her films at Paramount and he was at RKO. He went to see her, and, flattered by his interest, she explained the method to him.

It was an outgrowth, she told him, of the ingenuity of her mentor, director Josef von Sternberg. Von Sternberg was a master artist in the use of light—on props, on sets, on people's faces. Marlene told my brother, "When von Sternberg found me in Berlin, I hadn't done very well, either on stage or in films. I was overweight and very unsure of my talent and my looks. But he insisted anyway in starring me opposite Emil Jannings in *The Blue Angel*. It was to be Joe's biggest film up to that time. I have a broad Slavic nose that was accentuated by the fact that I was too heavy then. My body weight didn't bother von Sternberg at all, but my nose did.

"One day he got me onto a bare sound stage, pulled out a small vial of silver paint, and drew a line right down the mildle of my nose. Then he climbed up onto a catwalk and adjusted a tiny spotlight to shine directly on the silver line from above my head. It was like a miracle. When he made a film test, I realized that he had reduced the width of my nose by nearly a third."

As a bonus, at that meeting with Ern, Marlene showed him another extraordinary trick. She took the saucer from under the cup of coffee she was drinking and held it about four inches above the tabletop. Then she lit a common wooden kitchen match and let it burn just beneath the bottom of the saucer. When she turned the saucer over, there was a black smudge of pure carbon in the indention of the saucer's bottom. She then poured a few drops of baby oil into the indention and, with her finger, mixed the oil with the carbon deposit from the match. With the same finger she began to apply the mixture to her eyelid. She started just above her eyelashes, where she allowed the black color to be the heaviest. Gradually she blended the "shadow" up toward the outside of her eyebrow, where it subtly faded away.

Ern was amazed. He told me he'd never seen an eye so beautifully and naturally "framed." Everyone else was using heavy black greasepaint on the eyelids.

Ern adopted both of these techniques he had learned from Dietrich, and so did the rest of us Westmore brothers, We used the line-down-the-nose, sometimes white instead of silver, on Colbert, Ginger Rogers, Hedy Lamarr, Barbara Stanwyck, and many others. As recently as 1952, when I did Marlene's makeup for *Rancho Notorious,* I was still using the match trick. Today, of course, more subtle eye shadows have come on the market and the saucer bit is no longer necessary. But I still wouldn't hesitate to use it in an emergency.

Ern was head of the makeup department at RKO from 1929 until 1931, when his tumultuous personal life caught up with him again and he was fired, leaving a gap of four years before he bounced back impressively as chief makeup executive at 20th Century-Fox in 1935. In his last months at RKO, Ern was drunk and absent for days at a time and his personal life was a mess. He and his first wife, Venida, were divorced in 1929, and when he married wife number two, Ethelyne Claire, in 1930, Venida attracted newspaper coverage by showing up at the wedding clad in rags, their little Molly in her arms, to emphasize the alleged state of poverty in which Ern had left her.

His second marriage to Ethelyne foundered the same way (once again there was a daughter, Lynn) when he acquired another drinking buddy, Errol Flynn, who, if anything, was even more of a carouser than the John Barrymore-W. C. Fields old guard. Mont said that Flynn actually goaded Ern into slashing his wrists in that suicide attempt just before I went to work for Ern on *Elephant Boy* in 1937.

According to my wise sister-in-law Edith, Ern's temporary downfall from RKO at the peak of his creativity in 1931 came about because he was the most sensitive of the brothers and the most guilt-ridden over what had happened to our father. Others saw it as retribution, but beginning in 1926 George had gone into a decline from which he never emerged. After DeMille's *The King of Kings,* and with his four oldest sons doing superbly well at the major studios, the old man opened a new salon on Hollywood Boulevard, convinced that he would be the *super* movie makeup czar to whom his sons—and everybody else—would have to come with major problems. But nobody came. Even the stars, including Douglas Fairbanks, to whom George had been closest, now preferred the sons to the father. So George sat and waited—and deteriorated.

Late in 1926, Paramount, the biggest and most important studio of its day, decided that it, too, had to have a Westmore as the head of its newly formed makeup department. The old man took it for granted that Jesse Lasky would call him. Instead, Lasky picked my brother Wally, then only twenty, for the job he was to hold for forty-three years.

Similarly, in 1928, George expected a call from RKO. The nod went instead to twenty-four-year-old Ern.

In 1931, the Motion Picture Academy awarded its Cup—forerunner of the Oscar—to Ern as the most distinguished makeup artist in the industry for his remarkable work in the now-classic film *Cimarron,* starring Richard Dix. A few weeks later, George committed suicide and Ern went on a monumental drinking binge. His guilt still showed six years later when I heard him discussing my father's death with Mont, who had come to pick me up from my teen-age labors on *Elephant Boy*.

Ern said, "The old man picked the most painful possible way to kill himself. It took four days for that bichloride of mercury to eat its way through his guts. I felt that even in the way he chose to die, he was punishing me for my success."

PERC suffered from no guilt feelings. Even when I was only eight, during that brief interlude when he took me out of military school to live with him for a few months, I was conscious of no emotional reaction in Perc to my father's death, other than an automatic presumption that he was now head of the family. At fourteen I was made acutely aware that he was indeed King Perc of the Westmores—with no challenge from any of my other brothers. In his seat of power, Warner Brothers, any of his dozens of subordinates who made the mistake of mispronouncing his name "Perk" instead of "Purse" faced instant dismissal. In the family, he arranged the obligatory gatherings of the clan (such as the dinners with personalized ivory chopsticks at Don the Beachcomber) and moved us around like chessmen.

It was Perc, for example, who farmed Bud out at thirteen to live with Ern and then, after perceiving that Ern's drinking habits were not exactly salutary for the youngster, clapped him back into military school. When Bud was fifteen, Perc allowed him to live with Wally and took him in as an apprentice in his own Warner Brothers makeup department. It was Perc who had talked Wally himself into becoming a makeup artist (instead of, possibly, a stock-broker) and had then recommended him to Paramount to head the makeup department instead of my father, the logical choice.

And it was Perc who, after forgiving me for running away from his jurisdiction to live with Mont and Edith, insisted that I be pointed in the proper direction of future Westmore makeup fame. After school and during vacations, I was expected to begin to learn the profession with one or another of my brothers, as I did with Ern on *Elephant Boy*. I was delinquent in this regard, preferring girls and football to rouge pots and hair lace. Everyone indulged me in these digressions—except Perc. When he phoned me at Mont's house to come over to Warner Brothers of an afternoon, I went.

Perc was a strange and complex man, as I learned more and more in those afternoon sessions with him. Like my father, he was a born manipulator of people, with a built-in compass that directed him unerringly toward the centers of power. Yet in his personal life he was almost fanatically moral—*un*like my father. He married Tommy—Virginia Thomas—in 1924, the year after he had become the nineteen-year-old head of the makeup department at First National, and as far as I knew he remained faithful to her almost until the time she divorced him in 1936. Before the divorce Tommy told Edith that she never believed the rumors of Perc's affairs with Ann Harding, Kay Francis, or Thelma Todd (who died mysteriously of carbon monoxide poisoning in the garage of her Malibu restaurant and whom Perc made up for her final public appearance in her casket). But even as a child I could see that Perc was a forgetful and neglectful husband. "I really lost Perc to Jack Warner," said Tommy.

Perc zeroed in on Jack Warner as a future giant of the industry even in the five years before Warner Brothers bought out First National in 1928. After that, Perc was in the highest councils of the company, alongside Jack Warner, and was always seeking out more moguls to conquer.

In 1931, for example, the ultimate in status was to be invited to lunch in Marion Davies's fourteen-room "bungalow" erected for her exclusive use on the lot of her studio, Metro-Goldwyn-Mayer. The ultimate ultimate was to be there when newspaper tycoon William Randolph Hearst was playing co-host. One rough index of Perc's eminence in the industry was that he was a frequent guest at these ultimate-ultimate bashes at a rival studio. As with everything Perc did, he had an ulterior motive in mind.

Marion's idea of a perfect shooting schedule was five hours for lunch and three before the cameras. It was, of course, not an ideal schedule for Louis B. Mayer, the autocratic head of MGM, or for Irving Thalberg, his young resident production genius. Both, however, never dared refuse to attend one of the Davies-Hearst noon-to-five pre-soirees. After all, it was Hearst who financed not only Miss Davies's bungalow but her MGM films. Mayer preferred to eat in the Metro commissary, where his wife's chicken-soup-and-matzo-ball recipe was so good that the shrewd L.B. was able to keep his stars on the lot for lunch instead of in the surrounding bars. However, once he entered the lavish Davies premises, it was hard to get him to leave.

One day, Perc, John Gilbert, Greta Garbo, and others were nibbling on caviar and drinking champagne in the mansionlike bungalow. Hearst was in an expansive mood. *Polly of the Circus*, which Marion had just completed, was, he knew, going to be the all-time box office hit. It was to be sneak-previewed that night in Riverside, California, and moguls Mayer, Thalberg, Hearst, and others were going from the bungalow to take a private "Big Red" trolley car to the screening. Since it was almost a three-hour ride, they would play pinochle on the way out and discuss the film on the way back. (It was Mayer's rather wise custom to hold his executives in creative captivity on the trolley car immediately after getting the feel of the real-life audience who would make or break their latest effort.)

But this time Mayer, his optimism increased by the unaccustomed consumption of large quantities of champagne, was more interested in singing sentimental songs, another of his favorite activities. He listed near the grand piano in Marion's living room, rendering his versions of "Eli, Eli" and "My Yiddishe Mama," the tears pouring down his cheeks. Thalberg kept saying to Mayer, "Let's go, let's go." Perc also saw Thalberg clap his hands over his ears as if he couldn't stand another bar of Mayer's off-key singing. Mayer was not to be deterred, however.

"Well," said Thalberg, "are we going or not?"

"Fuck you, I'm singing," said the mighty Mayer.

Eventually, however, they got on the "Big Red" car (Perc excluded because he was from another studio) and saw the sneak preview of *Polly of the Circus*. As was the case with all Marion Davies movies, it was terrible and she was terrible. L.B. blamed Marion; Hearst blamed Mayer; and Thalberg suggested that if his wife, Norma Shearer, had played the part, it would have been a smashing success. Stalemate. Except that in the course of the preceding revelry, Perc had planted an idea in Hearst's mind.

In the mid-thirties, Hearst—who with uncanny foresight had had Marion's bungalow constructed in breakaway sections—severed his connection with Mayer and Metro and transported Marion and her bungalow to Warner Brothers. The move across town took a fleet of ten flat-bed trucks. It was Perc's contention that Hearst could have made a deal with *any* studio but chose Warner Brothers because Perc was there to do Marion's makeup. A typical Perc exaggeration? It's hard to say. To this day, on the Warner Brothers' Burbank Studios lot, there's an unusual monument both to Perc's influence with Hearst and to Hearst's unbelievable profligacy in all matters concerning his protégée.

Here's how it came about: Elaborate musical numbers were very popular on the screen in movies in the 1930s, with a battalion of men and women in evening clothes tap dancing in unison onstage. One day in his Warner Brothers office, thoughts of such a spectacle stirred Perc's creative juices as he read the script of Marion's next picture, *Cain and Mabel*, in which she was to star with Clark Gable. Perc conceived the idea of a gargantuan pipe organ, the stops of which would open to spew forth dozens of tap-dancing young ladies playing violins and other musical instruments. In the midst of this holocaust of sound and motion, Marion and Clark Gable would get married. For the climax of the ceremony, the camera would pan up past the myriads of musician dancers and conclude the scene with a heavenly chorus of fifty little boys in angel costumes harmonizing from the heavens.

Perc rushed to Marion's bungalow with his idea. Miss Davies, her eyes misting over, adored it. She said, "Let's get W.R. over here right away." ("W.R." is what she habitually called Hearst.) The newspaper czar arrived, and when Perc acted out his grandiose plan, complete with tap dancing and imitations of musical instruments and heavenly choir, Hearst's eyes misted over, too. He said, "Let's get Jack Warner and that dance fellow, Busby Berkeley, in here."

After another performance by my brother, Warner said it was great and Berkeley applauded, albeit sadly. "It's all so beautiful, but I can't do it," the dance director said. "We don't have a sound stage high enough to fit it all in."

"Nonsense," said Hearst. Turning to Warner, he said, "How much would it cost to raise the roof of Sound Stage Seven?" Warner said about a hundred thousand dollars. "Done!" shouted W.R. And that's why, if you visit the Warner Brothers lot today, you will see an exceptionally tall, thin sound stage.

Even with Clark Gable's charisma and Perc's ingenuity (his dance concept, to tell the truth, was rather ludicrous on the screen), *Cain and Mabel* bombed. Marion made only one more picture, and then she was out of the industry for good. Despite Hearst's willingness to continue footing the bills, no studio wanted to be associated with such expensive flops any more.

It always saddened Perc during the years he was associated with her to know that even her friends made malicious fun of Marion's so-called career. She was an industry joke. Perc, though, understood the joke for the tragedy it really was—and as fictionalized in the movie, *Citizen Kane.* "Actually," he said, "Marion hated being an actress and only did it as a sop to Hearst's ego. He thought he could make her a star by the sheer weight of his millions. Instead, he gave her a drinking problem she battled all the rest of her life. She dreaded the camera, and in order to face it she'd belt down whole water glasses full of gin. When I'd try to reason with her and say she was going to ruin her beauty, she'd cry so hard I'd have to do her makeup all over again. All Marion wanted was to love and laugh and play."

Perc was an almost incomprehensible bundle of contradictions. His compassionate understanding of Marion's problems was often duplicated with many of the stars with whom he became involved. Yet he was capable of utter ruthlessness in the pursuit of power. This surfaced not only in his ability to manipulate his own family but even in his dealings with such autocrats as Warner and

Hearst. Mr. Hearst left a standing order with his influential newspapers to give Perc Westmore all the space he ever wanted for public-relations purposes or anything else. Louella Parsons alone devoted thousands and thousands of words to "this makeup genius," as he referred to himself and the other Westmores. In fact, he completely obliterated the less flamboyant names for our profession, such as "makeup man" or even "makeup artist." I grew up almost thinking that "makeup genius" was a part of our family name, because that's the way the newspapers and magazines always described us. (Perc generously did not restrict the term only to himself in his brilliant public-relations gambits.)

Bette Davis (who loved and understood him better, perhaps, than even we Westmores did) said, "Perc spent all his life caring, fighting, hated and hating. He came from a family of humble origins and he was always trying to better himself. He knew Hollywood respected power, and if he needed me in that regard, I adored him enough to let him use me. We never did have a physical affair, but if he wanted others to think that, what did I give a damn."

Although Bette came to Warner Brothers in 1932, the year after Ern had created her new mouth at RKO, Perc did not personally take over her beautification process until 1936, when she had become a really big star. For more than thirty years after that, they were the closest of friends. Perc was the one man she felt she could call on for advice about makeup, costumes, even scripts. She, in turn, helped him live through his divorce from Tommy in 1936, his subsequent reported engagements to Betty Hutton and Ann Sheridan, and his second marriage, in 1938, to starlet Gloria Dickson, who burned herself to death smoking in bed shortly after their divorce in 1940. Bette recently told me, "Perc was always there when I needed him. And I was always there to try to keep him on an even keel. It was amazing to me that a man who had such enormous ego and self-confidence in his own abilities could harbor such deep-seated doubts about his background and origins."

Perc even went so far as to try to invent some illustrious forebears for the Westmores. For quite a while he got away with telling people we were of "noble birth" in England. He came a cropper, though, when he ran head on into Charles Laughton, the brilliant English actor who was an expert on every name in *Burke's Peerage*. Together they turned the 1940 version of *The Hunchback of Notre Dame* into a sensational meld of makeup and acting, but when Perc tried his "noble birth" routine on Laughton, the distinguished actor said, "You're so full of shit, your eyes are brown." It was not the happiest of unions—Laughton and my brother—but it did contribute to Hollywood history.

In 1939 Jack Warner loaned Perc to RKO for *Hunchback* for the then unprecedented sum of $10,000. The Westmore conception of the hunchback differed considerably from Lon Chaney's 1923 version. Chaney always did his own makeup, and the hump he devised for himself weighed forty pounds. By the time Laughton got around to the part of Quasimodo, more pliable and lightweight devices had been discovered, mainly by Perc, who had found that six pounds of sponge rubber could be molded to look like a tremendously heavy mass.

Laughton decided that he couldn't possibly work effectively unless he was suffering under the same weight Chaney had carried. Perc's first battle with Laughton began when he suggested that Laughton simply conjure up the pain. "You know," said Perc, "*act* as if you're in agony." Laughton was outraged at such a suggestion by "a hired hand." Perc was outraged by that description of himself. Laughton went slamming out of the makeup department, declaring that he would have the film's producer, Pandro S. Berman, fire Perc at once. Perc slammed out after him in hot pursuit.

With Solomonlike wisdom, Berman placated both of them, but not before some rare dialogue passed between Laughton and Perc. In the course of a diatribe about my brother's "abysmal stupidity and lack of talent," Laughton said, "He is going about this makeup all wrong. You see, I must look like a pig with a very heavy hump."

"Don't give it another thought," said Perc. "You look like a pig *without* a very heavy hump."

Since Perc had yet to experiment with the very complicated

face makeup, Berman sent Laughton home to England for a two-week vacation. Perc returned to his lab, his nemesis temporarily out of range.

Before Laughton left, Perc took several molds of Laughton's face. He called them "death masks." Then Perc made twelve more copies of the original mask, trying out a different makeup idea on each mold. One of Perc's better ideas for deforming Quasimodo's face was to have a bloodshot eye just left of the mouth. Another was to place a misshapen ear near the other eye. In any case, by the time Laughton returned from England, Perc had twelve different makeup masks ready to try on the actor. It had taken him two weeks, working day and night, to achieve his results. It took Laughton exactly two minutes to reject them all out of hand. Perc had to start all over again to find the right combination of grotesquery.

Some of those nights when he was working late, he'd call me over from Mont's house to the studio to watch him. When he finally accomplished what both he and Laughton wanted, it was an absolute masterpiece of makeup engineering. For that false eye, Perc had built a sort of tiny copper bridge that fitted over Laughton's nose. He also had constructed a copper eyelid for the glass eye, covered over with rubber and painted to look like skin. Then he used a slender thread of catgut which he glued onto Laughton's own upper lid. When Laughton's real eyes blinked, so did the false eye located on Laughton's cheek. While everyone else on the lot was raving over what had seemed an almost impossible task, Laughton only grunted a monosyllabic approval. Perc smarted under the slight.

Then early one Friday morning, as I was getting ready for school, the telephone rang. It was Perc. He said, "Hey, kid, skip school today and come over to the studio and learn something really interesting."

I never needed to be urged to skip school. When I arrived at the studio, I went straight to the makeup department, where Perc was waiting for me. In his hands he held the six-pound hump. He laughed when he told me that in order to put on the hump, with its complicated arrangement of straps to hold it in place on Laughton's back, the dignified actor had to get down on all fours on the floor. "He sweats," Perc said unkindly, "like the pig he is, and he grunts like one, and the whole process makes him very thirsty. Anyway, this is something I want you to see for yourself." As we walked toward Laughton's bungalow, I tried to figure out what all that meant, because Perc rarely wasted words.

The actor was slumped on a long black couch, holding his head between his hands. Perc said, "Mr. Laughton, this is my fifteen-year-old brother, Frank. He's going into makeup, too, and I wondered if you'd mind if he watches me put on your hump."

Laughton looked at me balefully and, in acknowledgment of my presence, said, "I've got a toothache." But he didn't tell me to go.

I backed into a corner to be out of the way. Without another word, Laughton got off the couch and dropped to his hands and knees. I wanted to laugh, but I didn't dare. I watched as Perc unwound the straps from around the hump; for the first time I noticed he was carrying a bottle of quinine water. As he began to put on the hump, sure enough, Laughton started to sweat. Beads of perspiration dripped on the floor. Without looking up, he said, "Give me a drink, Perc."

"Yes, Mr. Laughton," said my brother. Deliberately he squatted down right in front of Laughton's face and vigorously began to shake that bottle of quinine water.

"No, Perc, no! You wouldn't!"

"Yes, Mr. Laughton, I *would*," Perc said, and he shot the whole fizzy bottleful right into the face of one of England's most distinguished actors. For good measure Perc then stood up, walked to the other end of his captive on the floor, and kicked him squarely in the ass. "That's for all the grief you've given me," said Perc. "I brought my brother today because I needed a witness to say this never happened, if you try to say it did. But you won't, Mr. Laughton, you won't." Laughton didn't. The makeup was finished, and Perc and Laughton never worked together again.

Strangely, Perc seemed to have most of his problems with fellow natives from the British Empire: Laughton and, earlier, Errol Flynn. Errol and Perc first met when Warner Brothers bought

Rafael Sabatini's swashbuckling novel, *Captain Blood*, in 1935. The role of Peter Blood, physician-turned-amateur-pirate, seemed a natural for the studio's biggest male star at the time, George Brent. But every time Perc put a long-haired wig on Brent for a makeup test, the virile actor looked like a beautiful girl. Even a flowing Moses-like beard didn't help; Brent still came across like a woman in pants. Then Jack Warner, present at most of the filmed makeup tests, said, "There's a handsome guy in England I saw on my last trip. He's a sort of actor, and he's got a perfect body because I watched him model men's bathing suits." The guy, Errol Flynn, was brought to Hollywood and tested for the part of Captain Blood. "He's in!" shouted Perc when he saw his makeup on the unknown actor, and "in like Flynn" soon became an accepted expression for those who make good very quickly.

For his major debut in motion pictures, Errol was moving in fast company—Olivia de Havilland and Basil Rathbone among others. He also moved in fast company after hours. There was hardly a night when he didn't go drinking and on the prowl for nubile females. In the morning he would report to Warner's makeup department, bleary-eyed and hung over, to be confronted by an immaculately white-smocked Perc Westmore, makeup tools in hand, glaring at him with clear-eyed virtue. Once when my brother was particularly pensive and quiet over Flynn's delicate condition, Flynn shouted at him, "Don't you ever do anything bad?"

"No," said Perc.

After that, to Errol, Perc became "Mr. No," some thirty-odd years before Ian Fleming dreamed up Doctor No.

When Perc had designed Flynn's makeup, he turned the actor over to one of his assistants, as was his custom. Flynn quickly subverted the assistant, persuading him to make certain substitutions in his makeup case, putting gin, vodka, Scotch, and bourbon in bottles labeled as skin cleanser, hair preparations, and the like. When Perc sniffed Scotch-flavored shave lotion one day and summarily fired the duplicitous assistant, Errol was not defeated. Every morning at six thirty he would make a big show of ordering "malted milks." Actually, they were Ramos gin fizzes, which consist of nine parts gin and one part beaten egg white. When his makeup and his "malteds" were finished, the handsome Flynn would swagger from his dressing room and onto the stage to swashbuckle as Captain Blood. But most mornings he tended to buckle more than he swashed. Perc caught him again, and no more "malteds" were given to Errol.

For sheer ingenuity, Flynn was the all-time champ. He was determined to come up with a gimmick that not even the dogged Perc could detect. Oranges began to appear in abundance in his dressing room. To Perc and Jack Warner, the fact that Errol was eating so many oranges was an encouraging sign of health consciousness; the fruit would supply Flynn with a lot of vitamin C and increase his energy for his athletic role. But Flynn's oranges had an extra ingredient; they were actually a kind of screwdriver.

The fruit was so "juicy" that a colorless liquid constantly ran down his chin, and the new assistant makeup man had to keep mopping Flynn's face, not understanding how he was getting himself so soaking wet just eating oranges. Every morning Perc, watching the rushes (rough film of the scenes shot the day before) wondered why Flynn still looked bleary every day. Jack Warner, with whom Perc sat at the rushes, didn't notice anything strange, but to Perc's trained eye Errol's own eyes always appeared a little out of focus.

Knowing that Flynn was getting drunk somehow, despite all his precautions, Perc slept one night in one of his department's makeup rooms. Very early the next morning he hid himself in the bathroom adjoining Errol's dressing room, and he was there when a fresh crate of oranges was delivered. Soon Flynn arrived with a heavy suitcase clanking with bottles. My brother watched as Errol began using a hypodermic syringe to inject the oranges with vodka. Finally Perc couldn't help himself; he burst out laughing. So did Flynn.

For the remainder of the picture, there were no more oranges, and a sober Flynn completed *Captain Blood* and got rave reviews. Perc's vigilance did not, however, permanently stop Errol from drinking—nor from commencing that extremely destructive relationship with Perc's already vulnerable twin brother. Until he died of alcohol and narcotics in 1959, when he was only fifty,

Errol posed a problem to Warner Brothers and to nearly every other studio that employed him.

It baffled Perc when Bette Davis, the queen supreme of the Warner Brothers lot, raved about "Errol's charm and enchanting ways" all during the filming of their first movie together, *The Sisters*, but Bette later explained that she adored working with Flynn "because he never really *worked*. He was just *there*." Errol provided a handsome foil for the temperamental actress without giving her any serious competition. However, the complexion of the Davis-Flynn pairing underwent a drastic change in 1939 when they began their second—and last—starring venture together. Bette was only thirty-one years old when she was handed what was to be one of her most difficult roles, that of portraying the middle-aged Queen Elizabeth I, who fell desperately in love with the young and dashing Second Earl of Essex, played by Flynn.

All the problems of this onstage and offstage mismatch fell on Perc's shoulders. The first problem had to do with Bette's makeup as the queen, which presented an enormous challenge to his ingenuity and skill. He had a prodigious amount of homework to do.

"Queen Elizabeth," he told me, "was anything but a beauty, even when she was young. In fact, there were some in her court who even considered the fact that she might be a man in disguise. Of course, she was not a man, but she did have an unusually high hairline. As she grew older, she began to get bald, and the hairline receded higher and higher. Also, Elizabeth never had any eyebrows. I was horrified at what I knew I would have to do to Bette in order to transform her into a historically accurate Queen Elizabeth: I was going to have to shave off most of her hair and all of her eyebrows. I just couldn't figure out a way to tell her, so I decided that in some way I would have to make her tell *me*."

Each morning prior to the start of filming, Perc would be ready for Bette with different types of makeup. On one day he bound her hair back tightly, covering it with a skinlike cap over which he used wig and headdress. Then there would be a filmed makeup test. Another day he covered her eyebrows with color-tinted mortician's wax, and they looked at *that* film. This type of experimentation went on for several days.

One morning Bette walked into Perc's department and said, "I just don't look right as Queen Elizabeth. Really, Perc, you should have known that my hairline is terribly wrong." Breathing a sigh of relief, my brother set to work with his barber's tools. When he had finished, the front half of Bette's head looked like a baby's bottom. She had lost her eyebrows, and she had even allowed Perc to trim her own beautiful long eyelashes.

"Pro that she was," said Perc, "all she did when we got through was to say, 'God, this is going to play hell with my sex life.'"

The second major problem was not cosmetic. It dealt strictly with ego—mainly Bette's. When principal photography began, the movie was titled *Elizabeth and Essex*. That was fine with Bette: top billing for the top star. But somewhere along the line, the Warner executives decided to capitalize on Errol's sex appeal in the film, and the title was flipped to *Essex and Elizabeth*. Bette was not going to stand for *that*. Perc relayed her forceful message to Jack Warner, so Warner changed the title to *The Knight and the Lady*. At that point, Bette tore off her Elizabethan ruff and her wig and marched bald-headed into Warner's office with Perc right behind her.

"You cannot," she roared, "give second billing to the Queen of England! Or to me! Change the goddam title or I'm walking out." And walk she did. There was no more shooting the rest of that day. To no one's surprise, when the picture was released, it was called *The Private Lives of Elizabeth and Essex*. (In her own private life, Bette had to wear wigs and false eyelashes for six months—until her own hair and lashes grew out again.)

Perc and Bette worked together in more than sixty motion pictures, most of which were untroubled by any untoward incidents. Perc used Bette and other big feminine stars to put across his philosophy of makeup to more women than he ever could deal with in person. He believed that if you *felt* beautiful, you would be beautiful, and that by creating his innovative makeups and hairstyles for actresses who would be seen on the screen by millions of moviegoers he could in effect revolutionize makeup and hair-styling all over the world.

In large measure, he succeeded. For instance, when he cut bangs for Bette to minimize her too-high forehead, after *Elizabeth and Essex*, Davis fans the world over had their hair cut in bangs. Some forty years ago he cut Claudette Colbert's hair in a short, curly crop, a style also adopted by millions of women and which Claudette herself hasn't changed to this day. Silent actress Colleen Moore's Dutch bob, which Perc devised, is another flattering hairdo which is still worn. He tried orange lipstick on redheaded Ann Sheridan, with smashing results for other red-haired women who had been too timid to try something so radical. Again through Ann, he popularized the center part when he styled her naturally curly hair that way. He yanked up Katharine Hepburn's unruly, baby-fine hair and fashioned a little knot right at the top of her head; the "washtub hairdo," as he called it, is as good today— for women with Hepburnlike features—as it was then, and Kate still wears her hair this way.

Perc didn't limit himself to faces and hair. Shoulders, arms, legs —name it, and he could improve upon nature. There was only one area he didn't think of, but Carole Lombard rectified that.

One day she telephoned him and said, "Hey, Perc, can you think of something to make my tits look bigger?"

"Yes," said a shocked Perc. "Stuff socks in your brassiere and put one in your mouth, too. Your language—"

"Never mind my language," she laughed. "I'm over here at Columbia making a picture called *Lady by Choice* and I've got this low-cut dress, and my tits just don't look big enough."

My prim big brother gave the problem some thought and came up with a solution which he later wrote about, realizing that many women have psychological problems because they feel their breasts are too small.

What he told Carole to do was this: To give the smaller bust an illusion of more fullness, first highlight the upper part of the breasts by applying a very lightweight, light-colored liquid foundation. Then use flesh-colored powder sparingly over the foundation. Even more intriguing highlights can be achieved by using cold

Bette Davis as Queen Elizabeth, made up by Perc.

cream or a light film of Vaseline over the liquid foundation, instead of the powder, and toning it down with tissue. In either case, run a thin line of dry rouge, applied with a brush, down between the breasts, and you'll be amazed at how the cleavage seems deeper.

As late as 1958, when I was at Paramount doing *The Buccaneer*, Kim Novak was on the next stage shooting *Vertigo*. Every male with eyes at all could see that Kim not only didn't wear a bra but that her breasts were absolutely beautiful. But only *I* noticed she was giving nature a little help with the same technique invented by Perc for Carole Lombard way back in 1934. Kim had read about it in a Louella Parsons interview with Perc when she was an eleven-year-old kid in Chicago.

7

I remember September 1938 for two reasons. First of all, as I continued my normal life in the pleasant home of Mont and Edith, I entered Hollywood High School and had a ball attending classes with nice kids whose names were Jason Robards, Jean Peters, Alan Hale, Jr., and Jack Kruschen. Another student—a somewhat sporadic one—who caught my eye was full-breasted Julia Jean Mildred Frances Turner, later and better known as Lana. She already had made two pictures for Mervyn Le Roy at Warner Brothers, but the truant officer kept apprehending her and sending her back to Hollywood High for further learning. It wasn't until late that year, when Le Roy took her to MGM with him, that she finally finished her education at Metro's Little Red School House with Elizabeth Taylor, Mickey Rooney, and Judy Garland.

The second reason September 1938 stands out in my mind is that—in my educational series of after-school visits to my older brothers at their studios—I learned rather dramatically how different Wally was from the rest of the family. I walked into his office at Paramount one day and saw him working on what seemed to be a severed human hand. I examined the hand and realized it was made of latex rubber. The hand itself and three of the fingers were hollow; the thumb and index finger were solid latex. Being a knowledgeable high school sophomore by then, I recognized Wally's invention as a prosthetic device and asked him about it.

He hesitated for a minute and then decided to tell all, if I promised to keep secret what he was about to divulge.

The hand, he said, was for his old friend, Harold Lloyd. The great comedian then was making a film—his next to last—called *Professor Beware*. At the time virtually no one knew, and very few people know even today, that Lloyd lost the index finger and thumb of his right hand when a faulty explosive prop blew them off in 1919 when he was at the old Hal Roach studios. For years—all through his celebrated pictures of the 1920s and 1930s— Lloyd had hidden his deformity by wearing a glove. Now, however, in *Professor Beware*, there was a scene in which Lloyd had to strip to his underwear, and there was no way the glove could go undetected. So he came to Wally and asked him to invent one of the first flesh-textured prosthetic hands. Wally did so, embedding wires in the latex so Lloyd could move the rubber thumb and forefinger of the remarkably lifelike hand by manipulating his own real third finger inside the hollowed-out part of the device.

I was not so much impressed with the ingenious craftsmanship of the artificial hand as I was with Wally's insistence that it all be kept secret (as it has been until I write it now). Even in 1938, I couldn't help thinking how Perc and probably Ern would have immediately trumpeted the feat to the world, via press release or, more subtly, through judicious leaks to Hedda Hopper or Louella Parsons.

Born in England in 1906, Wally was only two years younger than the twins and four years junior to Mont, but he was eons apart from them in temperament, in attitude, and even in physical appearance. He looked considerably different from the rest of us. All the other Westmores had broad faces with rather full jowls, dark wavy hair, and snub noses. Wally had a thin face, light straight hair, and a long straight nose. Until the day he died, my father habitually referred to Wally as "the bastard," an example of his irrational perversity.

Wally was conceived on a night when George had lingered late at the local pub. Instead of coming in through the door, he tried sneaking in a window. Ada was there waiting for him, and she hit him over the head with their own framed wedding picture. In a howling rage, the old man impregnated her with Wally. He then forgot the whole episode and was both surprised and annoyed at Ada's impending motherhood, accusing her of having an affair with the local fishmonger. How he could have thought his wife might possibly have the time to dally elsewhere is a mystery. Mont was a rampaging toddler, the twins were still in diapers, and Ada spent every hour of every day cooking and cleaning and doing laundry. I think the main reason for my father's distaste for Wally is that he was the only one who looked like Ada; the rest of us inherited his own facial characteristics.

Wally was also the only one of Ada's nineteen living births to be a breech baby. He came out feet first, and he stayed on his feet for the rest of his life, as witness the fact that Wally was the only Westmore brother to marry only once, and the only one to die rich. As I said, he was the cool and calculating one. When he left school at the age of fifteen, he contemplated going to work as a messenger for a stockbroker's office, but then, prodded by Perc, he rationalized that he could attain his goal of earning $10,000 a year much faster by trading on my father's reputation—even though the makeup profession didn't really appeal to him. He got a job at the old Brunton studio, then figured he could progress more quickly by capitalizing on Ern's reputation at the old Warner Brothers studio. So he went to work there, learned everything he could from Ern, and when Perc recommended him to be the head of the new makeup department at Paramount in 1926, Wally was ready. He went in and did a masterful job of selling himself to Jesse Lasky. At twenty, therefore, he more than doubled his original goal of $10,000 a year. It was only then that he married Edwina Shelton, his lifetime spouse, and had two children, James and Ann. Predictably, Wally later steered James into becoming a stockbroker, the career he had always wanted for himself.

The Westmores never were a close family (in my high school years I rarely saw any Westmore socially except for Mont, Edith, and their three sons); but Wally kept himself the most aloof of all—except from Bud, in whom he had taken a fatherly interest, much as Mont had done with me. Wally lived miles to the west of us on a fashionable street in Beverly Hills, next door to the wealthy par-

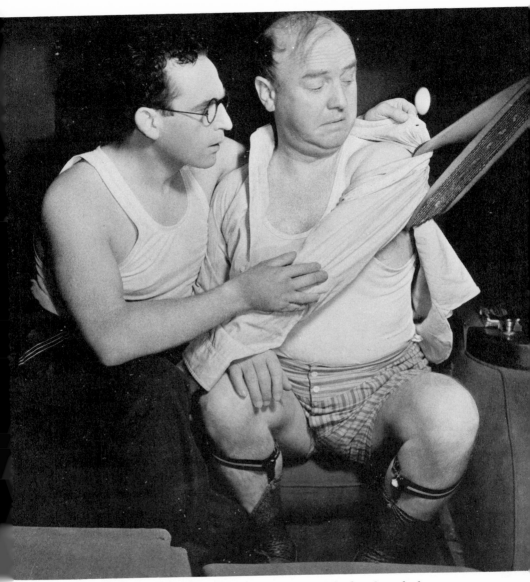

Harold Lloyd (left) wearing the false right hand made for him by Wally. The other actor is William Frawley.

ents of future star Elizabeth Taylor. We'd see him socially only at his annual Christmas open house and at the obligatory bimonthly family dinners that Perc badgered everyone into attending at Don the Beachcomber's in Hollywood. There, he was the only one to disdain the personal ivory chopsticks that had his name on them. He conversed very little with us as he ate with an ordinary fork and spoon. He had a habit of disappearing into the men's room just before the time came to split the tab. Once we had the waiter take the check to him in there. Then Perc and I stationed ourselves outside the bathroom door and wouldn't let him out until he paid.

Unlike Perc and Ern, Wally had few friends in the industry. His intimates were socialites, bankers, and realtors. The movie people to whom he was close, such as Bing Crosby, Harold Lloyd, Fredric March, Ray Milland, and Gary Cooper, were apt to be smart money men. They would give him stock-market tips, or tell him where to invest in land, and he'd never fail to take advantage of their advice.

Of all his movie friends, Wally was fondest of Bing Crosby. It did not, however, start that way. Before he came to Paramount in 1932, Bing had been one of the youths in Mack Sennett's stable of actors making two-reel short subjects. He had done six comedies, but he was better known as the lead singer in a group called the Rhythm Boys, and it was in this role that Wally first became aware of him. Wally and his wife, Edwina, had gone to the Cocoanut Grove in the Ambassador Hotel for an evening of dining and dancing. They picked an unfortunate night. Bing, standing at a microphone overlooking the dance floor, had overindulged and he became violently ill in full sight of the dancers, among whom was Wally.

When Crosby was placed under contract by Paramount, Wally at first refused to have anything to do with his makeup. He turned him over to his number-one protégé, Harry Ray. Harry made up Bing for his first two Paramount movies, *College Humor* and *Too Much Harmony*. Bing became a big star almost immediately. His salary took an astronomical jump, and by 1933, after *Going Hollywood* was released, Crosby was in the Top Ten of the Box

Office Poll. It was then that Harry Ray ran into a makeup problem with his charge.

Bing says his ears make him look like a taxicab with both doors open, and Harry had been pasting them back with spirit gum and adhesive tape. He would stick back the ears and then wrap Crosby's head with a turban until he was sure they'd stay pinned back. George Raft had the same kind of ears, but he had had an operation which flattened them permanently. Crosby categorically refused Harry's suggestion that he do the same thing, though he hated the daily ministrations.

In 1934, halfway through the shooting of *She Loves Me Not*, one of the scenes had to be more heavily lighted than the others. During one number, the heat of the lights loosened the spirit gum and out popped Bing's left ear. This happened no less than ten times. After the tenth time, Bing furiously refused to allow the errant ear to be stuck back. Wally was quickly summoned in the crisis. He burst out laughing when he saw Crosby's lopsided head, one ear flapping like an angry elephant's. Wally went to the head of the studio, then Emmanuel Cohen, who agreed with my brother's argument that Bing's ears had nothing to do with his extraordinary voice. Both Crosby ears thereafter were allowed to flap untrammeled.

There followed another struggle which Bing didn't win—the battle of the hairpiece, vulgarly known in the trade as a "rug," a "divot," a "scalp doily," or a "Bowser." Whatever the name, Bing loathed wearing it. He was prematurely bald, and Wally insisted that he couldn't appear on the screen without hair. "Flapping ears are one thing," Wally said, "but a skin-headed, flapping-eared romantic crooner is ridiculous."

To this day, Bing credits Wally—and his persistence in making him wear toupees—for the extraordinary longevity of his movie career. Recently Bing recalled to me the time he expressed his gratitude by drafting Wally to accompany him to Paris for the location of *Little Boy Lost*. Crosby claimed he needed Wally to glue on his hair. Actually, Bing knew Wally had never seen Paris and wanted his pal to come along for the free ride. Wally certainly "saw"

Paris. What he didn't see too clearly through the residue of a champagne evening was Bing's bald pate, as he made up the star one morning; he neatly and firmly glued on Crosby's wig backward. Bing didn't notice either, until the director returned the dilapidated duo to the dressing room for repairs.

However, Wally, unlike Ern, really wasn't a drinker, and he was dismayed when he was informed that he was to do John Barrymore's makeup personally for the 1938 film *Spawn of the North*. Barrymore had been in several movies for Paramount the year before, but Wally had always fobbed him off onto one of his assistants, complaining that the star's boozy early morning breath made him sick to his stomach. This time, though, Barrymore's makeup was much more complicated—a frozen beard had to be simulated, for instance—and the master's touch was needed. Although Barrymore never needed a reason to get drunk, in this picture he had a pretty good excuse to do so when he learned that he would be co-starring with a seal named Salty. He considered the pairing the grossest indignity, as I suppose it must have been for the formerly great Shakespearean actor. In any case, Barrymore's imbibing all through the picture was truly epic. Wally took to wearing a surgical mask over his nose for his morning makeup chores.

One day when he came reeling out of John's dressing room after completing Barrymore's makeup, Kenny Carter, the movie's press agent, was waiting for him in something of a panic. In response to Carter's question about what kind of shape the actor was in, Wally told him that, if anything, Barrymore was more smashed than usual.

"Oh, that's just great," said the despairing publicist. "*Look* magazine is here to shoot a five-page layout on him. What am I gonna do? I *can't* tell them he's too drunk to stand up. The studio would fire me."

Wally thought for a minute, then said, "Why don't I make up Salty the seal? Get him to my makeup department."

Ordinarily, Wally did no makeup whatsoever on the seal for his role in the picture. But *Look* didn't know that, and they went for the idea. Salty's trainer got the animal to sit in Wally's chair, where my brother bleached his whiskers, lightened his nose, and put makeup under his eyes, all the while keeping up a running commentary about how making up the seal was absolutely necessary to sustain the authenticity of the film and so on. Through the hour-long makeup procedure, Salty's trainer kept throwing the unhappy beast huge handfuls of sardines to keep him quiet, causing Salty to have the most hideous halitosis my brother had ever encountered. Wally never again complained about Barrymore's breath. And when *Look* came out with the five-page spread, my brother took one glance at it, turned green, and swore that even the pages smelled of fish.

Wally was secure enough to call in even the most formidable of his competitors when a makeup job stumped him. In 1936, he had a real problem on his hands. Akim Tamiroff, the superb Russian actor, had been hired to play a Chinese general in *The General Died at Dawn*. Gary Cooper and Madeleine Carroll, who starred in the movie, were both easy so far as makeup was concerned. But Wally had worked on Tamiroff before and knew that not only was he a stickler for visual authenticity, but he considered himself as much or more of an authority on prosthetic appliances, odd-shaped noses, or phony ears as Wally or any other makeup artist. Once when Wally had had to make Tamiroff up as Napoleon, the actor insisted on the devising of a totally new chin for him. In his heavy Russian accent, he had said, "Napoleon was strong-chinned man. I am weak-chinned man with strong will. Make new chin." Wally did so. But Tamiroff perspired so profusely into the fake chin that in the middle of a scene, while the camera was rolling, the entire appendage fell with a plop to the floor.

Now, as Wally puzzled over how to make Chinese eyes for Akim, he also wondered how Tamiroff, whose pronounced accent made him sound as if he were fresh from the steppes, could sound convincingly Chinese. While he was in his lab wrestling with the problem of Tamiroff's eyes, the grand old man of Paramount,

Adolph Zukor, wandered in. Wally voiced his concern about Tamiroff's Russian accent to Zukor, whose own speech inflections were anything but pure. "An accent's an accent," said Zukor. "Who's going to know the difference in Canarsie?" In the face of such indisputable logic, Wally went back to his eyes. Even a moviegoer in Canarsie could tell the difference between a Russian eye and a Chinese eye.

Wally had taken a cast of Tamiroff's face, modeled Chinese eyelids on the cast with clay, and then reproduced them in rubber. But applied to Tamiroff, the eyelids looked, in Wally's words, "like blobs of what they really were—rubber. Akim looked like a Russian actor wearing rubber eyes." Next, Wally called in a sculptor to model some Oriental eyes. When he reproduced the sculptured eyes in rubber, the results were even worse.

Then someone tentatively suggested that since Jack Dawn, the head of the MGM makeup department, had successfully turned Paul Muni and Luise Rainer into Chinese characters for *The Good Earth*, Wally might want to consult with him. "Consult, hell," said Wally. "Let's borrow him. I don't care how the job gets done, just *so* it gets done."

Dawn was brought from Metro to Paramount to work with Wally. As the two men toiled over Tamiroff, Wally was elated and felt sure that this time, when their subject left the makeup chair, he'd look Chinese. Dawn was doubtful. "I don't know," he said. "Muni and Rainer had good faces for this kind of transformation. Couldn't make it work on Jimmy Stewart."

Then he told Wally about the time James Stewart was tested for the part of Chang, Muni's *Good Earth* friend who survives a devastating Chinese famine. Stewart was under contract to MGM at a time when all studios had stables of actors who were brought along and developed in a succession of minor parts. Although Stewart had already made several movies for Metro and gave every indication of being a future star, he was difficult to cast because he didn't fit into the Robert Taylor–Franchot Tone mold of suave sophistication. Nor was he a Wallace Beery type of character actor. He was six feet three inches tall and weighed 135 pounds,

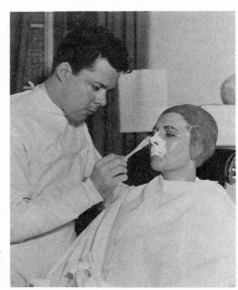

*Perc making
a face mold
of Ruby Keeler.*

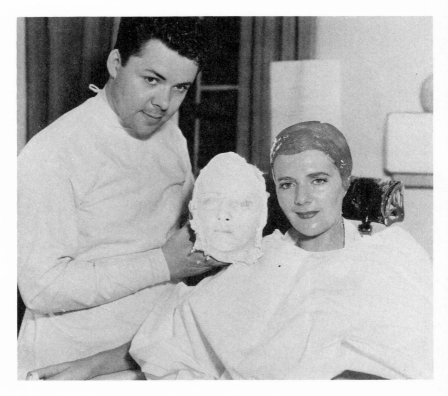

James Stewart as a Chinese. (He was not made up by a Westmore.)

and he really did say "wal" for "well." However, Louis B. Mayer said to test him for *Good Earth,* and so he was tested. (Later Stewart told me he thinks they wanted to use him in the film because he was the only man on the lot who looked as if he'd really been through a famine.)

Jack Dawn said he'd put a "bald cap" on Stewart's head, yanked up his eyelids with spirit gum, trimmed his eyelashes, and sent him to the set to test with Paul Muni. The first thing Muni said when he saw Stewart was, "That's one hell of a tall Chinese." So they dug a ditch for Stewart to walk in when he was near Muni. That didn't work because Muni, striding next to the gangling Stewart, tripped and took a header into Jim's ditch.

After three days of testing, Stewart, in his Chinese makeup, went into the commissary to have lunch. He passed by Mayer's table, where the studio head was enjoying his chicken soup. One of L.B.'s guests said, "Hi, Jim, are you testing for a part or something?"

Mayer looked up and flew into a rage. "Whoever thought James Stewart could look Chinese is a meshuganah!" he shouted, and the part of Chang went to a *real* Chinese actor.

When Akim Tamiroff rose from Wally's makeup chair with Jack Dawn's makeup on him, *he* didn't look Chinese, either. "He *did* look like a general," conceded Wally, "a *Russian* general." Then director Lewis Milestone stepped in. He called Wally to his office and said, "I hear you're having trouble making Akim look Chinese. Why don't you find a Chinese actor and take a mold of *his* eyes?" My chagrined brother did just that. He found a young Chinese performer named Philip Ahn, who sat with his eyes wide open while Wally made a mold from them with a jelly substance which doesn't hurt the eyes. Wally then transferred the jelly mold of Ahn's eye structure to clay and finally to rubber. The rubber partial mask was fitted to Akim—and at last Tamiroff became a Chinese general. What he sounded like was something else.

Such is the interlocking Westmore involvement in the makeup industry that nearly forty years later Philip Ahn's eyes were again under Westmore hands as I did his makeup for the television series

Kung Fu, in which he played the part of Master Kan, one of David Carradine's two Chinese-monk instructors.

In those days, when full face molds were made, ordinary soda straws were stuck into each nostril of the actor's nose so he could breathe through them when the plaster of Paris was poured over the whole face. I saw Wally perform this routine procedure on W. C. Fields with disastrous results during one of my after-school visits to the Paramount makeup department. Wally needed the mold to design a Humpty-Dumpty makeup for Fields. He greased Fields's face so the plaster wouldn't stick to the eyebrows; then he applied the plaster itself, leaving the nose area until last, as he always did. But when he began to pour the plaster around the soda straws inserted into Field's large nose, Fields went berserk. He began clawing at the still-damp plaster on the rest of his face, pulling it away from his mouth and emitting unearthly howls.

The hardening plaster began to adhere to Fields's hands, and he jumped from Wally's chair and struck them against the walls, trying to get the plaster off his fingers. The face mold was a crumbling mess around his still-shouting mouth, and his hands began to bleed. Wally realized then that Fields suffered from severe claustrophobia and quickly called the studio doctor. It took an injection of sedative to subdue the actor. Later, Fields admitted to Wally that he was so fearful of any kind of enclosure that he couldn't even stand to wear a ring around his finger. Neither could he bear to use an elevator. If he had to go to a room on the eighteenth floor of a building, he walked up the stairs. Wally told me that claustrophobia was only one of Fields's many mental disturbances, dating back to his childhood, and that any man carrying such a burden deserved forgiveness—even for such mistakes as his corrosive influence in abetting the alcoholism of our brother Ern. Wally eventually made the Fields face mold in two vertical halves, alternately leaving one eye and one nostril uncovered by the plaster.

The Fields incident added to Wally's reputation for compassion and understanding of actors—which was not entirely true.

101

He was a pragmatist. If he appeared to be close to important stars, he felt he had still another weapon to help him survive the unremitting political warfare which beset the upper echelons of the studio. (He survived forty-three years, outlasting nine studio heads, from Jesse Lasky to Y. Frank Freeman.) As a result of his be-nice-to-actors ploy, his makeup department—strategically located on the upper floor of the building housing the stars' dressing rooms—became the social center for the entire Paramount cast of characters. Ray Milland used to spend hours there, even when he was not working, playing klaberjass (a then-popular card game of Hungarian origin) with Wally. Both Bing Crosby and Bob Hope would hang around Wally's office practicing their putting. Susan Hayward used Wally as a father confessor to complain of her dislike of the Paramount brass for employing her more for cheesecake photos than as a film performer—and Wally would convince her that the road to future Oscars was paved with cheesecake.

Actually, Wally much preferred to discuss financial deals with his banker and real-estate-broker friends, and even at the studio he seemed to me to be most stimulated in his conversations with the stars when they brought up stock earnings and such. The only problem for Wally was that most actors couldn't stick to his favorite subject. I remember one afternoon, for example, when Henry Fonda came in to ask Wally's advice about hiring a business manager but soon digressed into a story of how he and James Stewart solved the mystery of skyrocketing milk bills when they were young actors sharing a house together. Fonda said that he decided to investigate the housekeeper's quarters to try to solve the financial mystery. A strange noise attracted him to the maid's bathroom. He opened the door and beheld one of the most shattering sights of his life. The bathtub was filled with milk, and, by his actual count, there were thirty-seven neighborhood cats happily gorging and disporting themselves in the tub. Fonda insisted to Wally that he was so stimulated by this scene of feline felicity that he stripped and got into the tub with the cats. He was inspired to do this, he told Wally, by a previous famous disaster at Paramount in which Claudette Colbert, playing Nero's wife in Cecil B. DeMille's *The Sign of the Cross*, bathed in milk for a scene which was before the cameras for three days. At the end of the three days, the milk had begun to curdle and Claudette's strongest perfume couldn't obscure the stench.

Even members of Paramount's publicity department hung around Wally's makeup office, recognizing it as a veritable wellspring of juicy gossip and ideas. One day press agent Kenny Carter dropped in to chat with Wally and mentioned that he had reached a point where he was totally devoid of ideas as to what to do to get newspaper space for Paramount starlets. The two starlets causing the immediate mental block were Susan Hayward and Evelyn Keyes.

Although he was swamped with his own work, Wally sat down with Carter, like a good company man, to dream up a fresh concept. He finally hit on one. "Take the two girls to the photo gallery," he said, "and put them in flesh-colored bathing suits. Then take this oil; I'll lend you a makeup woman to smear the young ladies with it. While she's doing that, you get two goosedown pillows. Cut them open—here's a knife. Then have the two girls engage in a pillow fight. The feathers will fly all over them and stick to the oil and they will look like chickens." Carter followed Wally's instructions to the letter. The world was simpler, or more simpleminded, in those days. The "chicken" photos were published in some twelve hundred newspapers and magazines all over the world.

Wally was resourceful, firmly entrenched at his studio, a power in the industry in his own right, and totally independent. It was something of a surprise, therefore, when my other older brothers asked Wally to join them in a revolutionary new enterprise and he accepted. The new enterprise, as yet unnamed, was to be undertaken by all of them as a sideline to their various posts as studio makeup department heads. Since Mont was then doing George Arliss's makeup on the picture *The House of Rothschild*, Edith said, "Why not call yours The House of Westmore?"

THE address was 6638 Sunset Boulevard. Today, the
two-story Tudor-style building prosaically houses the offices of
law firms, a union local, and a state senator. But on the evening of
April 13, 1935—opening night for the new House of Westmore—
the structure was the epicenter of glamour not only for Hollywood
but for the entire world, if one can believe the press reports of
the day.

Its golden doors opened with a fanfare rarely equaled even
by motion-picture-premiere standards. Hollywood newspaper reporters almost lost their collective minds trying to find the right
adjectives to describe the event. "Supergiganticcolossal" was, I
remember, one of them. (I was only twelve at the time and still
in military school but I read the clippings later that year, when
I settled in with Mont.)

According to one press account,

> Kay Francis, a reigning queen of the silver screen, turned a
> golden key which opened this magnificent salon of beauty.
> Joan Blondell threw the golden switch which flooded the in-
> terior of the salon with light, and everyone stood dazzled and
> dumbfounded by the spectacle that met their eyes. Claudette
> Colbert, gowned in gold, pressed a gold button to light the
> exterior.

Everything looked golden that night. Hundreds of screen
celebrities and other notables moved inside to congratulate my

brothers. The four of them in the receiving line stood united for once in the triumph of this evening. Perc was resplendent in his tailor-made dinner jacket; the frugal Wally was in a tuxedo borrowed from Paramount's wardrobe department; Ern was sober for a change; and Mont, who was then laboring on *Mutiny on the Bounty*, looked exhausted. Perc, the public-relations wizard, gave reporters and photographers something to record when he persuaded the bald character actor, Vince Barnett, to have the remaining four hairs on the top of his head permanent-waved. Charles Laughton—not yet estranged from Perc by the *Hunchback of Notre Dame* incident—was the first male customer to have his hair cut that night, and child star Jackie Cooper agreed to have his locks shorn in the kiddies' department, where fairy-tale scenes in pastel murals adorned the white and coral walls. Marlene Dietrich's daughter, Maria, was the female backup child. Ironically, although The House of Westmore was primarily dedicated to the beautification of women, my brothers could not persuade any of the big feminine stars to pose having their hair or makeup styled that night. Actually there were none left to be done. Marlene Dietrich, Joan Blondell, Claudette Colbert, Carole Lombard, Anita Louise, Kay Francis, Clara Bow, and Myrna Loy were among the stars who had spent the day, each one with her favorite Westmore brother, being coiffed, painted, and groomed (for free) for their appearances at the opening.

All this was not an overnight phenomenon. The House of Westmore concept had been incubating for a long time—mostly in Perc's mind. He got the idea when he and Ern were invited by the Max Factor organization to develop, in their spare time, the highly successful "Percern" wig, for which they were each paid approximately $50,000 a year. The Factors were—and still are—the principal manufacturers of movie makeup (as well as cosmetics for the general public), though they never worked in the studios as makeup artists the way the Westmores did.

After Factor's profitable merchandising of the Percern wig, the first commercial toupee utilizing my father's invisible hair-lace base, it was inevitable that it would occur to Perc how wasteful it was to be doing this for the benefit of anyone else but the West-

Two views of the lavish lobby of The House of Westmore.

(above) The Westmore brothers at the opening of The House of Westmore. Left to right: Perc, Mont, Wally, Ern. (below) Perc at the opening with Kay Francis, Una Merkel, and Claudette Colbert.

more family. It was also inevitable that his fertile brain would carry the concept further, beyond wigs, to a line of Westmore cosmetics and a pleasure dome in which to apply them. Although Perc, of course, saw himself as the High Lama of The House of Westmore, he also saw his brothers, Lower Lamas though they might be, working together as friends at last, each brother grasping a corner of a vast four-cornered canopy, wrapping up the whole world in Westmore wigs and cosmetic wizardry.

The cost of this temple of beauty was astronomical. Wally was the only one who didn't have to scramble to get up his share of the money. Mont, Perc, and Ern went about garnering theirs each in his own way. Mont made a sensible loan at a bank, Ern borrowed money from John Barrymore and Errol Flynn (which he never did pay back), and Perc sold a piece of property he owned in Beverly Hills to W. C. Fields, for $40,000. The last was a very strange transaction. Fields delivered the money, in cash, all in small bills. He arrived at the escrow company lugging it in a huge suitcase, which caused him to tip to one side more than usual. It turned out that he had spent the entire morning going from one savings-and-loan association to another, withdrawing money from secret accounts he had opened under such names as Humbert Lompoc and Horatio Festenfeather. Because of some disagreement in his earlier years, Fields distrusted commercial banks. In his vaudeville days, he opened savings accounts in every town in which he played, so that the money would be there for easy withdrawal if he ever passed through again. To this day, it is said, there are hundreds of thousands of dollars of Fields's money on deposit in undetectable savings accounts, the names of which Fields himself had long forgotten by the time he died. Fortunately for Perc, he remembered enough of the names to deliver the $40,000.

For Perc, however, there still was not enough capital to open The House of Westmore. As I have said, Wally was the only Westmore with business sense, and he was appalled when he heard that Perc had spent $5,000 to have a genealogist trace the Westmore family back to the sixteenth century, so that the salon could be emblazoned with an authentic Westmore coat of arms. (He got it, all right. It is a lion *en passant* on guard above three lozenges, and it was the insignia of Thomas Westmore, Esq., Mayor of Lancaster in Preston County, England, from 1708 to 1718. Only it turned out that we were not related to that Westmore.) Other extravagances included floor-to-ceiling mirrors in the foyer, and peach-blush carpeting so thick you could break your ankle wading through it.

The decorators went just so far before they decided it would be prudent of them to collect the rest of their money. And that's what Perc was fresh out of. He was too proud to ask Wally to help, and he knew Mont and Ern couldn't. Then, one morning at Warner Brothers, he was making up Kay Francis for a movie in which she was starring called *Stranded*. He told me later that it probably was the irony of the name of the film which prompted him to tell Kay that his "monument," as he liked to call it, now would never be completed. Right then and there, with one eyelash on and the other still in Perc's hand, Kay reached into her purse, brought out her checkbook, tore out a blank check, signed her name at the bottom of it, and told Perc to fill in whatever amount he needed. He filled in $25,000, rushed to his decorators with the money, and the job was completed on schedule.

After the frenzy of the opening, customers had a better look at what Perc had wrought. There were pure white silk draperies with crystal fringe; bronze, coral, and white furniture graced each booth; every cubicle had its own white and gold telephone; and an announcer system crooned softly into your own booth, should there be a message for you. There were baby-sitters for customers with children. In the children's department, the chairs were fashioned into airplanes and hobby horses, and hot chocolate flowed as freely as imported wine did in the grown-ups' quarters. Perc's office on the second floor was paneled in solid oak. Next to it was his laboratory, with the newest and most modern equipment in the world, a lot of it designed by Perc.

About a mile away, in a separate building on Sunset Boulevard and Gordon Street, was the House of Westmore cosmetics plant. Its products were by far and away the most expensive beauty aids one could buy. The packaging was gorgeous: gold, black, and green containers housed lipstick, rouge, mascara, face powder, eye shadow, eyebrow pencils, everything then known to the cosmetic art. In addition to being used exclusively in The House of Westmore, the products were sold only in the fifty most soigné stores in the United States. For each such store, Perc designed a unique mirror which was surrounded with lights. When you flipped on the lights and observed your reflection, fine lines would appear on the mirror to help you decide which of the seven basic face shapes you possessed. Those seven basic shapes delineated by Perc and Ern—oval, round, oblong, square, triangle, inverted triangle, and diamond-shaped—are still studied and copied today by every makeup artist and major cosmetics manufacturer in the business. If, for instance, you determined (after peering into the special mirror) that you had a square face like Carole Lombard's or an oblong one such as that of Katharine Hepburn or Loretta Young, Westmore-trained cosmeticians would then suggest what Westmore makeup you should buy and how to apply it for the best results.

Both the salon and the cosmetics line—abetted by the magic mirror—took off immediately. Visitors coming to Los Angeles had heard and read so much about The House of Westmore that they went there as if it were a tourist attraction like the Disneyland of today. And they were never disappointed. On a given day they could see Laurence Olivier getting his hair cut, or Hedda Hopper and Louella Parsons, with open notebooks on their laps, collecting gossip for their columns and glaring at each other. When she was in town, the Duchess of Windsor was a customer, personally attended by Perc. Madame Chiang Kai-shek, too, was a special client of Perc's, and whenever her limousine appeared at the front door, a particular kind of oolong tea kept especially for her was immediately brewed. Rosalind Russell, Dolores Del Rio, Constance and Joan Bennett, and Barbara Hutton were often visible, as was Milton Berle, getting his hair dyed and not caring who knew it.

In the beginning of the salon's heyday, however, there were some stars who were not visible at all. They were mainly men who were either too embarrassed to be seen entering the front door of a beauty parlor or did not wish to be observed having fittings on their "scalp doilies" or seeking other means of enhancing their machismo. For them there was a special, partially concealed back entrance which led directly upstairs to Perc's private office. From that rendezvous point, a client could be escorted, unseen, to a section of hidden rooms the ordinary customer didn't even know existed.

George Raft briefly became one of Perc's back-door clients. For all his suave good looks and dashing grace as a dancer, Raft's body was shaped like the trunk of a stubby tree. His waist didn't indent at all. He was almost as broad through the middle as he was across the shoulders. One day at Warner Brothers, Raft confided to Perc about how he agonized over his waistline. Perc told him not to give it another thought; he had a "device" to solve Raft's problem. He told the actor to meet him at The House of Westmore the following Saturday, when he would be ready to give tough-guy George "a waistline as tiny as Shirley Temple's."

All week, Perc labored at Raft's device, constructing it of latex rubber topped with a four-inch band made of pure old-fashioned whalebone.

Saturday morning, wearing dark glasses and a hat, Raft entered the salon through the back door and slunk upstairs, where Perc fitted him into the contraption. It worked. Raft took one look at his new shape and was elated, even though the thing was so tight and rigid that the actor required instruction from Perc in how to breathe while wearing it. But when he put on his trousers, they were so copious that they slid down from his new Shirley Temple waist, and he left euphoric. All Raft's skulking about was for naught, however. Not only did Perc reveal to *Liberty* magazine the secret of the salon's back door, but he gave a joyous description of George's "device," candidly confessing that it really was nothing but a variation on the wasp-waist, turn-of-the-century lady's corset. Raft never spoke to my brother again.

Although my four older brothers were all financially involved in the salon, it was Perc who spent the most time there. He even insisted on a new clause in his lifetime Warner Brothers contract giving him leave to depart the studio every afternoon at

2 P.M., specifically so he could oversee The House of Westmore and its makeup plant. He actually got to resent the time he had to spend at the studio, because The House of Westmore had much more exciting backstage action. For example, Ann Sheridan, a regular customer, always came in to have her hair, nails, and makeup done during lunch, which she would order and eat while getting beautified. She always consumed the unusual combination of mashed potatoes and gravy and a hot fudge sundae. Once she and Hedda Hopper were there at the same time. That particular day, Hedda had written something snide about Ann in her column. The minute Sheridan heard that Hopper was there, she took her plate of mashed potatoes into Hedda's booth and dumped the whole mess right in Hedda's lap.

There was a fist fight in a House of Westmore booth between two suitors of my sometime schoolmate, Lana Turner. Often Carole Lombard would call for an appointment but would walk in through the front door and straight out the back and into the waiting arms of the still-married Clark Gable. Louella Parsons, constantly on the prowl in the salon for a good tidbit for her column, howled with laughter when she bumped into the always impeccably groomed Adolphe Menjou, parading around outside his booth in his undershirt, red suspenders, and spats, with an iced towel on his freshly dyed brown hair. She dutifully reported his deshabille in her next column, thereby starting a feud with Menjou. Another mini-feud began in the salon when Bob Hope saw his friend Jack Benny there and asked if he could borrow Eddie "Rochester" Anderson for his next movie, *The Ghost Breakers*. Petulantly, Benny said he couldn't rent, let alone borrow, Rochester. Hope used another actor, Willie Best.

One of the most dramatic happenings at The House of Westmore came about because Ann Sheridan refused Jack Warner's offer of the starring role in *Strawberry Blonde*. She didn't like the script or anything about the project. So Warner got the then raven-haired Rita Hayworth on a loan-out from her boss, Harry Cohn of Columbia Pictures, and told Perc to turn her into a strawberry blonde. Rita had begun her film career in 1935 under her real name, Marguerite Cansino, and had been rather unimaginatively publicized as "the black-haired beauty." Cohn had changed her name but not her hair color. He had hopes that she might become his prime competition to another "black-haired beauty," Hedy Lamarr. Perc had no idea what color strawberry blonde really was, and when he went to Warner seeking some sort of clue as to what the studio had in mind, Warner snarled, "Just take a strawberry and make it blonde."

At 8 A.M. on a Sunday morning Perc, his chief Westmore colorist, Helen Bore, and Rita arrived at The House of Westmore. The job was, Perc knew, far too complicated for him to tackle alone at the studio, and he had chosen a Sunday so that he and his assistant could work undisturbed. Eleven hours later, the trio left the salon. The metamorphosis of Rita Hayworth was complete. Her hair was now bright blond with unique red highlights. The dramatic hair-color change not only hypo'd her previously lethargic career but her entire outlook and personality as well. The hitherto almost inarticulate young actress became, by comparison, almost bubbling. In his *New York Times* review of *Strawberry Blonde*, Bosley Crowther described her performance as "the flirt who got away from James Cagney, a *classic* one." Thus stimulated, she got up the courage to divorce her first husband, a man much older than herself named Edward Judson, and married Orson Welles. To this day, Rita says that if it hadn't been for Perc and her strawberry-blonde way station to redheadedness, she never could have done her wildly uninhibited role in the movie *Gilda* (probably her most famous part), for which she was nominated for an Academy Award.

Because I was so young during the early years of the salon, I learned of most of these occurrences secondhand from Mont. Occasionally, on a Saturday afternoon, I'd go to The House of Westmore to gawk at the celebrities like any tourist. From time to time, when I was still only fourteen and not legally licensed to drive, I was drafted for service at the wheel of the gold-and-white Westmore truck, making the delivery run between the cosmetics plant and the shop. I knew I was being prepared for more responsible duties. Bud, only five years older than I, was already working at the salon as a makeup artist on weekends and after his daily work at Paramount, where he was apprenticed to Wally. He was nineteen; he already had married and divorced Martha Raye; he had flown the family coop two years before and was living in his own apartment as an active man-about-town.

I was still very much in the family coop—Mont's, that is. During my junior high school years, my easygoing eldest brother did not press me to work regularly at the salon, perhaps because he felt my learning process was proceeding satisfactorily through my after-school visits to the Westmores at their various studios. Then, after I got to Hollywood High in 1938, Mont wasn't around very much to press me into doing much of anything. He had gone to the Selznick-International Studio as head of the makeup department, and he was engaged in the monumental task of doing research for David O. Selznick's *Gone With the Wind*. I was on the Hollywood High football team, and Mont—when I did see him—tried to display the proper interest in me as I recounted my prowess on the gridiron. But he was so tired he would fall asleep in the middle of one of my sentences. He looked ill and at the point of exhaustion. He was struggling to keep up with the hyperkinetic Selznick and struggling to be a husband and father.

The last thing he needed was a problem, which I inadvertently provided. One day after a football game our team had won, a football-freak student offered another player and me a ride home in his yellow Dodge. We climbed into the rumble seat and were barreling down Sunset Boulevard when suddenly a police car, with sirens blaring, made us pull over to the curb. With their guns drawn, the cops told us to put up our hands and get out of the car. It's not easy getting out of a rumble seat with your hands above your head, but I managed. They lined us up and frisked us in full view of the dozens of cars which were slowing down to get a better look at what was going on. Obviously, we were in big trouble and I couldn't figure out why. When I opened my mouth to ask what we had done, my voice came out soprano. Then the kid whose car it was said, "I'm sorry, guys, but I stole this buggy."

The police piled us into their car, drove to the Hollywood

police station, and booked us. Then they started calling our parents. When they got to me, they phoned Mont's house and Edith answered. Mont had stayed home sick that day and I was scared to death. Even from where I was standing I could hear her gasp and then shout to Mont, "Frank's in jail." Then I heard him shout back to her, "Good. Leave the little son of a bitch there." He was joking, but I didn't know that until Edith and Mont, Jr., brought me home. Mont told me my escapade had given him his first belly laugh in a year.

However, directly after that episode, my big brothers had a council of war and their unanimous decision was that I should be kept working during all my spare time. From then on, after the football season was over, I went to The House of Westmore every afternoon and every Saturday. My first regular job was at the plant, cleaning wigs. In contrast to the salon, the plant was a stark, unadorned building which housed the elaborate equipment used in the making of Westmore beauty products. The biggest piece of machinery was the grinding mill. It consisted of three huge brass rollers, each eight inches in diameter, which crushed the solid makeup components into powder. The head of the cosmetics manufacturing operation was a Czechoslovakian chemist named Doc Fisher, a natty dresser who always worked in a proper business suit and tie.

One day, while I was laundering hundreds of Indian wigs for a Western picture, I heard a horrible gagging sound and turned to see Doc Fisher slowly being strangled to death by his own tie. He had bent over the grinding mill to check the color of a mixture he had prepared, and somehow the neckpiece had got caught between two of the rollers. For a paralyzed second, I watched as his head sank lower and lower into the churning vermilion mess that was destined to become lipstick. Just as his nose and mouth were being pulled into the rollers, I came to life, grabbed a scissors, rushed over, and cut off his tie. I was just in time. We nearly had a chemist who was both dead and red.

It was two years after the Doc Fisher incident before I was rewarded with a transfer to the salon, where under the tutelage of my brothers I became expert enough at makeup techniques to be able to handle some of the overflow business on Saturdays. Before long I was building a list of my own Saturday clients. One of these was Virginia Hill, bag woman for the Mafia and mistress of Bugsy Siegel, the mobster who had come from New York to build the Flamingo, the first syndicate hotel in Las Vegas. To unsophisticated Hollywood, Virginia got away with calling herself an "heiress," and she gave elaborate parties in her rented Beverly Hills home for such guests as Cary Grant, Jack Warner, Barbara Hutton, and Jean Harlow, godmother to Siegel's two daughters. Virginia was unmasked in 1947 when Lucky Luciano, then the boss of bosses of the Mafia, ordered Siegel's execution. Four slugs from a carbine nearly parted Siegel's head from his body as he sat reading a newspaper in Virginia's living room.

Long before that, however, I was doing her makeup. One day in the salon she wanted a chicken sandwich and a Coke. I called the restaurant down the street, and the order was delivered to the booth by a pimply-faced young soda jerk. Virginia fished in her purse and came up with a whole fistful of loose thousand-dollar bills. I was still staring at them when she handed one of them to the boy. He evidently thought it was a dollar bill because he said, "This isn't enough." She shook with laughter. Then the kid took another look and went pale. He said, "Christ, lady, I can't change this!"

I offered to pay, but Virginia had a phobia about accepting money from anybody. "I don't borrow dough from anyone, not even for five minutes," she said.

Once again she fished into her handbag. This time she brought out a tiny Derringer pistol with a hand-wrought gold handle. She laid it on my counter next to the makeup brushes and said to the boy, who was still holding the thousand-dollar bill, "Change it."

To this day I don't know how he did it because it was a Saturday and all the banks were closed, but somehow, somewhere, he managed. For his trouble Virginia gave him a hundred-dollar bill, saying, "Learn to count the zeroes, buddy, and you'll get to be somebody." When she left that day, she gave *me* a hundred-dollar bill, too. "Try to forget what you saw today, Frank," she told me. You forget things like that the same way you forget how to breathe.

All told, my part-time work in The House of Westmore made me, at seventeen, a strange mixture of sophisticate and yokel. In the yokel category, I'd still drop my brushes and gape when a big star walked in. But sometimes I didn't realize who I wasn't gaping at.

There was a new young actor named Ronald Reagan, for example. Thirty-five years later, in January 1975, just two days after he relinquished the governorship of California, Reagan told me how he had come to Hollywood as a baseball announcer for the Chicago Cubs, how he was signed by Warner Brothers, and how his makeup fell under Perc's jurisdiction. The Governor said, "I was the rawest of newcomers, and apparently I was too big a problem for Perc to handle at the studio. So he sent me to The House of Westmore on a Saturday for what turned out to be a joint consultation with his brothers. I still remember how they circled around me as if I were a racehorse. They spoke only to each other, not to me. I recall their saying such clinical things as, 'What are we going to *do* with him?' and, 'With his hair parted in the middle like that, he looks like Joe E. Brown with a small mouth.' "

Eventually it was Perc with whom Reagan became good friends. My brother cut and reshaped Reagan's heavy thatch of hair (parting it on the left side), and consoled him when all his scenes in his second movie for Warners, *Submarine D-1*, were considered so bad they were left on the cutting-room floor. Often Perc and Ronnie, as everyone called him in those days, double-dated, dancing and dining with their dates—Perc had now divorced his second wife, Gloria Dickson—at places like the Trocadero, the Biltmore Hotel, and Ciro's.

Reagan was cast in subordinate roles in at least twenty films at Warner Brothers until 1941, when he got his big break in the movie *King's Row*, based on the best-selling novel. He played Drake McHugh, a young man who was hit by a train and whose legs were amputated by a sadistic surgeon. The picture was one of Warner's most daring and ambitious dramas, starring Claude Rains, Ann Sheridan, Robert Cummings, and Charles Coburn. The studio even secured the services of the great director Sam Wood, of *Goodbye Mr. Chips* fame.

For this film, Perc himself made up all the stars, but he categorically refused to apply any makeup at all to Ronald Reagan's visage. And he had a battle royal over it with Wood. Wood asked Perc just who in the hell he thought was directing this picture and why was he refusing pancake on Reagan?

Perc said, "*I* am directing the makeup on this picture, and for the Reagan character to be believable, he cannot go around looking like a department-store dummy." Perc won the fight. Wood backed down and Ronald Reagan never forgot that his makeup artist friend, by *not* making him up, helped him stand out in one of the few memorable performances of his career.

Working in The House of Westmore as a youngster, I was inspired by the creative work done on clients such as Reagan, but I was both amused and appalled by other events that were taking place before my adolescent eyes. Because of laxity in management, the salon sometimes resembled a precursor of today's massage parlors. Any woman who needed an illegal abortion knew in just which booth to go to find out whom to call for the necessary service. Appointments were being made not for hairdos but for assignations conducted behind locked doors during business hours. On the more amusing side, Ern, who frequented a night spot called the Florentine Gardens—where Sally Rand and her legion of strip-teasers performed—persuaded Sally and company to come to The House of Westmore for free beauty treatments. A grateful Sally, in a silver-bound brochure that advertised the Florentine Gardens and displayed a huge picture of Miss Rand in the altogether, proclaimed in print directly opposite her portrait that "the hairstyling and makeup of my twenty-three girls is very important, *too*. All was executed and achieved by Ern Westmore of The House of Westmore." Polly Adler, probably the best-known madam of her time, became a customer. "Where else would I go," she declared, "but from one House to another?" None of this was the kind of publicity Perc had in mind.

Neither did he relish the headlines which accrued when The House of Westmore became the hapless victim of an industry-wide labor dispute, the origins of which long preceded the opening of the salon but nearly wrecked it. Back in the early 1930s, the Painters Union had managed to absorb the makeup artists, on the rather ingenious grounds that painting faces was related to painting buildings. This eventually led to a massive jurisdictional strike in the movie industry, beginning on April 30, 1937. One main issue was whether the makeup artists would continue under the jurisdiction of the labor federation to which the painters belonged or would be taken over by the International Association of Theatrical and Stage Employees (IATSE). At that time, IATSE was run by two labor extortionists (later convicted and given ten-year sentences in Federal court, where they admitted they were installed in office through the influence of the Chicago family of the Mafia). It was inevitable that there would be a lot of breaking of heads on the picket lines. Perc, Wally, and Mont—who as management were not on strike—remained inside the studio walls and slept in their offices in order to avoid disarrangement of their profiles.

One night, however, two goons broke into The House of Westmore, which, uptown on Sunset Boulevard, was far from the scene of battle. The intruders bound and gagged the terrified night porter. Then, obviously aware of the pride my brothers felt in the beauty of the white and bronze and coral furnishings in the shop, they smeared creosote over every wall, all the silken draperies, the desks, chairs, carpeting, the hair dryers, the crystal chandeliers, the accounts-receivable and appointment books, even the clean white uniforms and towels. After the disaster, and until the strike was settled, a police officer was stationed in every Westmore home each night for fear of more reprisals to their families. The shop itself was closed for nearly three weeks, at an enormous loss of revenue, and it cost $20,000 to clean up the mess.

While they were cleaning up one mess, my brothers wisely decided to clean up the other—the laxities which had besmirched the reputation of their establishment. They previously had hired a talented makeup woman named Ola Carroll who, they discov-

*The Westmore brothers at one of their lavish
Christmas parties at The House of Westmore.
From left: standing, Bud, Perc, Ern, Mont, Wally;
kneeling, myself and Mont, Jr.*

Ola Carroll applying makeup to starlet
Shirley Deane at The House of Westmore about 1938.

ered, also had extraordinary business and disciplinary talents. They made Ola both manager and housemother of the salon. She took over with a vengeance and put an immediate halt to any and all extracurricular activities not having to do with the business of beauty. Bouillon and hot tea replaced the free wines and other alcoholic beverages; the most daring thing she permitted behind closed booth doors was to let a woman seer named Louise Lockridge come in, by appointment, to tell customers their fortunes.

Ola was in her early thirties then, blond and as beautiful as any of the movie stars who patronized the salon. She had a great influence on my brothers, especially Perc, whose profligacy, along with Ern's, nearly bankrupted the salon in its first two years. Wally kept aloof from the family operation, as usual, and only was worried about having made a bad investment; Mont was too busy with Selznick to get involved.

Perc and Ern, however, kept spending their shares of the profits so wildly that the entire enterprise was endangered. They paid $35,000 in cash for a 65-foot yacht called the "Minx," which they rarely, if ever, used. They bought their wives and betweenwife lady friends mink coats, emeralds, and rubies. Although he seldom went to the track, Perc played the horses with relentless inefficiency, making his bookie a rich man. (The one time he got lucky, he won $30,000 on a horse via a tip from an associate of gangster Mickey Cohen. Out of that windfall, he paid back Kay Francis the $25,000 he had borrowed from her to open the salon; then he bet the rest of the money on another and lost it, plus $10,000 more.) Ern mainly was drinking his share, paying out vast sums for alimony to his two ex-wives, and supporting maybe half the hookers and bartenders in Hollywood. In desperation, Ola finally persuaded Perc to hire a business manager to come into The House of Westmore. After the business manager's first appalled examination of the nearly bankrupt state of the seemingly thriving salon, he induced the brothers to sell the retail cosmetics line outright, along with the Gordon Street factory, and agree to allow the Westmore name to continue to be used on the products. (An inexpensive line of Westmore cosmetics is still marketed in variety chain stores such as Woolworth and Kress.) Next, the efficiency expert sold minority blocks of stock in The House of Westmore to wealthy people, mainly from the movie industry, with my brothers still owning more than enough shares to retain solid control. And he tried, but failed, to put Ern and Perc on stringent personal budgets. They still could not or would not comprehend that the Niagara of money pouring into the shop, plus the steadily increasing income from their studio positions, might cease. All Perc needed to see was that the salon was back on an ever-increasing cycle of profitability. His life-style, and Ern's, continued unchanged.

Every year at Christmas, for example, The House of Westmore gave a lavish catered party—costing thousands—for the employees and their families. It was always a raucous, no-holds-barred affair. One such party stands out in my mind. Perc was in love with Ola and she with him, though neither acknowledged it for sometime thereafter. He was soon to divorce second wife Gloria Dickson in the coming year, 1940. Perc was dancing with Ola when Gloria suddenly smashed her highball glass and jammed the sharp edges into Perc's face. As I watched the blood pour down Perc's cheeks, I recalled hearing about a similar incident between George and my mother, Ada, and I couldn't help thinking that the Westmores seemed to repeat their own history.

9

THE first fissure in the façade of The House of Westmore came with the stunning and unexpected defection of Ern.
This most sensitive brother finally began to disintegrate in 1937
under the pressures of alcoholism and the breakup of his second
marriage to Ethelyne Claire, during which he made his first attempt at suicide by wrist-slashing. When that didn't work, he
pulled himself together for a while and somehow managed to
keep functioning as head of the makeup department at 20th Century-Fox. His innate talent preserved his job despite lost weekends
and even entire lost weeks. The studio needed him, so they put up
with his lapses. Even drunk, he was better than practically any
other makeup man in the business sober. The same was true of his
work at The House of Westmore.

Then came his second suicide attempt, in which I became involved—not a pleasant experience for a high school freshman. It
began when Ern was trying to drive home from a night of revelry
at W. C. Fields's house. Without even knowing it, he sideswiped
an entire row of parked cars and was arrested as a hit-and-run
drunk driver. Wally had to go downtown to the city jail to bail
him out.

When he was released, Ern refused to go either to Wally's
house or to his own. Instead he checked into a tenth-floor room at
the Hollywood Plaza Hotel. Wally had to get back to Paramount,
but he was terribly worried about Ern's mental condition, so he

called Mont's house. I was the only one there because it was Washington's Birthday and I was home from school. The other kids were shopping with Edith. Wally told me to get down to the Hollywood Plaza immediately to make sure that Ern was all right.

I had no way to travel the two miles except on my bicycle. By the time I arrived, Ern had managed to order more drinks from room service and was in terrible shape. When I walked into the room, he glared at me and told me I was interrupting something. I didn't know what that something was, but I felt it was going to be bad. I was frightened and decided that the best thing to do was to keep him talking. Ern poured out his problems to me, and I answered as best as I could with my fifteen-year-old understanding of such complex matters. Finally Ern got to the point. He said over and over again that he was going to jump out the window and kill himself. I was desperately trying to figure out what to do, and perhaps instinct caused me to hit on the right antidote. I walked over to the window and called his bluff, reasoning that the shock of it would maybe sober him down. I flung open the window and said, "You're my brother and I love you, but if that's what you really want to do, go ahead. Jump." The strategy worked. Ern collapsed on the bed crying. I finally managed to get him to Mont's house in a taxi. He went to sleep and didn't remember a thing in the morning.

During Ern's diatribe in the hotel room, I got some idea of how deep-rooted his problems were. He kept talking about George and Perc as if they were the same authoritarian person. Not quite understanding the psychological complexities of this puzzle, I discussed it with Mont, who explained how my father had encouraged and fostered a bitter, often vicious competition between his mirror-image twins when they were youngsters. Perc was the strong one and pleased my father by casting himself in his image; Ern, weaker-willed, fell behind in the competition. Perc loved the challenge; Ern hated it, hated my father for forcing the rivalry, and transferred his hatred to Perc, who took over as head of the family after my father's death. The fights between the twins became so corrosive they often wouldn't speak to one another for months at a time.

125

The battles mainly were instigated by Perc. He was jealous of Ern because, while he struggled and studied and battled to be the best in the business, Ern's natural ability was so great that makeup miracles were easy for him. For example, Ern's highly acclaimed work in 1936 in a single picture, the aging of Sam Jaffe and Margo in *Lost Horizon*, eclipsed anything Perc had done that year.

Also, Perc was a moralist and the self-appointed guardian of the family reputation. Whenever he learned of Ern's more spectacular binges with John Barrymore or W. C. Fields or Errol Flynn, he'd bitterly castigate Ern for dragging the name of Westmore in the mud. Ern would just laugh and go out and punish Perc with more drinking—indirectly punishing my dead father as well. Curiously, Perc and Ern would both undergo periods of guilt for their actions toward one another, and there were interludes of genuine fraternal warmth between them.

One such interlude was shattered when Ern, again driving while drunk, struck a newsboy with his car while the youngster was in a pedestrian crosswalk. Luckily, the boy suffered only minor injuries, but Ern's driver's license was permanently revoked by the Department of Motor Vehicles (he never drove again) and he was given a suspended six-month jail sentence. Perc's inevitable diatribe over these events caused Ern, now totally out of control, to do something that can only be described as irrational. He sold his shares in The House of Westmore to the Max Factor organization, apparently believing that his defection would give majority control to the non-Westmore stockholders and thus bring down Perc as the head of the operation. Fortunately for the family, his mathematics were incorrect. More than fifty-one percent still remained in Westmore hands.

Ern sulked for a while, inevitably lost his job at 20th Century-Fox, and suddenly took off for Europe in January 1939. Using the money he had realized from the sale of his stock, he launched lavish Ern Westmore salons in London and Paris, both patterned after The House of Westmore in Hollywood. His two new salons had barely opened their doors, however, when World War II erupted in September. Ern fled for home on the S.S. *Presi-*

dent Harding. Not only had he run out of money and backers, but as a British subject—he had never bothered to take out U.S. citizenship papers—he could have been drafted for military service in His Majesty's Royal Army.

It took a long time for Perc to forgive Ern for his treason to The House of Westmore, but as always in their hot-and-cold relationship, he eventually did. He and Wally got journeyman makeup jobs for Ern at various studios and even allowed him to work occasionally at The House of Westmore, as he dried out and began to move back up again to the top of our family's profession.

That period, 1939–1940, was a bad one for me personally. I dearly loved Mont, in whose house I now had lived contentedly for five years, and it pained me to see what was happening to this kind, decent man. I'd come home from my after-school duties at the booming House of Westmore (for which co-owner Mont had no time at all) and watch him struggling to the point of exhaustion over the mounds of paperwork he had brought from his job as head of the makeup department at Selznick-International.

David O. Selznick had observed Mont's fine work with Clark Gable and Charles Laughton on *Mutiny on the Bounty* at MGM, and when the dynamic executive left Metro to found his own studio, he had induced Mont to give up his carefree and successful free-lance career to become his chief makeup executive. It turned out to be a bone-crushing job for Mont. He found himself working on three difficult pictures at once: *Rebecca* with Laurence Olivier and Joan Fontaine, *Intermezzo* with Ingrid Bergman and Leslie Howard, and *Gone With the Wind* with Clark Gable, Vivien Leigh, and a cast of thousands. All three films have become classics —and, in our profession, lasting tributes to Mont's makeup wizardry.

The problem during the preparation and production of the pictures was that Mont and Selznick were two hard-nosed perfectionists who simply did not get along. In temperament, Selznick was the direct antithesis of Mont. It was the producer's nature to badger, belittle, and berate his employees. Obviously there were those who withstood the now-famous torrent of Selznick memos (some of which ran to ninety or more pages), but my sensitive, inarticulate eldest brother suffered under the unceasing barrage. Edith begged him to quit, but of course he refused to do so. And in a perverse way he had a profound respect for Selznick's passionate attention to every detail in a film. Night after night Mont would study the communiqués he had brought home from the studio. The famous makeup artist Ben Nye, who trained under Mont and later became head of the 20th Century-Fox makeup department, recently told me that most of those memos to Mont were outrageous, blaming him for foul-ups that had nothing to do with Mont or his forty assistants. But my brother never shrugged them off, as did more hardened souls such as Alfred Hitchcock. At home I'd watch him puzzle over them, sometimes writing out an answer, sometimes tearing them up with uncharacteristic fury. One memorandum I remember in particular was about Ingrid Bergman, whom Selznick had imported from Sweden to star in his version of *Intermezzo*. It said something like, "Monty, I have just learned that Bergman is 69½ inches high. Could she possibly be? And is there any makeup you can use to make her look shorter?"

Mont's neatly typed reply said, "Mr. Selznick: No."

When Mont was doing Joan Fontaine's makeup for her test as Scarlett O'Hara in *Gone With the Wind*, one of the producer's memos said, "You have got those damnable false eyelashes on Miss Fontaine and they stick out like multi-antlers on a freak elk. Further, there were no false eyelashes during the Civil War. Take them off."

Again Mont's reply was brief. "Those eyelashes are," he wrote, "Miss Fontaine's *own* lashes."

During Mont's years with Selznick, there was hardly a night when the telephone didn't wake him. Since there was an extension phone in my room, I'd try to get it on the first ring, but Mont was so conditioned to the disturbance that he usually answered anyway. Eavesdropping once, I heard Selznick's studied voice. "Monty," he began (he always called him Monty), "I hope I'm not disturbing you."

Mont said, "Why, no, Mr. Selznick, it's only three in the morning. What would make you think you were disturbing me?"

That particular call was again about Joan Fontaine's eyelashes. Now she was starring in *Rebecca*. Said Selznick, "I was just running today's rushes and I *still* don't like Joan's lashes. Can't you trim them a little?"

Mont said, "You want someone's natural and beautiful lashes trimmed, cut 'em yourself." And he smashed down the phone so hard my ears rang. So must Selznick's. His retaliatory memo on the subject of Joan Fontaine read, in part:

> Even if they are her own eyelashes, they are made up in such a fashion as to look fake, and her eyebrows are all plucked out to a point at the end, so that the whole idea of this sweet young girl being at Manderley fighting a memory of the sophisticated Rebecca is materially hurt. Please correct this for the future, and immediately. And what can I do to get you makeup men to throw away your kits and your tweezers? The public is so far ahead of you all and is so sick of your makeup that you are managing to contribute to the destruction of stars.

Principal photography began on *Gone With the Wind* in December of 1938. Mont, however, had been at work on the picture for nearly a year, doing filmed makeup tests of almost every actress in the business, plus some unknowns uncovered in a publicity-oriented worldwide "search." He told me Vivien Leigh said that by the time she got around to putting on the Scarlett O'Hara costume for her test, so many actresses had tried it on it was still warm. Mont also filled me in on the casting of Clark Gable, obtained on loan-out from MGM under rather unique circumstances. Gable's second wife, Ria Langham, had finally agreed to let him divorce her so that he could marry his long-time love, Carole Lombard. But Ria was asking for a huge monetary settlement of $286,000, which Gable didn't have. Selznick, knowing Gable's tremendous box-office magnetism, accepted a deal proposed by his wily father-in-law, Louis B. Mayer: Gable would agree to do the film only if part of the loan-out fee would be applied to meeting

Ria Langham's demands. MGM, in return for putting up less than half of the financing of the picture, would receive full distribution rights and 50 percent of the profits.

But the settling of the vexing casting problems did not stop the avalanche of memos and nocturnal phone calls from Selznick to Mont. Selznick even revived the disproved old saw about Gable's ears being too big. He complained that Hattie McDaniel "looked too dark," that Butterfly McQueen "looked too shiny," that Leslie Howard "looked too Jewish." The biggest flap came over the color of Vivien Leigh's eyes. In Margaret Mitchell's book, Scarlett O'Hara's eyes were characterized as green. Selznick became obsessive over that description. He wrote memo after memo to Mont, raging that in various scenes Miss Leigh's eyes were not green but "violet, gray, blue, tan, and nearly every other color in the spectrum."

Mont finally took care of that problem with the help of the wardrobe department. He arranged for Vivien to wear colors that would highlight the green in her multi-hued hazel eyes, and he supplemented the effect by an extravagant use of green eye shadow. Selznick never could figure out how Mont wrought the Miracle of the Green Eyes.

On December 15, 1939, *Gone With the Wind* premiered in Atlanta, Georgia. Four months later, in April of 1940, Mont entered Hollywood Hospital for a simple tonsilectomy but died there of a heart attack following the surgery. In an interview with the Hearst newspapers, Mont's physician, Dr. William Branch, was quoted as saying, "Westmore had been in a weakened condition for some time as a result of his arduous work in charge of the makeup of the stars in *Gone With the Wind*."

Mont was only thirty-seven years old. He was buried at Forest Lawn, not far from our father and mother, and over a thousand people attended the services. Mont's was the most lavish funeral for a Westmore before or since, probably because he was the most noncontroversial and best liked of the brothers. The cortège was thronged with stars, directors, producers. David O. Selznick was not, however, among them. My brothers all were genuinely stricken and stood together again at the gravesite. I tried to control my own grief by helping Mont, Jr., support and console Edith (her other two sons, Marvin and Michael, were still little boys). When we got home after the funeral, we two seventeen-year-olds took over and tried to fill in for Mont as heads of the household.

10

MY eighteenth year was a blur of schoolwork, graduation, helping Edith and my three nephews recover from the shock of Mont's death, and more work at The House of Westmore. Through my contacts with my surviving brothers at the salon, I realized how deeply affected they were by Mont's tragic and sudden demise. Subdued and frightened, they all went to their doctors for physical examinations and learned that there was a congenital heart weakness, undoubtedly inherited from our mother. They tried to slow down their activities.

At Paramount, Wally began to devote himself mainly to his administrative duties and hired more assistants for the grueling creative work. He spent more time with his wife, Edwina, and their two children. At Warner Brothers, Perc, too, became more of an administrator than a creator; at The House of Westmore he gave increased authority to the bright and tough Ola Carroll. Everyone expected him to marry Ola. Instead, he briefly took the more placid Julietta Novis (divorced from actor-singer Donald Novis) as his third wife in 1941. Then, in 1942, he married wife number four, Maggie Donovan, a fiery redhead who reminded me in appearance of my stepmother, Anita. Ola married someone else.

Ern, temporarily off the bottle, continued his comeback as a free-lancer in demand at many studios and was also active in the marital market. We could hardly believe it in 1940 when Ern's third wife turned out to be no less than Peggy Kent, referred to in the newspapers as "the merry madcap daughter of Sidney Kent, operating head of 20th Century-Fox in New York." Though Ern, in effect, had married his former boss's daughter, the mating did not restore him to the executive job he had lost at 20th before his precipitous flight to Europe. In any event, the marriage hardly lasted long enough for any such result. It was over in five months and then, in 1941, Ern married a beautiful Busby Berkeley dancer named Betty Harron. She was his fourth and last wife, and she patiently lived with him through all his further tribulations over the next twenty-seven years.

Handsome Bud, twenty-three years old in 1941, married his second movie star, Rosemary Lane. This relationship was much more permanent than his tempestuous three-month first marriage to Martha Raye, and Bud and Rosemary soon had a darling little daughter named Bridget. Bud by now had graduated from his apprenticeship under Wally at Paramount and was a full-fledged makeup artist with Guy Pierce, who had succeeded Ern as head of the department at 20th Century-Fox.

After my graduation from Hollywood High School, it was my turn to become a licensed apprentice, also under Wally at Paramount, on the Dorothy Lamour picture *Beyond the Blue Horizon*. It was in that movie that I had my mortifying run-in with Muck the chimp. With my banishment as Muck's makeup artist and my daily ascent up a ladder to paint elephants, I had a wonderful bird's-eye view of the entire set. From my vantage point I witnessed a scene which helped salve my own embarrassment.

The makeup man for both Miss Lamour and her co-star, comedian Jack Haley, was Harry Ray, one of the all-time great makeup artists. After I had goofed so badly with Muck, Wally asked him to help out with the nonhumans in the cast. Harry's new star was Sylvia, and she was a crocodile.

In the script the scene called for Haley, playing an explorer in the wilds of the jungle, to come to a stream, see a log on the bank, and say, "My feet are killing me. I'll just rest them here on this log for a while." The log, of course, was Sylvia. When Haley's feet touched her, she was supposed to give a sudden lunge, tumbling Haley into the water. Sylvia was gently tranquilized, but Haley understandably was worried about Sylvia opening her mouth and having him for lunch.

To soothe Haley, Harry had the special-effects man tie the animal's mouth shut. The director, Al Santell, called for action, Haley said his lines and put his feet on Sylvia's back—and absolutely nothing happened. Sylvia just lay there, half stoned and happy. So Santell told Ray to untie her jaws; maybe she was being inhibited by having her mouth tied. Harry wasn't happy about messing around with Sylvia's mouth, but he and the special-effects man obeyed. They did the scene over. Again, nothing happened. Sylvia was now sound asleep.

An electrician came by and said, "I know how to fix this little lady. I'll rig an electric charge under her tail, and then, when you're ready, I'll press down on my plunger, and I guarantee Sylvia will move."

There was no SPCA member on hand to prevent what might be construed as cruelty to an animal, and Harry told the electrician he thought that was a splendid idea. However, the electrician did suggest that Harry again have Sylvia's mouth tied shut. This time Ray ordered the special-effects man to use a thin piece of wire to do the job. Everyone waited while the electrician did whatever it was electricians do to rig an electric charge under a crocodile's tail. When he announced he was ready, Al Santell called for quiet, then, "Action!"

Haley, by now fairly blasé about old Sylvia, said his lines, put his feet on her back, and the electrician pressed his plunger. Sylvia shot at least ten feet into the air and snapped the wire around her jaw, which hit Jack right in the mouth. Instead of tumbling *into* the stream, Haley was propelled over the water and landed upside down on his head in our phony jungle foliage.

After her magnificent performance, Sylvia went back to sleep, Santell got a much better scene than he'd planned, and Harry Ray got an extra workout. For the rest of the picture, he had one hell of a time keeping Haley's facial bruises covered with makeup.

Directly after the movie was completed, Harry Ray enlisted

in the Navy. World War II was raging, and Harry said he could not be electrifying a crocodile's tail while everyone else he knew was entering the service. When the recruiter asked what his profession was, he was too embarrassed to say he was a makeup artist, so he said, "I'm in powder." The Navy put him to work loading bags of black-powder explosives.

Before *I* made the grand gesture, I needed some money to tide me over, so for two months I worked at the Douglas Aircraft plant. Then I enlisted in the Coast Guard. Ern, Perc, and Wally all had had boats—or yachts—on which I was allowed to crew from time to time, so I was an accomplished sailor by then. However, I did not count on climbing up a slippery ladder and falling through a hatch. I smashed my coccyx and had three operations at the Long Beach Naval Hospital. The place reminded me of all my years in military schools and I was miserable and unhappy.

I had been a patient for several months when the USO came to visit. I had been napping on my belly when I felt a light touch on my shoulder. Kay Francis was standing by my bed saying, "Frank? Frank Westmore? Is it really you?" Not too many weeks later a Coast Guard commander summoned me to his office. I'll never know how or why it happened, but the commander informed me I had been assigned as chief makeup artist for *Tars and Spars*, the Coast Guard's touring serviceman's show for civilian audiences—similar to *This Is the Army* and the Air Corps' *Winged Victory*. As we moved from city to city, I seemed to be the one who was getting more and more publicity. The stars of the show, Coast Guardsmen Victor Mature, Gower Champion, and Sid Caesar, shared honors with me and my makeup case. Westmore was a magic name. Every woman wanted to look like Ann Sheridan or Claudette Colbert or Kay Francis. They all thought I could tell them, or show them how to put on their makeup and achieve instant beauty, and they swarmed to the radio stations, newspaper offices, and shopping plazas where we did preshow publicity to attract audiences to *Tars and Spars*. I still have the newspaper clippings of that tour; one of the picture captions calls me "the youngest brother of the famous Westmore family of makeup artists, who for years have been plying their art in Hollywood, making the cinema lovelies appear a lot lovelier than they really are."

I plied my art all over the United States, gaining experience and stature as a war hero as *Tars and Spars* gained in reputation. Falling down the hatch gradually became translated in the newspapers as "wounded while doing anti-submarine patrol." My rank as Boatswain, Second Class, provided me with enough clout and money to spend all I wanted on the hundreds of girls I met and made up as we toured. For almost two years "the youngest brother of the famous Westmore family" became one of the most publicized. I began to think there was something in a name after all. Yet I found that what I really wanted was to be up there on the stage with Vic Mature and the other performers. Once again I experienced the same teen-age yearnings to be an actor I had felt when I dabbled with painting "native" extras for Ern in *Elephant Boy* in 1937.

For reasons of age and health, no Westmore brother (except for myself and Bud, also a Coast Guardsman) devoted much time to military service. Wally escaped the draft simply because he had a draft number which never came up for men of his age with two children. In one of those strange quirks of the Selective Service System, Ern was deferred in 1942 because of his age (thirty-eight), while the Army grabbed his twin, Perc, born on exactly the same day. Perc's experience in uniform was disastrous for both him and the War Department. He spent all his time in military hospitals with both real and psychosomatic ailments—at considerable cost to the taxpayers—and he and the Army parted company in less than six months via a medical discharge for, of all things, sinusitis.

In or out of uniform, however, the Westmores all did their specialized bit for the war effort. The House of Westmore threw open its doors to Wacs, Waves, and Spars, giving them beauty treatments and makeup advice for free. Also, Wally, Ern, and Perc staged a permanent makeup show at the USO's Hollywood Canteen. One or the other of them would be there every night (Perc more than the others), delighting the military audience by making up stars to look like other stars. On one still-talked-about evening, Perc converted Mickey Rooney into a miniature Clark Gable, and Bette Davis into Bela Lugosi as Dracula.

In addition, Perc and Ern used the Canteen to educate the masses to their seven-basic-face-shape concept. They would illustrate—and entertain—by calling servicewomen and the wives and girl friends of servicemen to the stage as models for their lectures. Sometimes a famous movie star with the same face shape would be worked on, side by side with the delighted "model." It always made a great show. I still remember Perc and Ern's characterizations of the seven face shapes and their tips for enhancing them:

THE ROUND FACE (*Olivia de Havilland*). Round hairline, round chin line. *Don't* use a straight eyebrow line. *Don't* slick the hair back severely off the forehead. *Don't* put rouge on in a circle. *Don't* overemphasize your mouth with your lipstick. *Do* wear your hair waved softly off the forehead. *Do* arch your eyebrows slightly. *Do* rouge only the outer portion of the cheek to shade the jaw. *Do* make up your mouth delicately but as wide as possible.

THE SQUARE FACE (*Joan Blondell*). Straight hairline, square jawline. *Don't* pull hair back tightly at the temples. *Don't* apply rouge in a straight manner, and never put any color on your chin. *Don't* wear sharply arched eyebrows. *Don't* make up your mouth in an extreme arch or make the lower lip too full. *Do* dress hair softly at the sides to minimize the sharp angle of the jaw. *Do* place your rouge back toward the ear and down the jawline. *Do* use your natural eyebrow line arched only slightly. *Do* make up your mouth with upward curves at the corners.

THE OVAL FACE (*Janet Gaynor*). Forehead is slightly wider than chin. *Don't* wear bangs. *Don't* wear any rouge if your hair and eyes are dark. *Don't* arch your eyebrows too high. *Don't* use a heavy, dark shade of lipstick. *Do* draw the hair back from your forehead. *Do* use rouge (if your hair is fair), but blend it toward the temple in a tricircular field. *Do* start your natural eyebrow on a line directly above the inside corner of the eye. *Do* make up the mouth full and follow your natural lip line with a softly colored lipstick.

THE OBLONG FACE (*Loretta Young*). Long narrow face with hollow cheeks. *Don't* dress your hair high on your head.

Don't bring rouge in too close to your nose or far out on the sides of the face. *Don't* arch your eyebrows too high. *Don't* use eye shadow if you have deep-set eyes. *Don't* widen your mouth too much or attempt a cupid's bow. *Do* get width into your face by fluffing hair at the sides of the face, or full behind the ears. *Do* use the lightest possible rouge for your coloring in a carefully blended circle in the center of your cheeks. *Do* use your natural eyebrow line and do not extend it. *Do* make your lower lip full at the corners with your lipstick.

THE TRIANGLE FACE (*Alice Faye*). Narrow forehead, wide jaw and chin line. *Don't* cover the forehead with even a suggestion of bangs. *Don't* use heavy rouge. *Don't* use a straight line for your eyebrows, or carry eyebrow line too far out on the temple. *Don't* arch the upper lip above its natural outline. *Do* brush the hair back from the temples to create the illusion of width in the forehead. *Do* apply rouge in a modified triangle shading to the temple and under the center of the jawline. *Do* arch your eyebrows only slightly. *Do* create a natural-looking wide mouth to reduce the apparent width of the jawline.

THE INVERTED TRIANGLE FACE (*Geraldine Fitzgerald*). Wide forehead, narrow chin line. *Don't* draw the hair back tightly or too snugly above the ears. *Don't* carry your rouge down the jawline or too far toward the center of the lower cheek. *Don't* raise the eyebrows or extend them or use an angular eyebrow. *Don't* use a wide mouth or make the lower lip too square. *Do* dress your hair in an easy effect on top, beginning the fullness at a point above the ears. *Do* place your rouge on the highest point of the cheekbone. *Do* keep your eyebrows natural and not thin. *Do* arch your mouth slightly, but don't widen the corners.

THE DIAMOND FACE (*Ann Blyth*). Narrow forehead, broad jawline, narrow chin. *Don't* have the fullness of your hair at the cheekbones. *Don't* use rouge on the lower part of your face. *Don't* use angular eyebrows or extend them too far out on the temple. *Don't* use a wide, full lip makeup, or a straight line. *Do* keep the fullness of the hair above and below the ears, and dress the hair snugly at the cheek line. *Do* apply your rouge at the highest point of the broad cheekbone, blending carefully in a circular field. *Do* arch the brows slightly. *Do* use a natural, lightly colored lip makeup, not too wide, and gently curved.

Since more sophisticated cosmetics still had not been invented in the 1940s, my brothers used rouge for shadowing. Today, merely by substituting the word "blusher" for "rouge," or by using a darker shade of makeup foundation instead of rouge, these same seven-basic-face-shape tenets still apply. I use them, and so do all other modern-day makeup artists.

It was these fundamental teachings of my brothers that got me through my Coast Guard stint as makeup man to the cast of *Tars and Spars*. It was about all I knew, having learned it daily at The House of Westmore. Not much more was required to enhance the appearance of attractive young people performing on a stage. But it was different when we got to Hollywood in 1945 to make the film version of the show at Columbia Pictures. After all, I had done only minor makeup work in just two pictures, and I underwent sudden ego deflation at the realization of how little I actually knew about the complex scientific aspects of the movie makeup art. I was gloomily thinking about my deficiencies and wondering if the Coast Guard would find out and transfer me, when I heard a newscaster announce on the radio that the Japanese had surrendered. I finished the picture with the help of the pros at the studio who were friends of my brothers, and I got my discharge from the Coast Guard. Although I still harbored acting ambitions, there was no question in my brothers' minds as to what my first civilian job would be. I went back to Paramount again as one of Wally's apprentices.

My first assignment was on a Cecil B. DeMille epic called *Unconquered*. While I was puttering around Wally's department waiting for the picture to get under way, I met Betty Hutton, then a big Paramount star, and we quickly became good friends. Betty was a warmhearted girl. One thing led to another, and in one of our conversations in the studio commissary I blurted out that I was torn by my hidden desire to be an actor.

I reported to the set of *Unconquered* on the first day of shooting, makeup box in hand. I was dazzled by the array of stars assembled. There were Gary Cooper and Paulette Goddard; Boris Karloff, wandering around looking for a chair to sit on; Ward Bond, Cecil Kellaway, Sir C. Aubrey Smith. I was also dazzled by DeMille. It was the first time I had met him.

Unknown to me, Betty had told DeMille about my acting ambitions and begged him to give me a screen test. She even offered to be in the test with me. But after we had talked together on the set, DeMille told me, "I don't need to run a film test on you. Your looks are just right for the part of the young lieutenant. It's a week or ten days' work without a lot of dialogue. If you do it well, I'll sign you to a standard seven-year contract." My role in *Unconquered* was to begin a few weeks after principal photography got started. Meanwhile DeMille wanted me to continue doing makeup.

After C.B. offered me the acting job, I was so excited I spent the rest of that day dropping powder puffs and generally forgetting everything I ever had learned about makeup. I couldn't wait until I could get off the set and back to Wally's office to give him the news. When I finally saw him, he was livid with anger.

"How dare you impose on *my* friendship with DeMille?" he yelled. "And how dare you decide to be an actor? You're a Westmore!"

"Damn right I am," I yelled back at him. "An *acting* Westmore!"

That very night, while I still was savoring my victory, the doorbell rang. In came Wally, Perc, Ern, and Bud. The Westmore cabal was again in session. Perc was the spokesman. First he tried sweet reason. "A lot of actors are out of work, Frank, and a lot more are coming out of the service to resume where they left off. You wouldn't want to be just another out-of-work actor, would you?"

I tried sweet reasonableness right back. "Mr. DeMille is going to give me a seven-year contract," I said. "I'll take my chances, because I think I can be a good actor."

When he delivered the coup de grace, Perc did it with the subtlety of a coyote cornering a jackrabbit. "All right," he shouted, "go ahead and be a goddamned actor, you ungrateful little son of a bitch! You *were* part of the Westmore Dynasty. Now just forget that you have any family at all. Take a good long look at us, because this is the last time you'll ever see us again!" And all four brothers marched out, slamming the door.

The next morning I went back to the set of *Unconquered*, again with makeup box in hand. I sighed as I thanked Mr. DeMille for his offer but told him I couldn't accept. Rightly or wrongly, I had made an irrevocable decision.

I took my place in the Westmore Dynasty.

THE crucial decision having been made, there was much for me to learn. Most important of all was the realization that being a Westmore makeup specialist was a considerably more elevated profession than the simple cosmetician's craft of daubing powder and color on faces, as I had done in the Coast Guard. All the Westmores were a unique combination of sculptor, painter, researcher, anthropologist, and creative theoretician—sometimes even engineer and psychologist.

As I progressed in my apprenticeship at Paramount, I found there was no better textbook example of the blending of all these scholarly skills than Wally's pioneering artistry with Barbara Stanwyck in *The Great Man's Lady* in 1942.

Barbara was only thirty-four years old then, but in the film she played a hundred-year-old matriarch recalling her life in flashbacks. Before production began, she had a long argument with Wally. To shorten the number of hours she knew she would have to spend in the makeup department every morning, she suggested a return to the old greasepaint technique then still used on the stage.

Wally explained to her that a face made ancient with greasepaint would look credible to audiences sitting twenty-five to a hundred feet away in a live theater, but in huge close-ups on the screen, with a magnification of her face of perhaps two hundred times, she'd look like a clown. Each line would show up for what it was: a streak of paint, not a wrinkle. He told her that our father,

George, had done away with greasepaint as far back as 1917. Barbara was finally convinced. So Wally began the laborious process of not only making her *look* old but also making her *feel* old—from top to bottom, inside and out.

First, Wally and Barbara went on an excursion to the Masonic Old Ladies' Home in Santa Monica. On the way he told her what to look for—how, for instance, an elderly woman doesn't just sit down in a chair the way other people do. She will first hold onto the chair, to steady herself, and then lower herself into it with her back and legs bending almost simultaneously. She will almost always choose a straight chair, not a long or overstuffed couch from which she cannot rise by herself. Once at the home, both Barbara and Wally listened carefully to the speech inflections of the old ladies and carefully studied their lurching gait.

Back at the studio, Wally sketched a kind of harness for Barbara to wear and the wardrobe department made it—a complicated series of leather straps which were connected around her legs just below the knees. These straps were hooked to a leather girdle around her waist. The harness prevented Barbara from moving freely because she couldn't straighten her legs when she stood up. Wally added a small rubber hump between her shoulder blades which forced her head forward.

He was truly inspired when it came to aging Barbara's hands. He had her curl her hands into fists and then smeared the tops with spirit gum, over which he placed ordinary toilet paper, crumpling the tissue as he applied it. When the spirit gum dried, he lightly stippled pancake makeup on the toilet paper with a sponge, using several different shades to achieve a mottled color. Since the picture was in black and white, he drew veins on the paper with a gray pencil. When Barbara opened her hands, there was the loose, discolored skin of a hundred-year-old crone.

For her face makeup, Wally elected to use foam rubber instead of the then more commonly used liquid rubber, which he considered too opaque and too inflexible. He was one of the first—if not the first—to discover that if liquid rubber is whipped with an electric eggbeater, it comes out frothy and light and really looks like skin. He took the obligatory plaster-of-Paris face mold of Barbara

and, using modeling wax, sculpted onto it all the old-age characteristics, including great wattles under the chin. Then he made a
mask of the sculpture, using the whipped foam rubber, which he
baked in a hot oven for six hours. He held his breath, he told me,
when finally he fitted the mask to Barbara's face. He told her to
smile. That was the crucial test. When the smile radiated naturally
through the rubber, he knew that the experiment was an indisputable success. Barbara looked at herself in the mirror and said
exultantly, "My God, I look just like an old tintype of my great-
grandmother."

The Great Man's Lady opened at the Paramount Theatre
in New York on April 30, 1942. The *New York Times* critic,
Theodore Strauss, was constrained to make a rare comment about
the importance of Wally's contribution to the credibility of an
otherwise not-so-credible film. "As an aged lady," Strauss wrote,
"Barbara Stanwyck does no violence to a marvelous makeup."

The 1940s saw similar peaks of artistry for all the Westmores.
The House of Westmore prospered as never before. Perc, at
Warner Brothers, contributed to the winning of Oscars by Jane
Wyman for *Johnny Belinda* and by Joan Crawford for *Mildred
Pierce.* My brothers even stopped marrying and divorcing and re-
mained with the same wives throughout the decade. Bud had pro-
gressed to the point where he was hired by a small new studio,
Eagle-Lion, to become the head of its makeup department in 1946.
Ern, the family teacher, had now rebounded to the point where he
was working with James Cagney's company and other independent
producers. It was now just a matter of time, we all thought, until
Ern would be grabbed up by the next major studio that needed a
department head.

The studio was Universal. But we didn't count on Perc's deep-
seated resentment of his twin.

When Perc learned that Universal was about to hire Ern, he
phoned his brother and asked him out to dinner to celebrate. Ern
was pleased at Perc's solicitude after their many years of intermittent feuding and accepted, innocently unaware of what Perc

really had in mind. At dinner they chatted pleasantly about how Ern should handle the interview with Universal's studio head, William Goetz, the next morning. Ern drank very little at dinner, but Perc knew his brother's weakness. He insisted on one toast after another once they had finished dessert, and then, all night long, he dragged Ern from bar to bar throughout the Hollywood area. There wasn't a single after-hours club they didn't hit.

The result for Ern was calamitous. He showed up for his interview as drunk as he had been in the Barrymore days, just as Perc had planned. Needless to say, Ern did not get the job. At Perc's suggestion, Goetz, who still wanted a Westmore, hired the much younger and less experienced Bud. Ern recovered sufficiently to take over Bud's job as the head of the Eagle-Lion department for a few months, but his night on the town with Perc really marked the end of his comeback. Within a year he was out of the movie industry completely, though his personal tragedy still had twenty more years to play itself out.

It was Bud's turn to prove himself in the Westmore hierarchy, which now had an octopuslike grip on the makeup departments of four of Hollywood's seven major studios. Bud immediately proved that he was not just the handsomest of the brothers. He demonstrated that he had the administrative know-how of Wally, along with enough of the imaginative skill of Mont, Perc, and Ern, all of whom had trained him at one time or another. Bud never liked the routine makeup chores and relegated most of them to his subordinates. But just as he was fascinated with the intricacies of interior design in his personal life (he was a superb decorator), so was he fascinated with the scientific miracles he could fashion out of plaster, plastic, and rubber in the Universal makeup laboratory.

Bud's first big test came in 1948 when Universal threw a seemingly insoluble problem at him. He had to convert a beautiful young actress into a believable version of a fish—or, at least, a half fish. The actress was Ann Blyth, and the problem was hardly a matter of makeup per se. Bud used the essentials he had learned from our brothers, but at the other end of Miss Blyth. The film was *Mr. Peabody and the Mermaid*. Ann played the part of Lenore the Mermaid, who suddenly turns up in the bottom of the swimming pool of a stuffy Boston Brahmin, marvelously portrayed by William Powell. In trying to determine just what a mermaid really looked like, Bud discovered that mermaid sightings were rare indeed. Mainly they were seen by fishermen returning to land with their boats loaded with empty beer bottles. Bud consulted an ichthyologist, who told him that, in ancient times, sailors who had spent years on end aboard their ships fantasized so much about women that they saw mermaids sunning on rocks when they really were looking at manatees, or sea cows, which are large relatives of the seal. Thus relieved of the need for scientific accuracy, Bud went to an aquarium, sketched the tail of a fish, added a few fancy fins of his own, and was ready to cast the first plaster-of-Paris mold of the lower torso of Miss Blyth.

Bud told me that when Ann arrived in his laboratory at five one morning for her first fitting she seemed unduly nervous. The tail problems began when the actress informed him that just three years before, after she had finished her role in *Mildred Pierce*, she had fallen off a toboggan and broken her back. She had spent an entire year in a stationary cast which extended from her neck to below her knees. Bud sent her home and devoted the remainder of the day to enlisting the services of two surgeons to stand by while he and Jack Kevan, his lab assistant, poured the heavy plaster.

The next morning, reassured by the presence of the doctors, Ann relaxed and lay on her stomach on a surgical table, wearing only a brassiere and a tiny pair of panties. Having first coated her legs, bottom, and waist with grease, Bud poured on the plaster. According to Ann, "The stuff got hotter, harder, and heavier, and I felt my back was cracking again." So eight hands—Bud's, Kevan's, and the doctors'—quickly pried her out of the not-yet-hardened mess. It fell apart and out went mold number one.

Two days and three molds later, using less and less plaster, Bud finally had a perfect impression of his star's nether regions. From the plaster impression, he cast an exact sculpture of Ann's legs and hips. By spraying and baking the sculpture with the same whipped foam rubber Wally had used on Barbara Stanwyck's face, Bud obtained a hollowed-out rubber coating which snugly fit Ann's lower half.

Then came the really tough, time-consuming part. Originally Bud had estimated that the tail would cost about $500 and take him three weeks to complete; instead, fourteen weeks and $18,000 were spent by the time he was finished. The tail hung on a hook in the lab, where Bud painstakingly shaped and reshaped the outsized fin by hand and individually carved thousands of fish scales. Then he made a slightly less detailed duplicate for Ann's stand-in.

Of course, Ann had to learn to swim with her new tail. On the Universal lot there's a huge water tank with outside portholes through which the cameramen can photograph underwater action. Every morning, after the three hours necessary to affix tail to girl, Ann, immobilized from the waist down and naturally unable to walk, would be carried to the tank by Bud and Jack Kevan and lowered gently into the water by a winch. At first she was suspended in the water near the top of the tank and just moved her body to cause the tail to swish back and forth. During all those harrowing days—for Ann—Bud refused to leave her. He constantly made adjustments to the tail as needed. Eventually she became a veritable Flipper in that tank, and Bud was free to go about other studio business—almost. Whenever Ann had to go to the bathroom, Bud was summoned. He spent a lot of time in various ladies' rooms around the lot, removing and then replacing Ann's tail. "Finally," Ann told me, "Bud forbade me to consume any liquids after eight o'clock the night before. That helped. For the last two months of shooting, I stayed firmly inside the tail for the entire day."

With Bud becoming more and more solidly established at Universal, my first choice was to work there with him after I finished my apprenticeship in 1947. As much as I admired the skills of my older brothers, Bud was closer to me in age, and, having grown up together, sharing the miseries of some of the same military schools, we spoke the same language. Nevertheless, whenever Perc called me from Warner Brothers, Wally from Paramount, or Ern from Eagle-Lion, I was always available to help out on their pictures. Now adequately trained, I did the makeup on Hedy Lamarr in *Let's Live a Little*, on Ginger Rogers in *Storm Warning*, on Barbara Stanwyck in *All I Desire*, on Marlene Dietrich in *Rancho Notorious*, among others. I had become a full-fledged member of the Makeup Artists Union, making upwards of $250 a week and on call for jobs at all studios in the industry. With my newfound affluence, I also fell into the marital trap that had ensnared Perc, Ern, and Bud in their early years. I married Fran Shore, whom I met while she was working as Diana Lynn's stand-in during the filming of *My Friend Irma* at Paramount. Fran was pretty, with ambitions to be an actress. Our relationship never worked out. We were married in November 1950 and divorced a few months later. I think my first venture into matrimony was simply because I was twenty-seven years old and afraid of being regarded as the old maid of the Westmores.

I was back to full-time concentration on my career, mostly under Bud at Universal, when one day Wally summoned me to Paramount "for ten days' work." I reluctantly went crosstown, hoping to finish up whatever minor chores Wally had in mind and then get back to Bud at Universal as soon as possible. It didn't turn out that way. Though I didn't know it, I too was about to make it as a Westmore.

Wally kept stalling me, giving me little to do during those ten days. That surprised me because the studio was bustling with activity. Cecil B. DeMille was preparing to go to Egypt to begin filming his remake of *The Ten Commandments*. I expected to help Wally stock his trunks and assemble the paraphernalia he needed to head the makeup staff for DeMille, as he had done on sixteen of the director's previous films and as Mont had done before him. Instead, Wally had little time for me. He seemed engrossed in his administrative duties and wasn't preparing for field duty at all.

On the afternoon of the tenth day, Wally nervously gathered me up and hustled me into DeMille's office. I still remember the old man sitting there, looking quietly amused. Wally said, "I appreciate it that you understand how my executive work here keeps me from making the trip to Egypt with you. But you wanted a Westmore.

You remember my kid brother, Frank. He's as good as the rest of us now."

"He'd better be," said Mr. DeMille, still smiling benevolently.

I nearly collapsed with an attack of combined anxiety and exhilaration, as I realized I was about to embark on one of the greatest adventures of my life.

12

ON October 14, 1954, I boarded a plane from Los Angeles to make the thirty-six-hour multiple-stop flight to Cairo. I didn't sleep at all during the grueling trip; every time I shut my eyes, I had a waking nightmare about the myriads of supplies I might have forgotten to send to Egypt. Since our production schedule indicated we would be spending more than $8,000 for every working hour, a mistake would be disaster. Mr. DeMille permitted absolutely no errors by anyone in his employ.

In the period between the conference I had had with DeMille in his Paramount Studios office and my actual departure, I was so busy ordering and shipping everything I thought we would need for the makeup department that I actually forgot that he would be there, too, realizing *his* greatest adventure. (For the 1923 version of *The Ten Commandments*, Paramount head Adolph Zukor wouldn't allow DeMille to go to Egypt because it would have been too expensive, and C.B. had had to built his version of ancient Egypt in Mexico.) But after that meeting, which Wally attended with me, my brother had warned me to expect a daily chewing-out by the old man, no matter how efficient I was.

Sitting on the Cairo-bound plane, all my youthful arrogance deserted me as I mentally recapped that day in DeMille's quarters. I hadn't seen DeMille in eight years, ever since *Unconquered* and my aborted acting career. He hadn't changed much. He was almost seventy-three years old, and the fringe of hair above his ears had gone from sandy to silver. He had been preparing *The Ten Commandments* for three years, and his face looked pinched with tension. Otherwise, his upper torso, developed from years of underwater diving, looked as powerful as ever. (Seated, DeMille looked as if he would be six feet tall, but he had short legs.) The only addition I noticed to the decoration of his Spartan working quarters was a replica of South Carolina's pre-Revolutionary War flag, the famous one with the coiled rattlesnake and the legend "Don't Tread on Me," a warning generally heeded by the Paramount brass.

He was seated behind an enormous cluttered desk, one corner of which seemed to sag under the weight of what looked like hundreds of Bibles. He handed one copy of the Old Testament to each of us and said, "I want you to read the Book of Exodus religiously." Then he permitted himself a small smile.

Neither Wally nor I said anything. We just stood there until he asked us to sit down. He indicated by an imperious wave of his hand that I was to take the chair near his desk. Wally sat behind me on a beat-up leather couch.

"So, young Frank, we are to be together again," DeMille began.

"Yes, sir," I said.

"Are you as good as your brothers?" he asked me.

"Yes, sir," I repeated. I knew from prior experience with him —and had heard the same thing from Mont and Wally—that the most disastrous way to answer one of DeMille's questions was to start by saying, "I think . . ." The old man didn't want you to think. He expected you to know.

He asked, "Remember on *Unconquered* when you suggested to me that the tips of the Indian feathers be dipped in red paint so they would photograph better?"

I was amazed that he remembered, although I shouldn't have been. He had a phenomenal memory, and he was taking the opportunity of reminding me of it. Before I had a chance to "Yes, sir" him again, he continued.

151

"We won't be concerning ourselves with feathers this time, young Frank. We will be working with thousands of people and thousands of animals under terribly adverse conditions." Then he asked me for a report of exactly what makeup and hair supplies I had packed.

Thank God I was prepared to answer. I had brought with me three large looseleaf notebooks filled with still pictures of every one of the two hundred and fifty people who were to have speaking parts in the movie. Also, I had a complete list of everything I had felt was needed for the makeup department, right down to how many bars of soap I'd sent.

It must have taken me an hour to read that list to him. He listened intently and interrupted me only once. "Three hundred and fifty Santa Claus beards," I had read. "Santa Claus beards?" he roared. "This is the Exodus, and there's no 'Ho, ho, ho' about it!"

Quickly I explained the term. It simply meant that the beards could be hooked on over an extra's ears with flexible wires, quickly and easily, and that this type of beard was to be used only on those far in the rear of the line of thousands. "Continue," he said.

When I had finished, DeMille rose, shook hands with Wally and me, and loaded us down with more Bibles, which he instructed us to distribute to anyone even remotely concerned with the production; then he said to me, "We shall meet soon at the Gates of Tanis." If I hadn't been staring at his stocky body, I would have sworn I had just heard the voice of God.

It was toward those DeMille-devised Gates of Tanis that I was hurtling en route to Cairo on the harrowing flight through darkness and light and numerous time zones. According to biblical history, C.B.'s gates were erected on the same spot as those built by Ramses II, about 2900 B.C., to guard the ancient city of Tanis, the capital of the despotic Pharaoh and other Egyptian kings of the XIXth Dynasty.

My black mood lightened, however, when the big plane put down at Cairo Airport at four in the morning, because someone was there to pick me up. As I went through customs I saw a handsome young man holding a sign with my name on it. I waved to him and he waved back. Then, burdened with my three suitcases, I hurried to him as fast as I could. To my horror, this strange Egyptian threw his arms around me and kissed me right on my lips. I would have decked him on the spot if I hadn't been so laden with luggage. Instead, I just made sure to ride in the back seat of the car as he drove me to the Mena House Hotel, in the Cairo suburb of Giza, which was to serve as our headquarters for the next few months. His name, he told me, was Fouad, and he was one of the assistant directors on the film. Amid a steady torrent of chatter, Fouad pointed out sights I really couldn't see at that hour. What I *did* see was that Fouad was planning not only to show me Egypt but a considerable part of himself as well.

When we reached the hotel, I jumped out of the car and raced into the lobby. Andy Durkus, one of the American unit managers and a close friend of mine, was waiting for me. After our handshake greeting, I asked him if my shipment of makeup supplies had arrived. Andy said they hadn't. Then he said, "So why don't you spend a few days with Fouad, and I'll let you know when your stuff does get here." I knew then that I had been set up. After he finished roaring with laughter, Andy admitted he had told Fouad that I was a "sweet makeup boy." "You marryin' Westmores have to see another side of life," he said. At the time, I felt like decking him, too. Instead, I went to my room and slept for fourteen hours.

The next day I drove the eleven miles to the set in a World War II jeep. The location was at Beni Youssef, a primitive village squatting on the flat, windblown desert. There were more sheep and goats and water buffaloes than there were people, no electricity, and no running water, so the sight of our "Gates of Tanis" was all the more overwhelming. They towered 108 feet above the desert floor. In front of the gates were four plaster reproductions of 45-foot-high ancient Egyptian gods. Basically, the gates were only a façade, supported from behind by a jungle of scaffolding. At the very top of the gates was a platform on which our chief cameraman, Loyal Griggs, had mounted his camera, complete with a camera lens which would "see" for an area of three miles. That would encompass the exodus itself, with the more than twelve thousand extras DeMille was planning to use, plus the always breathtaking sight of the Sphinx, the huge pyramid Cheops, and the two lesser ones, Menkure and Chephren. After deciding to have my makeup department built directly behind the gates (which would afford some shade and a little protection against the wind), I accepted Griggs's invitation to climb to the very top to look at the view. I did it, but only that one time. The sight was spectacular, but getting up there was like scaling a ladder to the roof of an eleven-story building.

The almost ceaseless wind, and the sand it carried, was a problem. The sand was a gritty, fine powder which seemed to permeate even my pores, not to mention my ears, nose, mouth, hair, and everything else exposed to it. But, sand or not, by the time my first assistant makeup man, Frank McCoy, got to Egypt a few days later, I had supervised the erection of a rough but serviceable makeup building. Our supplies arrived a few days after that. McCoy and I worked double overtime because we wanted to be fully prepared by the time DeMille arrived. He was making the trip in grand and leisurely style via the S.S. *Constitution* to Cannes and an equally luxurious Italian liner to Alexandria. In his retinue were several members of his family, including his daughter Cecilia and his nineteen-year-old granddaughter, also named Cecilia but nicknamed Citsy.

When C.B. finally showed up, we were ready, but it hadn't been easy. We had to have running water in our department, so I improvised and put a water tank on the roof and then cut a hole under it. Frank McCoy and I went to an Arab flea market looking for something faintly resembling a makeup chair. We found eight barber-chair relics. They were short-legged by American standards, so I built boxes on which to put them so they would be high enough to do the makeup without acrobatics. To add a little color, we painted the chairs green. We bought yellow curtains and some fat, brightly colored pillows. My headquarters were still pretty ramshackle, but it was the best I could do.

By comparison with my crude 25-by-30-foot wooden structure, C.B.'s central command post seemed the height of modern luxury. Not only did it have a chemical toilet, but there was real grass growing outside, even a few bushes. How that was accomplished I can't even imagine. Perhaps, in deference to a near-equal, Allah himself had responded to the Egyptian gardeners' pleas.

The day the old man was to come to the set for the first time, McCoy and I got to the makeup building at 4:30 A.M. It was immediately evident that the desert wasn't going to be in awe of C.B., even if we mortals were. The wind was howling; the sand was churning; miniature dunes collected on every surface, no matter how fast we dusted. Nearby, the wardrobe people were in worse trouble. They had left thousands of costumes hanging on long racks outside their building. The wind had blown down the racks one by one like so many dominoes, and piles of clothing littered the entire area. That was the first sight which greeted the director.

The famous DeMille rage almost outblew the desert. We watched from a window as the sturdy body paced back and forth through the debris. Then he stood still, assuming the familiar De-Mille stance: stoop-shouldered, hands clasped behind his back, mouth open in a perpetual roar. As usual he wore a crushed felt hat, twill riding breeches, and handmade leather gaiters above glossy brown boots. It was a funny sight (had we felt like laughing), watching the wardrobe employees chasing costumes and then running back to stand in front of DeMille to catch more hell. Luckily for them, he couldn't keep up his harangue too long. Sand was getting in his mouth.

By the time he reached our department, both his anger and the wind had subsided. He told me he was pleased at our effort and ingenuity. Then he flabbergasted me by saying, "Citsy would like to go dancing tonight in Cairo, Frank. Will you take her?" Naturally I said I would; he wasn't asking me, anyway, he was telling me. In any case, it would be no hardship to spend time with Citsy. She was a knockout—gorgeous red hair, a great body, and lovely gray-green eyes. Still, I was puzzled. One was not lightly invited into the personal circle of the DeMille family.

The next morning C.B., along with our Moses, Charlton Heston, and accompanied by four of the ten assistant directors and part of the crew, left for the Mount Sinai location, some two hundred miles southeast of Cairo, to film the sequence where Moses received the tablets of the law. For the few days DeMille was away, I was swept into a frenzy of activities preparing for his return and for the start of the shooting of the Exodus itself. Our production managers hired whole villages, which included all the inhabitants and their animals. The initial batch of extras numbered over five thousand. Eventually, there would be twelve thousand. They were billeted in tents pitched all over the desert. The location was beginning to resemble the staging area for an invasion.

I stirred up huge batches of light-colored foundation body makeup which I practiced applying by spray gun on the extras, since the Egyptians were too dark to look like Hebrews. With assembly-line precision, we got to the point where we could spray hundreds of men, women, and children in less than an hour. Abbas Bougdadli, a major in the Egyptian Army, was there with two hundred cavalry troops, training his men to use their horses hitched up to chariots constructed by our crews. Dozens of house painters from Cairo were swarming over the Gates of Tanis, toning down colors which DeMille had pronounced too garish.

The wardrobe department painted three shacks: one red, one blue, and one yellow. Then the extras were handed corresponding colored cards so they would know where to line up to be given the proper wardrobes and props after they left our makeup department. We believed that by precise timing, and by starting the day at 4 A.M., we could complete our part of the operation in four hours. (My mind boggled when I thought of the additional seven thousand extras who would take part later.) We spent the remainder of each day preparing beards made of carded wool, using rubber face masks as models for the faces of the extras who would wear them. By the time our Leader got back, we had completed two thousand beards.

For Frank McCoy and me, rehearsal day for the first phase of the Exodus filming dawned early. We were in the makeup building shortly after 3 A.M. It was black and freezing cold on the desert, but we shuddered with more than the cold as we contemplated our work. We had to body-spray and slap beards on some four thousand men. (The other thousand or so were women and children who needed only face makeup.) Even with the forty makeup assistants I'd rounded up in Cairo, I wasn't sure we could do the job. I had awful visions of improperly applied beards falling off and blowing away in the wind while the cameras were grinding. I was grateful for those Santa Claus beards I'd brought; at least *they* would stay on.

By 4:30 A.M. I began to feel a little better. Loyal Griggs and the five other cameramen were there, the wardrobe department was aswarm with people, Major Bougdadli and the cavalry were working with the chariots, and it was starting to get warmer. Amazingly, I could hear almost none of the usual joshing. Even the Arabs were unusually quiet. Only the hundreds of different animals—pigs, goats, water buffaloes, and those foul-breathed balky camels—were kicking and groaning and snorting. Little did they know that DeMille was apt to fire them, too, if they didn't perform properly.

When the sun rose, McCoy and I and our helpers were working like automatons, mindlessly spraying bodies, faces, and hands and gluing beards. Somebody even put a beard on a little boy. I started to pull it off, but the kid cried out in pain, so I left it on, delighted at how well the glue had adhered. I figured if DeMille noticed him, I'd say he was a midget.

At eight thirty, we saw C.B.'s car approaching at top speed, the sand spurting up in misty clouds as the vehicle's wheels made the turns. It looked unearthly, and so did the old man when he leaped from the passenger seat. He advanced through the billowing sand like an apparition, wearing his usual attire of wide breeches, gaiters and boots, and a floppy loose shirt. Around his waist was his gun belt and holster which held a forty-five pistol. (For mob scenes, he would fire a shot into the air to indicate the starts and stops, instead of trying to yell "Action!") A white pith helmet protected his bald head. His face wore a look of surprise. I think he had figured we couldn't be ready, but we were. Thousands of people, costumed and bearded, stood in ragged lines behind the towering gates. With military rigidity, the major and his two hundred horsemen waited near the chariots. The wild mélange of livestock sounds, and the cackling and honking of thousands of ducks and chickens, provided a background for the miracle we had jointly accomplished.

It was the director's custom to deliver a speech of admonition and warning to his company before each day's work. What he said was not meant to reassure but rather to tip everyone a little off balance so that no one would lapse into complacency. But the seventy American crew members, as well as three times that many Egyptians, were spared that morning because C.B. couldn't make himself heard above the animal noise.

I waited until I saw him heading toward a conference with Loyal Griggs, and then I decided to walk down the aisles of extras and check beards again. Suddenly I spotted one extra with his beard sticking straight out from his forehead. I reached him at a gallop and, through my interpreter, asked him just what in the hell he thought he was doing. He was one of those on whom I had put a wire Santa Claus beard. He had pushed it up, he said, to shade his eyes from the sun. I looked around and saw at least a dozen other men with their Santa Claus beards jutting out of their eyebrows. I ran back toward the makeup department, shouting and screaming for Frank McCoy. Believe me, *I* made myself heard above the animal din. We just managed to change all the Santa Claus beards to wool ones before DeMille's pistol shot rang out and the rehearsal got underway.

Those of us not actually in the scene were given long wooden paddles to swat the recalcitrant camels on the rump when they refused to move into the shot. On my first swipe at the rear of one of the hump-backed creatures, it kicked its back legs and almost crippled my left arm. I passed my paddle to an assistant and abandoned camel-beating. Instead I devoted my time to chasing wandering chickens back into line.

The sequence we did that day was the gathering of the Israelites around Moses as he prepared to lead them to the Promised Land. Charlton Heston was out in front of all these people, and, as DeMille waved them toward him, they closed in so fast I thought he'd be trampled. All day long, DeMille's forty-five cracked as he began a scene, then stopped it, then started it again. From where I was situated, I couldn't see well enough to understand why he was shooting the pistol so often. Then someone who had been up front told me. There were two wagons in the procession which were loaded with the same kind of unleavened bread which Moses and his people actually took with them on their trek. By the time one of the wagons rode under the cameras, the bread —or matzos—had disappeared. The extras nearest to the wagons were looking fatter and fatter. They were taking the matzos and stuffing them under their costumes. Who could blame them? Those Arabs were poverty-stricken, working all day under the broiling sun for a paltry twenty-eight cents. Still, C.B. had to photograph the meal which was to sustain the Hebrews, so he designated six of the biggest extras to guard the replenished wagons, at least until they had passed before the cameras. But as the wagons came by again, not only the bread had disappeared; so had the matzo guards.

While DeMille filmed the gathering of the Exodus, another camera unit moved a few miles away to Abu Ruwash to get ready for the scene showing the parting of the Red Sea. C.B. had chosen a long flat stretch of desert and ordered the prop department to mark the way with boulders. As far as we were concerned, that particular scene would simply be a continuation of what we already were doing. After we returned to the studio, the special-effects people would take over the film to insert shots of the sea opening for Moses and his followers.

Meanwhile, the old man wanted the sand to seethe with movement and the costumes of the extras to blow wildly as the still-imaginary body of water parted. So one of the cameramen found ten old airplanes without wings and had them hauled on huge flat-bed trucks to the location. Then the propellers were started, the sand churned up, and a hellish man-made sandstorm was in progress. In addition to the natural wind, the extra wind generated by the propellers caused a number of unforeseen problems.

One of the extras, who was carrying a burning torch, tripped

On the set of The Ten Commandments *with my "surrogate father," Cecil B. DeMille.*

*In front of the pyramid Cheops during a break
in the shooting of* The Ten Commandments.

in his haste to escape the blast of sand and fell into a little girl marching in front of him. The flaming fuel sloshed out and set her clothing on fire. Luckily I was standing just a few feet from the child. I reached out, jammed my arm inside her costume, and literally tore it off her body.

Some of our Egyptian extras were bitten by scorpions blown out of their burrows in the sand, and one man was bitten by an Egyptian cobra. The company's doctor, Max Jacobsen, administered first aid and rushed the victims to a hospital in Cairo. Otherwise, considering the masses of extras, now some nine thousand in number, the shooting went remarkably smoothly.

Of our company, only Henry Wilcoxon, once an actor and now DeMille's staunch right hand, met with any trouble. The endless columns were unruly and not too well controlled by the assistant directors in the field, so C.B. sent Wilcoxon out, in costume, to try to create some order. Henry took off his shoes and went plowing through the sand to join the lines. The old man now was using a loudspeaker to make himself heard over the roaring of the airplanes, and Wilcoxon kept turning around, both to hear him better and to watch DeMille's gesticulations. While doing so he stepped into a huge pile of fresh green water-buffalo dung, a mishap which shook him so badly that he was out of action for the rest of the afternoon.

As exhausted as I was after that day's shooting was over, I was still chuckling about Wilcoxon as I got into my jeep and headed toward the hotel. The road to the Mena House ran alongside a large canal. As I tried to make a turn, the steering wheel wouldn't move. I was heading straight for the filthy water, into which sewers flowed and where horses and water buffalo bathed or died. I launched myself out of the jeep just about one second before it went hurtling into the water. Some of the crew in the car behind me picked me up and took me home.

I was in my room nursing my assorted bruises when the telephone rang. It was DeMille. Someone had told him of my near miss, and he sounded genuinely concerned. He made me assure him that I was all right. He asked if I wanted Dr. Jacobsen to come over. I said I really didn't need the doctor, that I only had some nasty scrapes. He talked a while longer about the picture, and then he said, "Please take care of yourself—for me." I hung up, deeply touched. As I thought about our conversation, I felt as if I might have been talking to a father who loved his son very much.

13

I was spending all my free time—which admittedly wasn't much—with Citsy. We shared many sunrises together, but not in the way I would have liked. She had taken to coming to the makeup department every morning at the crack of dawn, sometimes arriving before I did. She would have the coffee prepared and, more often than not, would be deeply involved in conversation with the handsome Major Bougdadli. Citsy was crazy about horses, like her mother, and our spit-and-polish Egyptian Army man was breaking all his own rules by letting Citsy ride his horses. Once he even allowed her to drive a chariot. For that he received one of DeMille's more classic chewing-outs.

So far, despite Wally's warnings, I had never been on the receiving end of a C.B. tirade. On the contrary, he went out of his way to be complimentary to me. Whenever he saw Citsy and me together he would beam with pleasure. Several times he invited me to dine with him and Cecilia and Citsy. Although he never said so, I had the impression that he would not object to me becoming his grandson-in-law. Actually I wasn't ready for another marriage, and it was hard to feel very romantic after the kind of working days we all put in. We barely had the strength left over for a shower, a drink, dinner, and bed—alone—in that order. DeMille worked harder than any of us. Every night after shooting, the day's film was packed in dry ice to protect it from the blazing heat and shipped to England for developing. Then it came back to the Mis'r Studio in Cairo, where the old man viewed it nights and weekends. Only God knew when he slept.

The rehearsal for the actual Exodus scene—with our ranks swelled to the anticipated twelve thousand extras—went badly. DeMille was furious with nearly everyone. His normal ill temper was magnified by frustration over the dilution of his rages into mild harangues by the Egyptian interpreter translating for the Egyptian crew members and actors. A great deal of his wrath was aimed at the English-speaking Major Bougdadli. I sensed that he loathed the major because Citsy spent so much time trailing after him.

The next day, despite the shambles of the rehearsal, DeMille was ready to shoot the Exodus. Once again Frank McCoy and I and the whole crew were at the location around 3 A.M.

DeMille himself arrived at six. He summoned all of us, some seventy American crew members and several hundred Egyptians, to the command post for the daily tongue-lashing. I listened for a while, drinking coffee and watching the old man. Then my mind wandered until suddenly I heard him shout my name. I didn't know what I'd done wrong, but I figured my turn had arrived. To my astonishment, he said, "Frank, I want you to put on a galabia and burnoose and lead this Exodus. I can't trust anyone else." He strode over and handed me a walkie-talkie.

I didn't dare refuse what essentially was a job for the assistant directors, who stood around glaring at me. Chico Day, one of DeMille's long-time assistant directors, accompanied me to wardrobe, where he helped me into a galabia, a sort of nightshirt, and a burnoose which I noticed had Victor Mature's name on it. Mature had worn it in *Samson and Delilah*. I tried to tell Chico I was sorry, that I knew this wasn't my job, but he told me to shut my mouth and do as I was told. Under the galabia I wore nothing but my underdrawers and paratrooper boots, hardly fit footwear for trudging across a desert. I concealed the walkie-talkie beneath my robe and went out to take my place directly to the rear of Charlton Heston. Behind us were the twelve thousand extras and what seemed like millions of animals. Moses tried to smile at me reassuringly, but I was frantic; all I could think of was that I had to go to the bathroom.

Through the two-way radio DeMille's voice said to me, "I will be at the top of the Gates of Tanis with a tied-down camera, Frank. I will be talking to you and letting you know if I want you to move faster or slow down, or go to your left or to the right. You will tell Heston what I relay to you. You will inform my assistants in the rear whether to catch up or go more slowly. The column must curve, and there must be no gaps. Do you understand me?"

"Yes, Mr. DeMille."

"Good," he said. "I am now starting up to the top of the gates."

The sun was high by then and scorching. My feet were swollen in my boots already, and we hadn't even moved. Then through the walkie-talkie DeMille shouted "Action!" and fired his forty-five. I told Heston to move, and we were on our way. Behind me I could hear the huge crowd jabbering in Arabic, kids giggling or crying, animals bawling.

After many hours and a dozen stops and starts, we had moved about two and a half miles into the desert. My lungs felt as if they were clogged with sand, and the calves of my legs ached. DeMille kept talking to me by radio from his distant 108-foot-high vantage point atop the gates.

At about five o'clock, I heard him say, "Frank will you please tell . . ." and then his voice stopped. I thought at first that my walkie-talkie had gone dead. Then the shocked voice of John Fulton, our special-effects cameraman, crackled over the radio. "Something's happened to Mr. DeMille. Repeat. Something's happened up here. Turn back, Frank, turn back."

I quickly told Heston what I'd just heard, and we both wheeled around. For a minute or so I pondered the enormity of the job of leading twelve thousand people—what I calculated to be about half the population of the city of Beverly Hills—back to our base at the gates. But all twelve thousand extras suddenly dropped their props (spears, paddles, torches) and raced off across the desert. Later I learned that it was sundown, the beginning of a Muslim religious holiday. When the Egyptians saw Heston and me start back, they figured their working day was over.

Without the hordes to hinder me I got back to the gates in about a half hour. It was easy to tell where DeMille was by the knot of excited people clustered around him in the shade. At the edge of the crowd Citsy met me. I was sure the old man was dead, but she said, "He's alive, Frank, but he's had some sort of heart attack." I asked her how they had managed to get him down from the top of the 108-foot-high scaffolding. She said that he had come down himself, with an assistant cameraman supporting him from below with one hand in the small of his back.

I moved closer. Dr. Jacobsen was with DeMille, trying to wave everyone away except C.B.'s daughter Cecilia. DeMille looked terrible. He was slumped in his director's chair, his face an odd shade of gray and shiny with sweat. I wasn't even sure he was conscious, but he fixed an eye on me and beckoned me to come over to him. In a weak, almost inaudible voice he asked me, "What happened out there?" I told him all the Arabs ran away when I stopped getting orders over the radio and Heston and I turned back. He sighed and said, "That's all right, Frank. I got the shot."

DeMille was carried to his car on a stretcher and driven to his apartment in Cairo. He refused to go to a hospital. I was frantic all evening and kept phoning Citsy for any scrap of information she could give me about his condition. Finally about eleven o'clock she came out to have dinner with me. She told me her grandfather's heartbeat had now stabilized and that he had not really suffered a classic coronary attack. It was a seizure brought on by exhaustion of the heart muscle, damaged many years before by rheumatic fever. Citsy also said that Dr. Jacobsen and two Egyptian cardiologists had suggested to C.B. that if he stopped working and rested for six months he'd be all right. According to Citsy, the old man replied to the doctors, "I will be on the set tomorrow morning."

And he was. He credited prayer for his ability to do so, but in all truth, he was very restricted in his activities and departed for the United States a few days later. DeMille's daughter Cecilia and Chico Day assumed command for the rest of the location filming.

DeMille had been able to complete the Exodus shooting before he left, but we still had about four more weeks of filming in Egypt before we were scheduled to leave for Hollywood and the finish of the picture at the Paramount studio. Our location moved to Luxor, some 320 miles to the south of Cairo. Our large and unwieldy company seemed rudderless; without DeMille the excitement was gone. We did, however, have some excitement of another sort.

One day, for example, we finished shooting across the river from Luxor. On the side of the river where we had been working, roving bands of cutthroat robbers had gathered, watching for their chance to attack us. When the boat arrived to take us back to Luxor, they charged. The extras panicked; hundreds of half-naked people all tried to get into the boat at once. The bandits threw rocks, one of which hit me in the head. Blood poured into my eyes and down my shirtfront and leaked into my shoes. It took seven stitches to close the wound.

We had another uprising the night before we were to go home. Our paymaster had been giving the correct amount of money to each village chieftain, who in turn was supposed to pay his people. Instead, the sheikhs were pocketing most of the loot and the extras were getting little or nothing. They blamed the company. Fearing for our lives, we sneaked out of town by boarding a train in the dead of night, instead of the one we were supposed to take in the morning. We left just in time. A full-scale riot erupted as the train pulled out.

One of my overriding concerns was Citsy. No matter what her grandfather had planned for her, it was obvious that she and Major Bougdadli were madly in love. I knew I would be called to account for that when I saw the old man, even though there wasn't anything I could do about it. He had designated me as Citsy's escort for a trip through Europe before we returned to Los Angeles just before Christmas. He called it a "publicity tour" for the film, but obviously he was using me to try to distract her from her involvement with "the Arab," as he called him. The strategy failed. Soon after we got back to Hollywood (we'd been away a little under three months), Citsy escaped back to the Middle East and married her Arab.

Everyone who had been in Egypt was given a three-week vacation before the resumption of shooting on *The Ten Commandments* at the Paramount lot. DeMille was still recovering his strength in his isolated mansion on the edge of a park in the Los Feliz district of Los Angeles. After my return, I barely had time to unpack my bags when my telephone rang. It was DeMille himself. He invited me to come see him at his home the following night.

I was stunned, knowing that through all the twenty-five pictures Wally had done with C.B., he had never set foot inside the home of this reclusive man. Neither had anyone else with whom DeMille worked. It was a well-known fact that he loathed entertaining in his private domain, so I was both honored and apprehensive. I had been a dismal failure in my efforts to abort Citsy's romance, and I'd known all along that I would be asked to explain that failure to DeMille. But I had figured on a reprieve until we started filming again.

When I arrived on the dot at the appointed hour of 8 P.M., Mrs. DeMille herself opened the door almost before I had taken my finger from the doorbell. Although I had never met her before, she greeted me warmly and directed me upstairs to DeMille's bedroom.

At first I couldn't see DeMille at all. What I did see was what must have been every magazine, periodical, book, Bible, script, and letter he had ever received, stacked, tumbled, thrown, jumbled, and walked on. His bed was piled at least three feet high with papers. I thought maybe he'd gone to the bathroom, so I called his name to let him know I was there.

"No need to shout, dear boy. I'm right in front of you," said a voice I knew so well by now. I looked at the bed again and then I saw him. He was wearing a little pointed red cap. Then I noticed he'd cleared a path to his lavatory. Stacked high on either side of his walkway were more books, boxes, and scripts. Near his bed was a beat-up brown card table, sagging on wobbly legs under another load of newspapers and illustrations of the *Commandments* sets then being built at the studio; also there were a small sunburst of colored pencils jammed into a water glass and a yellow legal pad. Obviously he used the card table as his desk.

"Sit down, Frank," he said. I did, on the floor. There was no other place.

To my surprise, DeMille was very philosophical about Citsy's defection. We talked a bit about the "flow of true love," as he put it, and he assured me that he didn't hold me responsible for "not stemming its tide." He offered me fragments of nonpertinent advice: "Never give money to a woman. Make her borrow it." "Never settle for one woman." "Never be humbled by anyone." "You can determine almost everything you want to know about a person by examining his feet." (I had heard about DeMille's so-called "foot fetish" but had put it down as just another ridiculous rumor. Now I realized it was true. A psychiatrist once told me that a foot fetish often indicates a severe genital inadequacy coupled with a rigidly moralistic attitude. Certainly in C.B.'s case, the latter applied, but it was difficult for me to consider DeMille inadequate in any area.)

Not once did he mention his illness. Neither did I. We talked about the film—there were to be eight more months of shooting—but he was already planning his next movie. It was to be a comprehensive history of the Boy Scouts. I left with the premonition that the Boy Scout picture never would be made, that *The Ten Commandments* would be DeMille's last picture. As it turned out, it was.

The work resumed. DeMille appeared to be in good physical shape. His temper was as explosive as ever, and the familiar De-Mille bellow was heard throughout the Paramount back lot. However, his health did force him to make one addition to his normally large entourage. This retinue, without which he never made a move on the set, consisted of the ubiquitous Henry Wilcoxon, first assistant director Chico Day, two secretaries, and a script supervisor. Now added to their ranks was a new employee: the chair boy.

In order for DeMille to sit rather than stand during the long hours of daily filming, he ordered the prop department to make a set of four chairs for him. They looked like stools with backs, and all were of different heights. That was to ensure that no matter how C.B. adjusted the camera there was a chair tall enough or short enough so he could sit down comfortably to squint through the lens. The chair boy's only job was to carry the chairs, keep his eye on the height of the camera, and then slide the correct-sized chair under DeMille's posterior. DeMille never looked to see whether that chair would be under him. He just expected it to be in place.

The chair boy C.B. hired wasn't a boy at all. His name was Justin Buehrlen and he was in his late twenties. Justin had been both an actor and a director in his native Germany, but when he came to this country he couldn't get a job in those fields. After trying his hand as a garage mechanic, a dishwasher, and a street cleaner, he was finally hired in the mail room at Paramount. Every morning he delivered the mail to the DeMille office, efficiently and courteously. What impressed the old man most about Justin was that he didn't ask him for anything.

As Justin told me, DeMille was waiting for him in the outer office one morning. He said, "Justin, how would you like to be my chair boy?" Justin had no idea what a chair boy was, but he assumed it must be some studio terminology he had not yet heard. Figuring that being any part of the DeMille company would eventually get him a place in the American film industry, he told the old man he would love to be his chair boy. After C.B. explained what his job as chair boy was to be, Justin had serious misgivings. Still, he reasoned, it was his one chance to work near the great man and, at the same time, advance himself.

Justin was very good at his job. The crew quickly got accustomed to seeing him trotting doggedly behind DeMille, hauling the four chairs. Justin saw very little of us, though, because he never dared take his eyes off the camera lens, lest he make a mistake in judgment and slip a chair of the wrong height under DeMille's royal rump. Then one morning Justin had diarrhea and had to get to the men's room without delay. He asked a crew member standing nearby to fill in for him temporarily and took off in a hurry. The crew member was so enthralled watching a scene between

Heston and Anne Baxter that he forgot to watch the camera eye. So when C.B. lowered himself to where he assumed one of his chairs would be, it wasn't. Down went DeMille, flat on his back, his little pointy-toed boots aimed straight up toward the sky.

The entourage sailed into action to help him get up, but they couldn't get near him. He struggled unaided to his feet, flailing his arms and screaming with fury. Justin got back to the set just in time to hear that he was fired. Yet the next morning, Justin jogged onto the set juggling his chairs. Surprised, I asked him how he had managed to get himself reemployed.

"By explaining the necessity of my absence and then by quoting Goethe, my favorite German poet," said Justin.

"That," I said, "must have been some quote. What was it?"

" 'Nature has neither kernel nor shell; she is everything at once.' "

From that time on Justin, too, became a DeMille favorite. He is still at Paramount Pictures, having risen to become production auditor on such films as *Love Story, The Godfather, Part II,* and *Once Is Not Enough.*

Our production company was spread out all over Paramount Studios. Almost every sound stage was occupied with *Commandments* sets. The back lot was one enormous trench; it was used to depict scenes where Moses and his people made mud bricks for the building of Ramses's cities. Hundreds of extras swarmed everywhere, and the body-spraying at which Frank McCoy and I had become so proficient continued. Since the extras were Americans, not Egyptians, we now had to spray them with a darker shade of makeup instead of a lighter one. For the body-spraying and the laying of beards, we built two outside booths, one for women and the other for the men. Each booth had a window. When we realized that the extras were choking on the vapor the spray guns left hanging in the air, we installed oversized fans in the windows to pull out the excess.

That seemed to solve the problem, until Wally called me to his office with a complaint. The windows in our spray booths overlooked Hollywood Cemetery, and the vaporized body makeup sucked out the windows by our fans was turning the nearby tomb-stones a lovely shade of tan. When we applied beards to the men, little pieces of wool also flew out the windows and stuck to the sullied monuments. The cemetery attendants had tried to clean the markers but had been unsuccessful. Studio laborers were sent out with buckets of detergent and wire brushes to do the job. Meanwhile, we made canvas flumes, attached them to the fans, and then ran them down to the ground to guide the spray there. And that was the end of the problem of the suntanned, bearded tombstones.

The rest of the eight months of shooting went smoothly. I set some sort of record by having only one conflict with DeMille. It finally happened in the mud-brick trench. For several days Heston worked in the pit, spattered up to his Adam's apple with mud. Each morning I had to put the mud back on him exactly the way it had been the day before. In order to do that, I had the still photographer take 8-by-10 pictures of Heston each evening, just after the day's final shot. Then I worked from those pictures.

About the third morning, as Heston started climbing down into the trench, DeMille picked up his megaphone and shouted through it, "Frank Westmore, the mud is wrong on Heston's chest. Step out here front and center." As I started making my way through the crowds, he shrieked again, "The mud on Heston's chest doesn't match yesterday's mud on Heston's chest!"

I still was a good two hundred yards away from the old man, and I had no megaphone to yell through, but he and everyone else heard me when I hollered back, "Mr. DeMille, you are one hundred percent wrong!"

The set went dead silent. Hundreds of extras stopped moving. One simply did not tell DeMille he was in error about anything.

I saw Heston start to touch his body and I screamed, "Keep your lousy hands off my mud. I have to prove I'm right."

I held up production for at least ten minutes while I rushed to the makeup department to get my photographs of Heston and his mud, and I picked up a magnifying glass. When I finally reached DeMille, panting and terrified, he looked as if he were ready to kill me. I handed him the magnifying glass and the pictures. There he stood, the bright overhead lights glinting off the glass, staring first at the pictures through the magnifying glass, and then at Heston's chest. Heston was at least a foot taller than DeMille, and I could see his eyes fixed straight over C.B.'s head. Time went by soundlessly during the old man's minute scrutiny of the disputed mud. Then slowly, like a reluctant ballet dancer, he turned on both toes, squinted at me, and said, "You're absolutely right."

I had great affection for the old man who had designated himself my surrogate father. Of the hundreds of people who worked with him on *The Ten Commandments*, I was one of only fifty to whom he gave a small percentage of the profits of the film. (Wally, the businessman, was enraged at being excluded.) I was deeply touched when he died three years later and I learned that he had left instructions that I be included among his honorary pallbearers.

14

BEFORE I finished *The Ten Commandments*, I had to make a vital career decision. There were two options open to me: I could return to a studio with an eye to one day heading a department, or I could accept director Edward Dmytryk's offer to go to work as a free-lance makeup artist on *The Mountain* in France with Spencer Tracy. (Dmytryk had seen and liked my work in the DeMille epic. He also told me that if I could handle C.B. so well, possibly I could even control Tracy, although he seemed doubtful about that.)

I had witnessed at first hand Mont's disastrous experience with David Selznick after his happy years of carefree independence. I saw Wally and Bud practically having to abandon doing creative makeup in order to administer their large departments: recruiting and training small armies of makeup artists, assigning the right artist to the right job, buying and dispensing supplies, attending daily production meetings and weekly budget meetings, reading scripts, and not only making suggestions for new makeup ideas for a film but—a Westmore specialty—dreaming up publicity gimmicks for it. Only occasionally were they able to get out in the field and use their skills on an especially important project.

I came to the conclusion that being an executive was not for me. I wanted to work at my craft, unburdened by ordering seven thousand eyebrow pencils and such. But what really solidified my thinking and convinced me to remain a free agent was the almost

175

unbelievable downfall of Perc, who had been the very pillar of the family and the indispensable force at Warner Brothers, the studio he had helped make great for so many years.

As I have said, Perc had a lifetime contract with Jack Warner. To my knowledge, it was the sole agreement of its kind in the motion picture industry for a makeup executive. Only if Perc quit could the notoriously short-fused Jack Warner get rid of him. Yet secure in his belief that he was the irreplaceable man, Perc used his contract as a weapon. He threatened to resign with astonishing regularity. Every time something displeased him, Perc fired off a letter announcing his immediate departure unless what he wanted done, or undone, was accomplished immediately. Throughout the halcyon decades of the twenties, thirties, and most of the forties, Perc estimated that he quit no less than eighty times. With each "resignation" he received more money, more power, and more homage from the studio, which truly believed that without Westmore there would be no Warner Brothers. Unfortunately, Perc did not foresee that the upstart television industry, with its flickering ten-inch screens, would be his Waterloo.

For a while, none of the major studios thought they would be seriously affected, either. But increasing numbers of people were sitting at home in darkened living rooms in front of their television screens, fascinated in spite of the poor reception and even poorer programming. Gradually film box office receipts began to fall off. The moviemakers, determined to beat back this electronic interloper, started a concerted campaign to lure audiences back into the theaters. Movies Are Better Than Ever was the slogan. The fact was that they weren't better than ever. The entire industry had gotten fat and sloppy. By 1950, Hollywood had to acknowledge that the unwritten slogan was: Theaters Are Emptier Than Ever. Mass studio firings were taking place, and the studios cut back wherever they could.

Perc, with his enormous ego, paid no attention whatever to these ominous developments. In February of 1950 the biggest problem he thought he faced involved Jane Wyman's long blond wig for her role in *The Glass Menagerie*. Jane complained every morning that the hairpiece made her head look too big. Perc talked her into letting him cut her own long hair and designed the short, fluffy bob she has worn ever since. The wig fit smoothly over her shorn locks, and both she and Perc were happy.

While thus engaged in the minutiae of his specialty, Perc was blissfully unaware that Warner Brothers contracts were being reviewed by an efficiency expert. The expert's recommendation to Jack Warner: All high-salaried executives must take substantial salary cuts. When Perc was informed that his $1,250 weekly paycheck would be reduced by $500, he was outraged.

While he was trying to decide what to do, Perc received entirely different advice from Ola, at The House of Westmore, and from his wife, Maggie Donovan, at home. Maggie, a Warner Brothers hairstylist when she married Perc, had risen to become the head of her department. Maggie did not use our family name in her craft. Perc was wounded by this, but she was adamant. "I battled my way to the top of my profession as a Donovan," she screamed at him, "and I don't have to be known as a Westmore to stay there." That was typical of their acrid, childless relationship.

But Maggie went 180 degrees in the other direction on at least one occasion. One night, just before Bette Davis married artist William Grant Sherry, her third husband, Maggie and Perc stopped by Bette's house for a drink. Maggie spotted the handwritten wedding invitation list lying on the coffee table, glanced at it, and saw, among others, the name "Perc Westmore." She emitted a screech of anger and shouted at Bette, "Why doesn't this say 'Mr. and Mrs. Perc Westmore?' " Then she leaped to her feet, wrestled the startled Bette into her fur-coat closet, and locked the door.

While Bette pounded and pleaded to be let out, Maggie forced Perc to amend the guest list by adding "Mr. and Mrs." in front of his name. Then she calmly let Bette out of the closet and mixed a drink for her. For a change, Bette kept her own temper in check. "I was afraid of that Maggie," she later told me.

Apparently Perc was afraid of her too, because Maggie's was the deciding voice in the matter of what Perc should do when he learned that his salary was to be reduced. At the salon, Ola reasonably advised Perc to accept the decrease with good grace because she felt sure that when the industry got back on its feet the $500 would be restored. She also pointed out that $750 a week was hardly a pittance. At home, Maggie, on the other hand, was incensed over the fact that her husband, "the great Perc Westmore," should be forced to knuckle under to the likes of Jack Warner. She told him to quit at once. "Twentieth will snatch you up in one second," she assured him, adding, "Just be firm like you've always been. Warner won't let you go." Perc preferred Maggie's sound good sense, as he put it. He promptly dispatched his eighty-first letter of resignation to Jack Warner, left the studio, and went to his office at The House of Westmore to await Warner's usual panicky telephone call begging him not to leave.

It was a Saturday, the busiest day of the week at the salon. Ola was at the front desk, checking people in and out, answering the phones, making appointments, and keeping the place running smoothly. When a Western Union messenger delivered a telegram for Perc, she signed for it and set it aside until she had time to open it. About an hour later, she read the wire. It was terse and to the point. It said, REGRETFULLY ACCEPT YOUR RESIGNATION, EFFECTIVE AS OF NOW. SINCERELY, JACK WARNER.

Ola resealed the envelope, gave the lethal message to a maid, asked her to deliver it upstairs to Perc's office, and waited for the interoffice telephone to ring. After the expected summons to come upstairs, Ola diplomatically refrained from saying, "I told you so." Instead she consoled my numbed and shaken brother.

Perc was not snatched up by Twentieth. After several weeks of waiting, he realized that he wasn't going to be hired by any major studio at all. He was, in the words of one industry head, "overqualified," which Perc understood to mean overpaid. But business was better than ever at the salon, and Perc, maintaining the proud posture of a man in command of his own destiny, worked there at a frenetic pace, often spending as many as eighteen hours a day in his lab and with the delighted customers. (According to Ola, a woman from Iowa who was having her hair set became so overwhelmed by the sight of the famous Perc, when he popped into her booth, that she fainted. The incident gave his stricken ego a considerable boost.) He had no such balm in his home life. Maggie became as fiercely contemptuous of her husband as she had been proud of his power only two months before. She conveniently forgot that it was her own advice that had brought him down. The always-rocky marriage staggered on for another few weeks and then ended. The only good thing resulting from the fiasco of his final resignation from Warner Brothers was that Ola and Perc, in love for so many years, finally acknowledged it. In August of 1951 they slipped into Mexico and married each other—for a change. As Bette Davis, an expert on Perc's marriages, put it, "Ola became his fifth, last, most permanent—and best—wife."

Through his friendship with the stars, Perc managed to hang on in the industry. For example, when RKO cast Jane Wyman in *The Blue Veil* in 1951, she insisted that Perc be hired to do the complicated aging makeup for her role as a love-thwarted children's nurse.

As he designed the ingenious foam-rubber devices which would age Jane's face as she advanced in years, he seemed curiously lethargic. Jane said, "We used to have a silly little routine we did whenever we worked together on a picture. In the Warner Brothers days when I came to be made up in the morning, he would say, 'Be's you got bugs?' And I answered, 'Sure I are, everybody do.' When we started *The Blue Veil* at RKO, he didn't say it any more. Also I missed the thoughtful little things he used to do, like painting a picture of a beautiful poppy and propping it up on his table so it was the first bright and cheerful thing I saw at the start of the day. Then, about two weeks after we had begun shooting, I arrived at RKO and was told that Perc had had a severe heart attack and was hospitalized. I was shocked and saddened, but not altogether surprised."

Ola remembers that it was a Sunday morning when Perc had the first symptoms of his attack. They had boarded a commercial fishing boat at Malibu Pier and planned to spend the day hauling in halibut. Less than an hour after they had been under way, Perc complained of feeling very ill. "He said that his left arm and thumb felt numb and painful and heavy," said Ola, "and I told the captain to return to shore. Perc looked ashen."

The boat turned back and Ola drove him home. Perc got into bed, telling Ola he felt better and probably only needed some rest. He refused to let her call the doctor. The following morning he dragged himself to RKO to attend to Jane Wyman. About 4 P.M., he arrived at The House of Westmore, barely able to climb the stairs to his office. "That night, about two A.M., Perc woke me up and said he was sure he was having a heart attack," Ola went on. "I called our doctor and was told to rush him to Hollywood Presbyterian Hospital. A heart specialist was called. After the tests, it was determined that he had had a cardiac infarction—a real jolt."

Perc remained in the hospital for four weeks and then was confined to his apartment for four more weeks, attended by nurses around the clock. Remembering Mont, I was horrified and more than a little frightened at the sight of the giant of all the Westmores lying on the couch in his house, looking like a beached and shrunken whale. Ern and Wally sent get-well cards but didn't visit him. Bud, pleading the press of his own job, came by once and not again. Meanwhile, back at *The Blue Veil* set, Jane Wyman, leery of any other makeup man, was attempting on her own to apply her elaborate facial devices. She couldn't do it, and Perc asked Bud to take over for him. Bud arranged with Universal to be at RKO every morning to put on the Wyman makeup before going to his studio to do his own work. At the end of the movie Bud sent Perc a bill for $750 "for services rendered." I asked Bud how he could do something so crass, but I never received a satisfactory answer. I reminded him it was Perc who had gotten him his job, but he just laughed. Bud was changing—in a way I didn't like.

When Perc's convalescence was over, he was in pretty good physical shape, but mentally he still was among the walking wounded. His eight weeks of inactivity apparently had caused his how-have-the-mighty-fallen syndrome to fester within him. With his flair for publicity, he had previously arranged contracts with radio and television programs (among them Art Linkletter's *Houseparty* and Jack Bailey's *Queen for a Day*) to provide free beauty analysis and makeup to winning contestants on those shows. (Eventually, more than 2,600 Queens for a Day were thus glorified at The House of Westmore over an eleven-year period.)

Struggling to revive his ego in his post-heart-attack period, Perc decided to carry this basic idea even further. With the old-time fanfare, he announced that he, the greatest of the Westmores, now would "personally perform his moviestar magic" on the faces of all women who would come to The House of Westmore and pay him twenty-five dollars. Customers flocked to the salon, and the money poured in. He spent only a few minutes with each client before turning her over to an assistant. He did as many as thirty a day—and there was a long waiting list besides. But, in a few months, the unending succession of homely but hopeful faces became more than Perc could bear. What he thought would be his therapy turned into a perpetual nightmare. Gradually an astounding transition took place in my puritanical brother. He did exactly the same thing for which he always bitterly condemned Ern: He began drinking heavily, for the first time in his life. House of Westmore maids sneaked quarts of vodka to his private office despite anything Ola could do to prevent it.

One day in April 1952, a strong and resourceful black maid— Perc's chief co-conspirator in liquor smuggling—ran upstairs to her boss with a bottle hidden under her uniform. As she entered his office, she found Perc slumped over his desk, the previous vodka bottle lying on its side near his head, the remaining contents seeping onto the carpeted floor. A vial of pills, half empty, stood beside it. Although Perc's eyes were open and he was conscious, his breathing was labored and the maid immediately took it for granted he had attempted suicide. Fearing her exposure as Perc's supplier, she did not summon Ola or a doctor, but fortunately for him she knew what to do. Her own husband, in jail at the time for armed robbery, had tried to kill himself in the same way. She rushed downstairs to the kitchen, picked up a full pot of coffee, and raced back. Then, roughly yanking his head up by the hair, she pushed her fingers into his mouth and made him throw up and then forced the scalding coffee down his throat. Finally, she got him to his feet and started walking him back and forth, back and forth. After about an hour, Perc recovered to the point where he said he was hungry. The immediate crisis was over. Strangely, though, Perc told the maid that he wanted Ola and his brothers to know what he had done. "Why did I go through all this if no one knows about it?" he asked querulously.

A dramatic reversal was occurring in the roles of the mirror-image twins. It didn't happen all at once. In 1949, when Perc was still riding high at Warner Brothers, Ern had become virtually unemployable in the film industry after losing his job as head of the department at Eagle-Lion Studios. No studio could afford to take chances with his drinking, and he had run out of friends from whom he could borrow money, since he rarely paid anybody back.

Still, his reputation as a makeup wizard remained, and at least one entrepreneur thought Ern was salvageable. Sol Dolgin, a businessman involved in the movie industry, approached Ern and asked him if he would be interested in making a pilot television show loosely predicated on the Westmores' seven basic face shapes. Ern not only was interested in anything that would bring in some money, he was genuinely fascinated with the new medium and leaped at the opportunity. Dolgin warned him that if he got drunk and blew the deal, no one would ever hire him again in *any* industry. Ern solemnly promised that he wouldn't touch a drop. Reassured, Dolgin put up $100,000 of his own money and got two other backers to furnish the rest of the $250,000 of the pilot's cost.

On the last day of filming, Ern got drunk and disappeared. He was gone for more than two weeks. Dolgin tried to fake the ending of the film by photographing the back of another man similar in build to Ern, but it didn't work. The project was a disaster, and it didn't sell to any of the three networks. Everyone involved lost a small fortune.

When Ern returned home from his bender, he found that his

wife, Betty, was seriously ill with a number of maladies, not the least of which was an emotional dysfunction brought on by Ern's latest goof-up. She didn't chastise him. She simply asked him to help her. No one, not his two daughters, not even Betty, had ever asked Ern for support before. It always had been he who needed shoring up.

It was then that the reversal of the twins' personalities took place. Somehow Ern managed to dig up enough money to do another television pilot. This time he behaved and performed exemplarily, and The Ern Westmore Hollywood Glamour Show sold on local stations, first in Cincinnati and later in New York. Ern left Hollywood with Betty, escaping more or less permanently from the shadow of Perc. He stopped drinking and became relatively stable financially, at just about the time Perc began drinking and went into his career decline.

I didn't see much of Ern after he left town, but according to Shelley Hull, who directed Ern's New York show, the format was simple but effective. The simple set was basically a semicircular desk and a green velvet backdrop on which hung large sketches of movie stars—drawn by Ern himself. For the first ten minutes, Ern, wearing an impeccably tailored double-breasted blue suit, spoke to the live studio audience and dispensed makeup advice. Then his wife, Betty, went into the audience, picked out a woman, and brought her to the stage. Ern analyzed her face shape and completely redid her makeup on camera. The last few minutes were devoted to a male singer who warbled such snappy lyrics as "Baby, look at you now."

"No matter how often I heard Ern do that opening ten-minute spiel," Hull said, "I was always fascinated. He had some quality that almost hypnotized his audience. I swear if he had told those women to shave their heads, they would have done it. We never had to rehearse him, and with what seemed no effort on his part, he'd just stride out to center stage, slip behind that desk, and start talking. He was a natural showman, which he coupled with natural salesmanship."

Typically, in forsaking alcohol, Ern was unable to function without a substitute crutch. He discovered food, something he previously had more or less neglected, having preferred to extract his calories from the bottle. Now he ate to excess, just as he had once drunk to excess. On one occasion, Hull saw him eat six whole pies topped with ice cream. His weight soared to three hundred pounds, and he looked much like Jackie Gleason at his most obese. He suffered from chronic indigestion and, in keeping with his compulsive eating, he chewed something like fifty Tums a day. He looked so gross on camera that his series was canceled after about a hundred airings. He had literally eaten himself off his show. Shortly after that, Ern suffered excruciating chest pains. Like his twin on the West Coast, he was rushed to a hospital. His heart condition was diagnosed as angina pectoris. Nitroglycerin pills replaced the Tums.

In reviewing the plights of ex-studio department heads Perc and Ern, plus the job constrictions of studio department heads Wally and Bud, my decision to remain a free agent in my profession seemed less a decision than a fact of self-survival. Once again, as I had when I went to Egypt with DeMille, I assembled my gear and boarded a plane for Paris—and thence to Chamonix in the French Alps—to do the makeup for Spencer Tracy, Robert Wagner, Claire Trevor, and E. G. Marshall in *The Mountain*. I was young, healthy, and independent, and I intended to stay that way. I had made another unfortunate foray into matrimony in 1955, this time with Johnnie Fay Rector, a young girl I had met when she came to visit *The Ten Commandments* set. My second marriage created some sort of record for instant incompatibility by lasting only ten days.

I figured that if my emotions could handle that disaster—*and* Cecil B. DeMille—I was ready to take on even the fearsome Mr. Spencer Tracy.

15

THE Terrible Tracy had made his reputation long before I got to Chamonix, but I knew all about it. As far back as 1933, when he was still with 20th Century-Fox, there was an incident which established his trademark, though as usual it was hushed up. Tracy got into a fight with director Winfield Sheehan and went on such a drunken rampage that he had to be locked inside a huge sound stage until he passed out and could safely be handled by the studio doctor. Before he reached the blessed state of unconsciousness, he tore down sets and systematically smashed thousands of dollars' worth of lights on the stage.

He calmed down somewhat when his acting brilliance made him a superstar at MGM in the twenty-year period from 1935 to 1955. As is well known now, his relationship with Katharine Hepburn helped to domesticate him. But just before he came to work in *The Mountain* for Paramount, he created one last monumental flap which sealed the end of his long and mutually profitable relationship with Metro.

It happened on a film called *Tribute to a Bad Man*. Perhaps he was feeling ornery because he didn't win the 1955 Oscar for his great performance in *Bad Day at Black Rock*; perhaps he resented still being under contract to MGM on a fixed salary that did not match the enormous sums being made by James Stewart and others who had left the studio and were working as free-lancers. Whatever the reason, Tracy caused trouble from the first day he was assigned to *Tribute to a Bad Man*. He didn't like the script. He didn't like his co-star, Irene Papas (Irene is nearly six feet tall and Tracy complained he'd look like Mickey Rooney standing next to her). On the first day of shooting, June 10, 1955, he arrived at the location in the Rocky Mountains near Montrose, Colorado, said he was going to his motel to take a nap—and disappeared for eight days. In the meantime, it was costing MGM approximately $30,000 a day just to keep the cast and crew in the field. The studio already had spent nearly a half million dollars to build nine ranch houses on a beautiful plateau about 8,000 feet up in the Rockies.

On June 19, Tracy suddenly reappeared and said, "Let's get to work." He worked only three half days, during which he pointedly disregarded all instructions of the director, Robert Wise. On the fourth day, Wise, one of Hollywood's best, who went on to win Oscars for *West Side Story* and *The Sound of Music*, had a historic confrontation in Tracy's trailer dressing room. Tracy demanded that the entire location, with its expensive sets, be moved from the 8,000-foot-level to the 6,000-foot-level. He said he couldn't stand the altitude. At that, the redoubtable Wise said, "You're fired. Get your ass out of here." To the amazement of the industry, the studio backed Wise, and Tracy was finished at Metro. James Cagney was hired to substitute for him in *Tribute to a Bad Man*. But the most ludicrous thing of all was that Tracy, who said he couldn't stand the altitude in the Rockies at 8,000 feet, signed to do his first free-lance picture, *The Mountain*, at Chamonix in the French Alps: altitude 11,000 feet.

I met Tracy for the first time the morning after I arrived at Chamonix by bus from Paris. The meeting took place early in the morning at the Hôtel des Alpes. Director Edward Dmytryk was breakfasting with his star and motioned me to join them. The minute Dmytryk introduced me, I knew I was in trouble. Tracy's eyes narrowed and he started a diatribe about makeup men. He said he didn't want or need makeup, adding, "My face looks like an outhouse door and nothing can help it, not even a Westmore."

I replied with some heat, "Mr. Tracy, I'm here to be of help to anyone who needs my services. If you don't want any makeup, I couldn't care less."

Dmytryk's eyes indicated that I'd be on the next plane back to the States. So did Tracy's. He said, "You arrogant son of a bitch, take your cap off when you yell at me."

"I can't take my goddam cap off," I screamed back, "because I look like a goddamned Mohican!"

With that I whipped off the cap, revealing a two-inch-wide bald strip down the middle of my head. I had bought a French gadget to trim my own hair and, not being able to read French, had put the cutting edge on backwards. Tracy cracked up, and so did Dmytryk. For the rest of the movie I had no further trouble with Spencer Tracy. That is not to imply that others didn't.

It was a very difficult location. Most of our working sites were far above the timberlines of those forbidding mountains and could only be reached by cable cars. Against the vast bulk of the 15,771-foot Mont Blanc, the funiculars looked like toys. At altitudes of more than 14,000 feet, it not only was difficult to breathe but we were burdened with layer after layer of clothing to survive the bitter cold. We wore crampon spikes on our boots to keep from slipping down the hidden crevasses and ravines. Often four of us were connected together by heavy ropes, so that when someone fell there were three others to haul him back. We came to dread the rending sounds of avalanches, which we could hear but usually couldn't see. Despite the fact that we had professional mountain climbers who preceded us when we moved from one location to another, I don't think anyone ever felt completely safe during the entire shooting of the movie.

Even the daily ride in the cable car was a nightmare. Our principal set was located on the very top of Aiguille du Midi, one of the highest peaks in the French Alps. It took two different cable cars to reach it. The first one wasn't so bad because, at the relatively lower altitude of 11,000 feet, the car wasn't so buffeted by wind and snow. But the second-stage car hung a full mile above the ground as it traversed the gap between the first mountaintop and Aiguille du Midi. The view from the car was awesome, if anyone had the stomach to look out the windows.

Tracy hated the funiculars and didn't hesitate to say so. But since he had no alternative, he gritted his teeth every morning and endured them. His deeply seamed face became even more wrinkled with every ride, making ludicrous the fact that he was playing Robert Wagner's brother in the film. He looked more like his grandfather.

One day Tracy didn't have to report to work until 2 P.M. He had told director Dmytryk he wouldn't come up to the set alone in a cable car, so first assistant director Bill McGeary was dispatched down the mountain to fetch him. On the return trip, according to McGeary, he felt a sense of foreboding in the first-stage car because the ride seemed unusually bumpy, but he said nothing to Tracy. They transferred to the second car. In the middle of the ride a cable malfunctioned. The car lurched to a sudden stop and both Tracy and McGeary were hurled to the floor.

From our viewpoint on the Aiguille du Midi, we could see the little car below us, swinging wildly from side to side and bouncing frighteningly against a now-slack cable. There was absolutely nothing we could do, so we just stood transfixed, barely able to make out the tiny figures of Tracy and McGeary hanging onto the safety bars in the car. It was as if they were on a damaged scaffolding at the top of a 500-story building and there wasn't even any way to communicate with them.

With a flurry of activity, technicians rushed to the cable house on our level and found that a cable had slipped its wheel. It took them two hours to get it back on. In the meantime, Tracy and McGeary swung in the wind, now facing the new and very real danger of freezing to death, since there was no heat in the funiculars. The repairmen finally restored the cable, and the car began to move toward us with maddening slowness. When it ground its way into the station, Tracy staggered out looking twenty years older than he had that morning. There was no more work that day, but poor Tracy had to get right back into the very same car and make the return trip to Chamonix.

I had to pack up my gear, so I left the mountaintop later, with Wagner and some of the crew. When we arrived at our hotel, Tracy was in the bar sitting at a small table, well on his way to drinking himself into a stupor. Wagner and I joined him. Strangely, he was very talkative and friendly, actually charming, telling all sorts of fascinating Hollywood stories, even as his head sagged lower and lower on his chest. He ordered another round of drinks.

I was sure this would be the one that would put him away and we could haul him off to bed, when suddenly, without reason, Tracy picked up his empty brandy snifter and hurled it at the approaching waiter's face. Wagner put up his right hand to catch the snifter before it hit the waiter. His hand closed reflexively over the glass, which shattered in his fist and cut his two middle fingers to the bone. Wagner's blood splattered all over the place. Tracy was oblivious to everything by then and didn't even know that he was being wrestled from his chair by members of the crew and hustled up to his room. I helped our company doctor as he stitched and bandaged Bob's hand, meanwhile pondering the practical consideration of how I could mask the gashes for the remainder of the film.

The next morning I fished around in my makeup box and found a bottle of collodion. This is a colorless liquid—actually acid-treated cotton fibers dissolved in a mixture of ether and alcohol—which I sometimes use to create an artificial scar on an actor's face. The substance is quick-drying and adhesive, and by applying it to, say, a cheek and then pinching the skin until the collodion hardens, I can produce what looks like a gash. I knew that collodion is antiseptic and is also used in the boxing ring, between rounds, to seal bad facial cuts sustained by prizefighters. So that morning (and for the rest of the movie) I applied collodion to Wagner's hand and covered it with makeup after it dried, neatly obliterating the stitches. A contrite Tracy watched the procedure, barely remembering what had happened the night before.

I used all the makeup procedures then in general use in the profession, but sometimes the abnormal conditions in the Alps made them difficult to execute. For example, there were scenes in which I had to fabricate frosted eyelashes, eyebrows, and facial stubble on Tracy and Wagner. It should have been a simple procedure but, like everything else on that location, it wasn't. To produce the frozen effect, paraffin is melted and then brushed onto the lashes, brows, and whiskers. When the wax hardens it turns white and looks like ice. The problem was that I had trouble keeping my can of Sterno lighted long enough to melt the paraffin. The wind and the lack of oxygen at that high altitude kept extinguishing the flame.

I had less trouble simulating rope burns on Tracy's hands. Using a technique resembling the one employed by Wally when he aged Barbara Stanwyck for her role in *The Great Man's Lady*, I stippled Tracy's palms with spirit gum, on top of which I stuck crumpled lens paper from my own camera equipment. Then, blending makeup base with liquid rouge, I smeared the red mixture on the paper. The trick was to do it quickly before the liquid congealed in the cold. By the time I finished, Tracy's hands looked as if rough rope had burned his palms raw.

Such comparatively routine techniques fascinated Tracy and gradually reversed his previously low opinion about makeup. After the glass-throwing incident he resumed his good behavior, not only to me but to director Dmytryk. He became particularly close friends with the then-very-young, relatively inexperienced Wagner. His tranquillity astounded us, until it dawned on the company that there was a specific reason for it. The reason's name was Margaret Shipway. She was an extremely proper young upperclass Englishwoman. At first we thought she was there as Tracy's secretary. But then it leaked out that Maggie, as we called her, actually was Katharine Hepburn's secretary, dispatched by Hepburn to our location to keep an eye on Tracy and help him stay on an even keel.

We didn't see much of Maggie the first week except at dinner every evening. There she was, impeccably dressed in handsome tweed skirts and cashmere twin-sweater sets and a single strand of pearls. She was always smiling and friendly and interested in everything that had gone on during our rugged days of shooting in the mountains, and not one of our hard-drinking, foul-mouthed company got out of hand in her presence. When she was around, the naughtiest word uttered was "darn." She was such a lady that she brought out the chivalrous side of all of us.

One afternoon we were forced off the mountain early because of a bad storm. There were gigantic rolls of thunder and lightning, and our guides insisted that we quit for the day. Our script clerk quit permanently. He had no toes on one foot and should never have accepted a job which required rigorous climbing. He further confessed privately that he was terrified of the storms which lashed the alpine peaks. He was to leave for Hollywood the next morning.

A script clerk is a vital adjunct to the director and must be at his side at all times. He follows the script and makes sure that every word and stage direction is adhered to, he's responsible for making sure everything looks just as it did in the preceding take, and so on. Dmytryk was frantic. To get a replacement from the States would take at least a week, and we already were a few days behind our schedule. I offered to try to learn the job. The departing script clerk and I sat up all night while he taught me the bare rudiments of his job. We both were physical wrecks by morning, but at least I felt I could carry on until a professional arrived.

As it turned out, our harrowing night was unnecessary. Tracy had told Maggie about the newest problem and she volunteered her services, revealing that she had been a script clerk on several major film productions in England. Since she hadn't brought the necessary garments for scrambling up Alps, everyone donated something from his own wardrobe: sweaters, parkas, men's flannel underwear, boots. In her bizzare outfit, she still managed to look like Princess Margaret on her way to tea, but she turned out to be a faultless, thoroughly professional script clerk for Dmytryk. (She also provided us with a continuing mystery we never could fathom. In the six weeks she was up there on the Aiguille du Midi, we couldn't figure out how and where she went to the bathroom. Since that basic function was a freezing, uncomfortable problem even for us men, Maggie's method became a topic of acute interest. We finally decided that her ladylike training either had provided her with an enormous bladder and iron intestines or she managed some sort of disappearing act which none of us could detect.)

It wasn't until the final day of shooting that an unexpected chink appeared in Maggie's patrician armor. Tied together with ropes, we were slipping, sliding, and clambering down a rock face to get back to Chamonix for the last time. My roped-together foursome consisted of Maggie, Tracy, a prop man named Carl, and me. Maggie was at the rear so that we three husky males could break her fall if she slipped. She did slip, banging ignominiously from one chunk of granite to another until the rope brought her to a sprawling, undignified halt. Opening her aristocratic British mouth, she said to me in normal speaking tones, "Oh, those fucking rocks." She did not count on the fact that we were standing in one of the world's great natural echo chambers, which picked up her words, magnified them, and sent them bouncing back: "... fucking rocks ... fucking rocks ... fucking rocks."

There was a moment of shocked astonishment. Then we all broke up. Even Maggie forsook her natural composure and guffawed along with us. But Tracy was out of control altogether. He laughed so hard he started to gasp in the thin air and we thought we'd have to carry him down the mountain. He was still laughing about the incident when we got back to Hollywood and finished the picture. I heard him tell the story to every visitor who came to see him on the set at Paramount, and I later learned that, until the day he died, he would cheer up Katharine Hepburn by bursting into their private parody of the hit song from *The Sound of Music*, "The hills are alive with the sound of Maggie."

16

WHENEVER I was away on location, it was my practice to write long letters to my family. Except for Edith, it was their practice not to answer. In Chamonix, I did get one letter from Wally asking me to buy a special lens for his camera if I went to Zurich, but of most interest to me was Edith's glowing comment that "Bud now is being called 'the new Perc' in the industry."

When I got back from France I found out why. Bud had emerged from his administrative offices at Universal and returned temporarily to his beloved makeup lab, where his work was the talk of the industry.

Like all studios, Universal still was suffering from the television-caused depression in moviegoing, though the company was surviving financially by joining the enemy and renting out most of its space for TV production. In the matter of film-making, Universal had made a brief foray into quality movies under William Goetz, who had hired Bud in 1947, but now the company reached the sage decision to turn back, in part, to the money-making days of the 1930s and 1940s when the studio was famous for its horror pictures: Boris Karloff playing *The Mummy* and *Frankenstein*, Bela Lugosi as *Dracula*, and literally dozens of variations thereof. In an attempt to counter television's free small-screen dramas, the studios had moved toward huge theater-screen processes (Cinemascope, VistaVision, etc.), and the Universal brass guessed that a new-style horror movie with a fearsome monster six hundred times normal size on the new big screen would be so deliciously terrifying that people would abandon Milton Berle and plunk down $1.25 at the box office. The studio came up with *Creature From the Black Lagoon,* and Bud was called upon to go back into the lab and use all his talents to create a monster so horrifying and realistic that it would outdo Japan's highly successful *Godzilla.*

Before Bud got into the act, the film's producer, William Alland, had assigned the special-effects department and the staff shop (which makes statues and other props) to develop his concept of what the sea creature should look like. The movie had a budget of only $650,000, and Alland was trying to circumvent the makeup department to save both time and money. For two months they wrestled with the problem. When they finished, a remarkable underwater stuntman from Florida named Ricou Browning (who was to play the Creature) put on their handiwork and got into the underwater tank on the back lot. Instead of projecting menace, he looked like a man swimming around in long rubber underwear with black hair stuck to it.

When Bud took over, he did so with the assurance of a Michelangelo. It took him four months, assisted by Jack Kevan and Tom Case, to complete his monster. He made the usual face and body molds of Browning but went one step further and did an entire plaster-of-Paris statue of the stuntman. Since he had a lot of sculpting to do, he wanted to work on the statue and not Browning. He researched all kinds of prehistoric animals, especially from the Devonian Age, about a half billion years ago, when most of the earth was covered with water and giant amphibians abounded. But since he didn't think any drawings of authentic Devonian creatures were ugly or terrifying enough, he made dozens of sketches, trying to come up with the proper combination of fearsome hideousness. Then he remembered the grotesque, still-existent Mexican iguana and knew immediately that this was what he wanted his creature to resemble—in gigantic form.

The basic suit for the monster was made of liquid rubber baked onto the statue of Browning. Bud, Kevan, and Case made hundreds of individual latex scales to glue on the suit, with some of the scales on the legs as much as an inch thick. To make it easier for Browning to swim, more pliant scales were added to the torso. But still the monster wasn't frightening enough, so Bud kept improvising. He devised a scaled and jagged dorsal fin, running all the way from the base of the skull down to the tailbone. A zipper and hooks and eyes were concealed inside the fin so Browning could get in and out of the suit, a necessary refinement after Bud's experience with Ann Blyth and her mermaid's tail. (Bud couldn't see himself carrying a six-foot-five-inch man to the bathroom.) The iguanalike head of the creature was separate from the suit. It, too, had individually applied scales and was surmounted by a matching spiny fin, also with a zipper inside. Bud built goggles into the head so that Browning's own eyes could be photographed wide open under water.

The monster's hands were unbelievable accomplishments of cosmetic engineering. They were long, thorny, and bony, had talons several inches long, and were completely flexible. Another fin ran around each hand, up the arm to the elbow, slipped on like a glove and then zippered tightly. In the movie, the creature falls in love with Julie Adams, who is taking a dip in his lagoon in a sexy white bathing suit. The script called for the monster to carry her off to his watery lair, so Browning had to be able to *use* the hands Bud made. Julie told me they were so soft and pliable that it felt as if she were floating on a water bed when Browning held her.

Richard Carlson, who played the scientist in the picture, often had to get into the tank with the creature, and he hated doing it. "That suit was so frightening and so real," he said, "that I'd forget we were play-acting. We'd be shooting at midnight in freezing cold water, and suddenly this thing would swim toward me. It took all my discipline to hold my position and let it come near me. Bud Westmore had so completely captured the creature's personality that once inside the outfit Ricou Browning turned in one hell of a performance. Since he wasn't really an actor, I'm not being facetious when I say that in this case the clothes made the monster.

"In our story, the creature meant no harm to anyone, yet he knew he looked horrible. So behind Bud's mask, Browning let us know with his eyes that he realized he was a lonely, ugly, sad creature unwittingly tossed into another time, another culture. He loved Julie spiritually while I merely loved her carnally. He deserved her more than I did, and every graceful, fantastic move he made inside his monster suit, and what he did with his face inside that head, made the whole ridiculous thing believable."

When *Creature From the Black Lagoon* was reviewed, Abe Weiler of *The New York Times* acknowledged that the monster suit was the real star of the film. He wrote, "Our Gill-Man was made up terrifyingly enough to make a Grand Banks fisherman take up tatting." The movie earned more than five times its cost, put Universal firmly into the black, and spawned a mini-cycle of equally successful monsters designed by Bud. In rapid succession the studio did *Return of the Creature, Creature Walks Among Us, Deadly Mantis, Tarantula, Mole People,* and a favorite of Bud's called *Land Unknown,* in which he created strange, huge-headed extraterrestrial beings with their brains exposed. Edward Muhl, then the head of the studio, gave Bud and set designer Alexander Golitzen much of the credit for saving the whole studio operation. Golitzen went on to win three Academy Awards for his work. Bud won nothing but praise, because to this day there is no fixed category for makeup awards in the Academy structure.

I was very pleased for Bud and told him so, but as I said before, he had changed—and not for the better. He *was* becoming "the new Perc," except that he was more like the old Perc at his worst: arrogant, power-driven, rough on his employees. Young Tom Case was one of his victims. Tom was almost a Westmore because he married the sister of Mont, Jr.'s, wife, yet after three years of working with Bud, Tom couldn't stand his caustic attitude and quit—at the height of the Creature triumphs. There was another makeup man, very famous now, whom Bud fired because, he said, "I couldn't stand the way he laughed." When I asked Bud to elaborate on this quixotic decision, he simply told me to mind my own business.

Most upsetting was his seemingly sudden determination in 1954 to divorce Rosemary Lane. They had been married for thirteen years and had been very happy, or so everyone thought, including Rosemary. When Bud said he didn't want to be married any more, Rosemary took him to court in Los Angeles where she filed for divorce, asking hefty alimony and child support for their daughter, Bridget. News reports showed her weeping and quoted her as still "very much in love with my husband." There were more pictures of her and Bud together, emerging from conciliation court, where each had promised to try to stay together. That reconciliation lasted about a week. When Rosemary finally admitted defeat, she did get her divorce from Bud. In 1955 he married Jeanne Shores, Miss California of 1952, whom he met while he was one of the judges in the Miss America Pageant. Once again I was struck by the fact that we Westmores tend to repeat our own history. Bud's final marriage to Jeanne was happy and successful, and Jeanne bore him four lovely children.

But at work, and in his relations with our family, Bud's behavior continued to be erratic, to say the least. He agreed to apprentice Michael, Edith's youngest son, shortly after he had refused to accept her middle boy, Marvin. (Her oldest, Mont, Jr., had studied under Perc at Warner Brothers and already was doing splendidly on his own.) Mike went to work at Universal believing Bud was some kind of god. It seemed like every other minute Mike reported to me a new act of genius Bud had executed. I didn't want to spoil his illusions because I felt sure Bud would eventually do that himself.

Surprisingly, Bud worked very closely with Mike for quite a long time and bragged about him almost as much as Mike raved about Bud. The two were inseparable, and Mike was learning everything Bud could teach him. Mike made his fatal error when he fell in love with a gorgeous model named Marion Bergeson. He spotted her at Universal wearing a wedding gown designed by Edith Head for a fashion show on the lot. Mike asked her to marry him about an hour after they had been introduced, noting that she wouldn't have to change clothes. Later, when Mike told Bud that he and Marion really intended to be married, Bud stopped speaking to him. "I'd seen him give that awful silent treatment to a lot of other people," Mike said, "but I never expected it to happen to me." The day before the wedding, Bud broke that silence: He fired his favorite nephew. Mike's mother, Edith, who never interfered in anyone's business, was so distressed that she phoned Bud to ask him to reconsider. Bud refused to accept her call, and Marion and Michael started their new life unemployed.

Outside the family, and to those who didn't have to work for him, Bud was a different man. He was witty, charming, and accommodating. If the wife of a Universal executive wanted a makeup job because she was going to an important party, Bud went to her house, makeup case in hand, although he categorically refused to visit a set with his equipment, deeming that beneath his dignity. Because of his remarkable good looks, he was a walking advertisement for his studio, and Universal periodically sent him on lecture tours around the country. Women fought to get near him. One year, when he was judging a Miss America Pageant, Walter Winchell wrote, "Bud Westmore is prettier than any of the contestants." He had a delightfully fey sense of humor when he chose to use it, and it was at those times that the brother I had known and admired briefly emerged.

For example, I was there one day when Piper Laurie came to Bud's department just to talk with him. Piper was a young actress, under contract to the studio, who suffered the indignity of then-prevalent "imaginative" publicity campaigns, such as one which proclaimed that in order to keep her complexion beautiful she ate gardenias. Piper, in fact, was highly intelligent and talented, along with having the most gorgeous naturally red hair I've ever seen. She adored Bud and he liked her, commiserating with her whenever she was dispirited. That afternoon Bud and I listened as Piper recounted a batch of complaints, mainly regarding her publicity.

"Let's have some fun with that department," said Bud. He outlined his plan to Piper, who burst out laughing and agreed to go along with what he had in mind. Hours later, having completed the preparations for his scheme, he called Gail Gifford, a studio public-relations woman they both liked, and said to her, "You may not know this yet, Gail, but we have a new actress under contract and the studio is sending you on tour with her all over the country to get the press acquainted with her."

"Fine," said Gail. "What's her name?"

"Ah Soo Lin," said Bud, adding, "There's only one thing. She's Chinese and doesn't speak a word of English."

Gail got to Bud's office in record time, and Bud introduced her to an ethereal-looking Chinese girl whose long black hair ended somewhere below her knees. Her slanted eyes were sparkling brown. She wore a cheongsam of lustrous silk, and when Gail held out her hand and murmured, "How do you do?" the Chinese girl broke into a torrent of unintelligible words and suddenly sank to her knees in front of Gail.

"What's she *doing?*" squealed Gail.

"That's the way she bows," said Bud.

"Well, my God, get her up," said the usually unflappable pub-licist. While Bud assisted the girl to her feet, Gail timorously asked him how long the tour with Ah Soo Lin was supposed to be.

"Two months," said Bud.

Gail turned away and groaned; the Chinese girl giggled. The laugh was unmistakably Piper Laurie's. Gail caught on and the gag was over. It didn't change things completely, but there were fewer "imaginative" publicity stunts for Piper after that.

It would take a psychiatrist to figure Bud out, but knowing him as well as I did, I don't think he ever got over feeling guilty about the way he had become the head of the Universal makeup department instead of Ern. Although Bud had not conspired with Perc to get Ern drunk the night before his interview, he had tacitly gone along with the ploy and said nothing in Ern's defense. Bud did his work as well as anyone else, but I could sense his insecurity. Whenever someone he had hired began to show signs of indepen-dent inventiveness, Bud would either fire him or resort to his fa-mous "silent treatment," making the makeup artist's life so miser-able in general that he would quit.

At our increasingly infrequent family gatherings, Bud ex-hibited outright contempt for Perc, oblivious to the agony Perc was going through after his fall from power or, perhaps, trying to compensate for his own guilt. Whatever the reason, it was uncomfortable to be present when Bud grew insultingly silent and wouldn't even answer a direct question from Perc. Even the usually impervious Wally squirmed. Fortunately, Ern wasn't around to witness Bud's caustic behavior; he was still in New York, now reduced to working as a salesman for Adorn Cosmetics.

Throughout the late 1950s, I was very busy on a succession of pictures, mostly for Paramount, such as *The Joker Is Wild*, *The Buster Keaton Story*, *Hot Spell*, *Houseboat*, which starred Cary Grant and Sophia Loren, and *The Matchmaker*, where I first met Shirley MacLaine. Also there was *The Buccaneer*. I got involved in that epic because it began as a Cecil B. DeMille project and the old man asked for me; but as it turned out he was too ill to do the film.

I was so preoccupied with my own work and my vigorous bachelor existence during this period that I saw very little of my family and kept in touch mainly by phone. I felt peculiarly disconcerted whenever I spoke with Perc. He sounded cheerful enough, telling me about pictures he did with Bette Davis (who kept insisting that any studio hiring her for a film also had to hire Perc as her personal makeup consultant), and he talked glibly about the thriving business at The House of Westmore. I knew it wasn't thriving any more. Occasionally I went to the salon on a Saturday to see Ola and Perc, and although the place still hummed with activity, I didn't see many of the big stars who used to frequent it. As the movie elite moved their residences away from Hollywood and westward to Beverly Hills, Bel Air, and Brentwood, the trek to The House of Westmore became too lengthy, and little beauty shops were springing up everywhere, severely cutting into the salon's patronage. Still, Perc stubbornly refused to move, believing the stars would come back after a taste of something lesser—just as our father, George, had once believed.

Ola was working harder than ever, keeping up morale at the salon and at home. She and Perc had been married for more than seven years, but they seemed like honeymooners. He was so in love with her that even when they were sitting in a restaurant he would reach out and touch her arm as if to make sure she really was there. He took to prefacing her first name with the pronoun "my," and new employees at The House of Westmore thought her name was "Myola." He still was doing the $25-per-face consultant work at the salon, hating it more and more but tolerating almost anything because Ola was with him. He stopped his heavy drinking, limiting himself to a cocktail or two before dinner. He even returned occasionally to Warner Brothers when Gordon Bau, who had replaced him as head of the makeup department, hired him for a special movie. His life-style, if a far cry from what it once had been, seemed at least to have stabilized. That's why his next and most publicized suicide attempt was all the more shocking.

May 20, 1958, had been a normal day. Ola drove Perc to the salon in the new Buick convertible he had given her for her birthday. They left their multilevel Hollywood apartment earlier than usual because Perc wanted to pick up some hair he had ordered from Korea for possible use in making wigs. They stopped at a wholesale beauty-supply shop and then, with the car top down, continued on Sunset Boulevard to The House of Westmore. Perc was quite sure that he wouldn't like the quality of the Korean hair, but as usual he was ready to experiment with anything new. The first of his $25-consultant clients arrived, and Perc winked at his wife and disappeared into a booth. He completed several more consultations before noon and then went upstairs to work on the new hair. Ola called him to ask if he would do a makeup on Jeanette MacDonald if she could get in before four. He was pleased and said he could. By 7 P.M. he had finished with Jeanette, the last $25 consultancy was over, and Ola and Perc left for home. A perfectly routine day.

The apartment was stuffy and Ola changed into shorts, a shirt, and an apron to prepare dinner. While she puttered about in the kitchen, Perc took off his tie, snapped on the television set, and mixed their usual before-dinner drink. When the meal was ready, Perc ate with his habitual gusto, though he was overweight and his doctor was constantly cautioning him to lose a few pounds because of his heart condition. He was always trying the latest fad diet, wildly enthusiastic for a week or so and then right back to eating rich foods again. This time he was between diets.

About eight thirty, Ola was in the kitchen doing the dishes. (Long gone were the days of the big houses and the servants.) Suddenly Perc called to her. She walked into the living room drying her hands on a towel. Perc was sitting on the couch with a drink in one hand and with his other hand, palm up and cupped slightly, extended toward her. She thought he wanted to give her something, but as she moved closer she saw that the cupped hand held what looked like at least two dozen red sleeping pills. He said, "See these? I'm going to take them." Before she could say anything, Perc gulped the handful of pills, washing them down with his tumbler of straight Scotch.

Stunned for a moment or two, Ola just stared at Perc. Then she rushed over to him and pounded him on the stomach, not really knowing what she was doing. She thought perhaps she could make him throw up, but he got away from her and moved to another chair.

"I'm sorry, Myola," he said calmly.

Ola picked up the phone to call the doctor but couldn't reach him. Hysterical now, she dialed the Fire Department, screaming that it was an emergency. While she waited for the paramedics to arrive, she cried and begged Perc to vomit and implored him to tell her why he had done such a crazy thing now, of all times. He just sat there looking at her sadly. It couldn't have taken the Fire Department crew more than six or seven minutes to get there, but as she waited for what seemed like hours, absolutely nothing was happening to Perc. Ola began to think the pills she had seen were placebos—sugar pills—that he had taken to frighten her. He looked just as he had all that day: tired, but rational and cool. Once she asked him what he was feeling. "Nothing at all," he answered.

Finally Ola heard the siren of the approaching fire vehicle. Since Perc was showing no effect whatever from the combination of pills and whisky, she calmly went to the door to admit the men. She told them what had happened but added that perhaps her husband had "been joking." The medics asked her what Perc had eaten for dinner. When she told them about the large steak and two potatoes Perc had consumed, the medics explained that a full stomach could delay the reaction of barbiturates and alcohol. Worried, they said to Perc, "Come on, Mr. Westmore, let's walk up the steps to the ambulance. We can work on you as we drive to Hollywood Receiving Hospital."

Perc came up with a classic black-comedy reply. "I can't walk up any stairs," he said. "I've had four heart attacks."

Still wearing her apron over her shorts, Ola climbed into the ambulance with Perc. As the paramedics had feared, he suddenly lapsed into unconsciousness even while they gave him first aid on the way to the Receiving Hospital. He was rushed into the emergency room where his stomach was pumped, but he was still in a coma when his doctor arrived and joined the team of physicians working on him.

When they had done all they could and his condition had stabilized somewhat, Perc's doctor had him transferred to a private sanitarium. He told Ola that Perc might not make it, that to try to save him he had to make sure he got round-the-clock intensive care. The doctor also said he wanted to avoid the publicity Perc always generated.

Perc hovered between life and death for three days but finally emerged from his coma, contrite and mortified over the pain he had inflicted on Ola. He was not so fortunate in the matter of avoiding unwanted publicity. The May 21, 1958, edition of the *Los Angeles Mirror-News* blared out the story, beginning, "Perc Westmore, 54, tried suicide by an overdose of sleeping pills, the second time in eight months. . . ." When I questioned Ola about "the second time," she admitted it was true.

Perc never tried suicide again. His last attempt may have been a closer call than he anticipated, and he became surprisingly mellow over the next few years. He seemed to have come to terms with himself, realizing that he had Ola's deep love along with his past reputation, which no temporary adversity could erase. Surprisingly, too, Perc and I became really good friends for the first time in our lives. Despite all his earlier faults, I now felt he deserved my respect and reverence for his vast contributions to the industry and our profession.

My other brothers had not reached that stage of regard for the fallen Perc. His twin, Ern, in New York, was still resentful over their lifelong rivalry. It was small consolation to him that Perc appeared to be emulating his own one-time instability. Wally, well established at Paramount, and Bud, well established at Universal, may have harbored fears that Perc might yet stage a comeback and threaten their personal empires. In any event, the family bickering continued right up through the next near-tragedy just two years later, in 1960, involving the virile, seemingly indestructible Bud, then forty-two.

It happened when I was working on a Paramount picture called *The Rat Race* with Debbie Reynolds and Tony Curtis. Although Debbie had made at least a dozen movies and was a big star, she was also a big makeup problem for any artist who worked on her. She is exceptionally pretty in person, and at first glance I thought she would be so easy a subject that I should pay Wally for letting me do her makeup. But the camera accentuates everything, and I soon discovered that her deeply set eyes seem on film to sink into her head. Wally insisted I come up with a new eye makeup to eliminate this particular problem. After experimenting, I found an easy solution. On her eyelids and on the inside corners of her eyes, I used a base two shades lighter than the makeup I had applied to her cheeks. I decided not to use any eyeliner. Instead I applied light, filmy strip eyelashes, in the palest brown color I could find, and then barely touched the tips of the false eyelashes with a light brown mascara. I was sitting in the projection room, looking at film which clearly showed that her eyes seemed bigger and happily accepting her compliments on my handiwork, when the telephone rang. It was Wally, telling me to rush to his office as fast as I could.

I arrived breathlessly and Wally said, "I just had a call from the director of the Miss America Pageant in Atlantic City. Bud has had a massive heart attack and is in the hospital in an oxygen tent. What'll we do?" It was September and, as usual, Bud was on the program as one of the Pageant's judges.

First I called the hospital to verify the facts. A doctor told me that Bud was dying and that Jeanne, his wife, had been notified and was already on her way to New Jersey. He suggested solemnly that a member of the Westmore family also be present. I glanced at Wally, who was listening on an extension phone, and he vehemently shook his head. I couldn't go because I was in the middle of a picture, so I called Ern in New York—he was nearest geographically to Atlantic City—and told him to get to Bud at once. Ern said he'd be happy to go but he had no money. I said I'd wire two hundred dollars, enough for him to fly to Atlantic City and check into a motel. Ern promised that as soon as the money arrived he would take off.

I still felt uneasy, possibly at my own guilt at having a legitimate excuse not to go to my brother's side, so I called my bank and had them wire fifteen hundred totally unneeded dollars to Bud's account at the hospital. While I was making these frenzied arrangements, Wally sat impassively behind his desk, checking off items on his makeup order list. At no point did he offer to contribute either his time or his money. I was outraged but not surprised.

Ern reached Atlantic City on Saturday morning, the day after Bud's coronary attack. Instead of checking into a motel, he went to the hotel where Bud had been staying and took over his luxurious suite. He informed a Miss America official that he was there and only then went to the hospital. He called me that night and told me Bud was still in an oxygen tent and looked terrible, but that he was conscious. Jeanne had been given a room in the hospital next to her husband's, and the outlook for Bud's survival was grim. That was when Perc decided that he, too, should go to Bud's bedside, and he left Los Angeles on Monday morning, arriving in Atlantic City that evening.

Tuesday morning there was another phone call to Wally and me from the Medical Director of the hospital, who told us there was such a disturbance outside Mr. Bud Westmore's room that his staff was at a loss as to how to cope with it. The doctor said, "Those twin brothers of yours are standing at the door of Mr. Westmore's room arguing so loudly about which of them the patient is happier to see that it is disrupting the entire floor. I don't know what to do, but we can't tolerate this kind of nonsense. We do have other sick people, you know."

For a second I felt an unbidden hysterical laughter welling up inside me. The incident was another example of Westmore black comedy. I choked back my impulse and asked the doctor to connect me with Bud's floor. I didn't have any trouble getting Perc and Ern to the phone; the floor nurse knew exactly who they were. I spoke first with Ern, who kept muttering, "Well, I was here first," and then to Perc, who said, "You know what this dumb son of a bitch did? He went to Bud's suite, which the Pageant pays for, and charged so much food and so many long distance calls to the room that they threw him out. And he's trying to tell *me* who's welcome and who isn't."

I suddenly felt like a father to the fifty-six-year-old twins instead of their baby brother. I made both of them promise to behave themselves, and only then was I able to find out how Bud was doing; Perc told me that with extremely good care he would pull through.

He *did* pull through. Five weeks later, Bud was taken by stretcher to a plane and flown home. Fortunately, both Perc and Ern had long since departed, and Wally, in his office at Paramount, was still saying things like, "D'ya think six hundred eyelash strips in assorted colors are enough for now?"

17

AFTER a fairly lengthy convalescence Bud returned to Universal, where he categorically refused to discuss his heart attack with anyone. Obviously he wanted what he called "just an incident" to be forgotten as quickly as possible, lest the executives get the idea that he was too sick to handle his demanding job. The strategy worked so well that even his own family's apprehensions about Bud's health disappeared. For a change, all the Westmores seemed to be intact and functioning well. No one was in jail or in a hospital. So in 1961, when Shirley MacLaine asked me to accompany her to Japan to do her makeup for the movie *My Geisha*, I saw no reason to stay close to home and said I'd love to go.

Shirley and I had worked together on five pictures since 1958 and had become close friends. In those days Shirley had not yet become a political activist. She had nothing on her mind but being a movie star and having fun. When I first met her she was a freckle-faced super-tomboy who hadn't yet developed the aura of stardom. I always regarded her as the rambunctious kid sister I'd never had. Like most redheads, she had a very short fuse to her temper, and her reactions were always physical—to hit, kick, run, express her emotions in action. Although she was—and still is—the wife of American entrepreneur Steve Parker and the mother of their daughter, Sachiko, her life-style was anything but conventional. Shirley was at least a decade ahead of today's so-called liberated woman. When Parker decided to live in Japan, Shirley, after a brief try at togetherness in Tokyo, declared that it was not the place for her and returned to the United States. She left Sachi with her husband and has been an intercontinental commuter ever since.

My Geisha was the brainchild of Steve Parker, who was to produce the film for Paramount, with his redheaded, unmistakably Irish-looking wife posing as a Japanese geisha girl. I liked the challenge because I knew I would have to use all my makeup creativity for the illusion to be believable. We started lab work with the technicians at Paramount before I left for Japan. The technique of making eye impressions has advanced considerably since the days when Wally struggled to transform Akim Tamiroff into an Oriental in *The General Died at Dawn,* but it is still one of the more delicate and uncomfortable of the highly sophisticated makeup operations. For the actor, it is more uncomfortable psychologically than physically. Once I sat for a mold of my own eyes just to see what it was like. I felt oddly helpless and dependent on the technicians. With Shirley the process became more complex, because it is next to impossible for her to sit quietly *anywhere* for any length of time.

When she came to the lab we were ready for her. Taking dental wax—the same rubberlike material a dentist uses in taking impressions of gums for dentures—we broke the substance into small pieces and melted it in a double boiler. We then applied it in a warm, semimolten state over Shirley's upper face, from her eyebrows to the tip of her nose. To give the wax additional strength, we covered it with casting plaster. When the wax had cooled and solidified, we removed it. I was delighted to note we had obtained an excellent impression of her eyes on the very first take. Shirley wasn't delighted. She stalked out of the lab in a temper at the indignity to which she had been subjected.

I blew a kiss to her retreating back and we began the real work of converting her Caucasian eyes to Oriental eyes. The technicians mixed a batch of dental plaster—a highly refined and smooth type of plaster of Paris—and poured it into the wax impression. When that hardened, we removed the wax and had a perfect reproduction of the top half of the familiar MacLaine face. It was on this model that we then proceeded to work with modeling clay, curving the eye to the desired Oriental shape. Through another series of wax impressions and dental-plaster castings, we were finally able to bake rubber eyepieces fashioned from the clay additions we had sculpted onto the plaster reproduction of her upper face.

These complicated procedures took four days, at the end of which time I summoned Shirley back to the lab. I glued on the eyepieces with spirit gum, and to give the eyes a further slant I glued an invisible flesh-colored plastic tab to the skin near each of her temples. Rubber bands, attached to the tabs and hooked together at the top of her head, under a concealing wig, pulled up the corners of her eyes. With brown contact lenses obscuring her bright blue eyes, Shirley looked as Oriental as the Japanese Empress. We sent still photos and movie film of my handiwork to Steve Parker and director Jack Cardiff in Tokyo. Word came back that they were pleased with the results. That finished the preliminaries in the States. All I had to do was pack an enormous location box with all the makeup supplies I thought I would need for the four months of filming.

When Wally heard how much I was ordering, he was very upset. "You're taking enough makeup for every woman in Japan for the next ten years," he grumbled. It was well known to anyone who ever worked with him that my brother was one of the world's champion hoarders. His makeup supply department was known as "the vault." When you asked him for a certain cosmetic, he'd keep you standing outside in the hall or, if you did get into the room, he'd half shut the cupboard doors so you couldn't see what he had in them. One day, while filling my requisition for Japan, he was rummaging in the clutter at the back of a cabinet when he discovered a large box of eyebrow pencils he had ordered long before World War II. When he pulled them out, they were covered with mold.

Two weeks after I had wormed my requirements out of Wally, Shirley and I boarded our Japan Airlines flight for Tokyo. I felt good. A dozen pairs of the Oriental eyepieces and tabs were securely locked in my makeup box, and Paramount's lab technicians had been instructed to keep molding replacements and

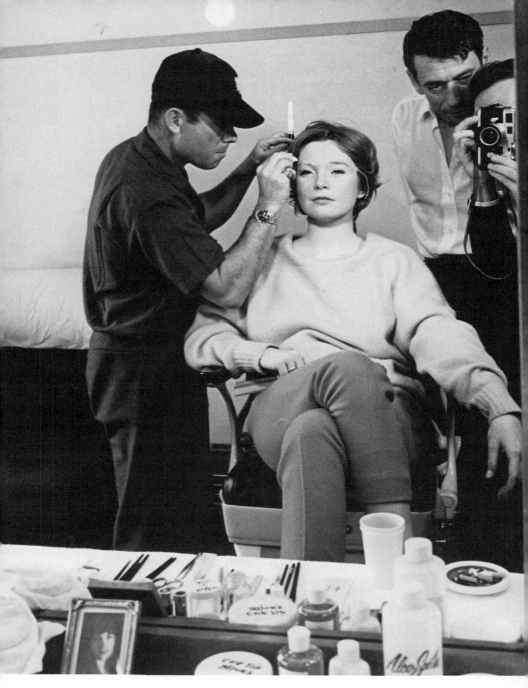

On the My Geisha *set, I begin the complex process*
of transforming Shirley MacLaine into an
Oriental, while co-star Yves Montand watches.

Applying Oriental eyelids.

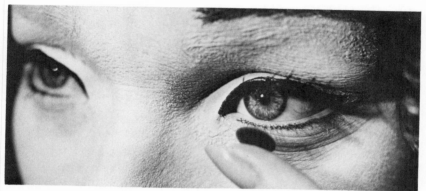

Shirley inserts the contact lenses which will change her blue eyes to brown.

The finished product: Shirley checks her full Oriental makeup as director Jack Cardiff and I watch.

sending them to Japan as we needed them. I settled down to enjoy the trip. The Japanese stewardess removed our shoes and jackets and helped us into the traditional Japanese "happi coats." We pulled down our trays and ordered drinks. Then Shirley, reaching for a napkin, knocked my tall vodka and tonic off the tray and into my lap. It was a freezing shock, but what was worse, I had to walk down the aisle of the plane looking as if I were headed for the bathroom but hadn't made it. A stewardess dried my trousers with a hand hair dryer. That was a taste of things to come.

We landed in Tokyo early in the morning and were taken by company car to the Takanawa Prince Hotel just outside Tokyo. The rest of the cast already was there: Robert Cummings, Edward G. Robinson, Yves Montand. Paul Godkin, Shirley's choreographer, was so glad to see her that he hurled himself upon his exhausted employer and both fell to the floor. Then Steve Parker and Jack Cardiff informed Shirley and me that more makeup tests would have to be made the following day. After Shirley had left to get some sleep, Steve and Jack explained to me that while Shirley certainly looked Oriental enough, she didn't look like a *beautiful* Oriental girl. I said, "Just making her face Japanese was a job in itself, but to make her beautiful—*that* she wasn't to begin with."

Steve may have reported my remarks to Shirley, because she was in a foul mood when she slipped into my makeup chair the next morning. She complained bitterly about the contact lenses, saying they hurt her eyes and made them tear. She blamed my eye tabs which, when I pulled them up with the rubber bands, caused her lids to press against the lenses. After nearly every take, she picked away at the eye tabs, ruining them. I kept putting on new tabs, worrying that I would run out before the replacements arrived from Hollywood. When I asked her to let me remove the tabs, she lashed out, "I'll do just what I please, schmuck." I was seething, too, but I knew the makeup was difficult to wear so I tried to keep myself in check. Finally, though, when she did ask, "How *do* you get these goddam things off?" I said, "Like this," and gave a mighty yank, peeling away a small patch of her skin as well.

She screamed with pain and yelled, "You son of a bitch," and started pummeling me. I ran out of the makeup room onto the sound stage with Shirley right behind me. The chase was on, to the merriment of the Japanese crew, but it was serious to me. Shirley had a right hook that could floor a heavyweight. When she realized she couldn't catch me, she sank to the cement floor and began to cry. I knew it was a signal that I was forgiven, but I had had all I could take. I skidded to a stop in front of her and suggested that she perform an anatomical impossibility on herself. We finished the day's work in sullen silence.

Not long after that, we moved to a little island near Hiroshima, to find that someone had neglected to reserve a room for me in the island's one hotel. I was about to head back to the mainland when Shirley unexpectedly said, "You can share my room with me." We spent the night with no physical contact except when I had to poke her in the ribs to make her stop snoring. But the crisis was over, and we were friends again.

The next three weeks were peaceful. Shirley endured the makeup with stoicism if not patience, and I learned to keep my brain moving three steps ahead of my hands so I could apply the eyepieces and tabs in forty-five minutes, Shirley's limit of endurance. By the time we returned to Tokyo, I was mentally and physically worn out.

On a Saturday, our first day off since we'd arrived in Japan, I was determined to sleep until noon and then see something of the exciting city. I was just barely awake when my phone rang around eleven thirty that morning. The caller was choreographer Paul Godkin. He said, "Shirley is in the beauty shop downstairs, but she doesn't like the shampoo they use here. Where is her own stuff you brought from the States?"

I told him the shampoo was in my makeup room at the studio, that each bottle of liquid was wrapped and labeled, and to be very careful not to disarrange anything. Apparently I insulted him because he abruptly hung up. I ordered breakfast and then went to the shower. A short time later the phone rang again. Godkin shrieked, "Come to the beauty shop immediately!" I tore into my clothes and arrived at the shop in about five minutes. There sat Shirley, her hair stark white and stiff as a board. She was speechless with shock. Instead of shampoo, Godkin had grabbed one of my specifically labeled bottles of clear plastic adhesive which turns white on hardening. The whole scene reminded me of my disaster with Muck the chimp. I used nearly a full gallon of alcohol to dissolve the glued-together mess of Shirley's hair, painfully burning her scalp in the process. This restored Shirley's use of her tongue and ended her period of self-imposed control. She blistered the air with expletives in combinations never before heard in that serene Japanese environment.

There were another ten days of comparative tranquillity. I knew Shirley's singed scalp ached under the heavy black geisha wig, and even with my constant adjustments to the eye tabs, there was still painful pressure on her contact lenses, so I went out of my way to be exceptionally kind and tender with her. I even negotiated an arrangement with director Cardiff for Shirley to work in forty-five-minute segments, with fifteen minutes off in each hour. During the rest periods, I removed her wig, unhooked the tight rubber bands, and took out the brown-tinted contact lenses. She not only appreciated this solicitude but worked doubly hard onstage, and the filming progressed at a much faster pace.

Then we got ready to move to the ancient city of Kyoto, some 250 miles southwest of Tokyo, and I had my next contretemps with the now fully recovered actress. To be sure Shirley would be ready to leave on the 6 A.M. flight for Kyoto, I ordered breakfast for both of us from room service the night before, asking that it be brought to my room at 5 A.M. Shirley arrived at 4:45. Breakfast didn't appear until nearly 5:10. The waiter rolled in the table, laden with a basket of fruit for our trip and fried eggs sunny side up, just the way Shirley and I liked them. The waiter was gone before we realized there was no cutlery on the table except for a single silver butter knife. With no time to send for forks, we had to eat our eggs with the one implement that was available. Did you ever try to get slithery fried eggs to your mouth with a butter knife? It was a shambles. On the first attempt, I spattered my suit with melted butter. Shirley dripped egg yolk all over the front of her dress. We left with Shirley in a fury. She grabbed the basket of fruit and stalked down the hall, insisting that it was my fault because she had to share the butter knife with me.

She continued scolding in the elevator, all the way down to the hotel lobby. Just before the elevator doors opened, an orange rolled out of the basket. As the doors hissed open, she stooped to retrieve the fruit. By this time I was so angry myself that I couldn't resist giving her a good kick in the rump, so temptingly vulnerable in her bent-over position. Maybe I kicked her a little *too* hard. She went out the doors head first and slid on her belly across the highly polished floor of the lobby, finally coming to rest with her head under a couch and her pantied bottom exposed to the world. Horrified, I rushed over. I pulled her out from beneath the davenport and discovered she was laughing so hard she scarcely could catch her breath.

Shirley and I played together and fought together like a pair of healthy puppies. Yet there were many other sides to her as well. For example, she has a deep reverence for foreign cultures, and when she took me on a tour of some of the eight hundred ancient temples and shrines in Kyoto, the historic center of the old Japan, I learned more than I could have absorbed in a two-year college course in the subject. Also, she has a fascinating built-in mechanism for loosening up otherwise staid people. She took Edward G. Robinson and Robert Cummings to the sumo wrestling matches and deliberately neglected to warn them that the arena's restroom facilities are unisex. Both Robinson and Cummings were startled out of their innate cocoons of reserve when they were mobbed by female Japanese fans and forced to sign autographs one-handed as they stood at the urinals.

Despite such disruptions, the filming went well in Kyoto, and there was only one other emergency that required any makeup ingenuity on my part. It was a problem I never had faced before, and it took some unique improvisation to prevent the production from closing down indefinitely. I looked in my makeup case on the second day of shooting and realized I was completely out of eye tabs. Shirley had torn off so many of them that first day of tests that my supply had run down, and the replacements shipped from Hollywood to Tokyo had not caught up with our move to Kyoto. Without the eye tabs, Shirley's eyes wouldn't slant and the footage wouldn't match previous shots of her face. The director, Jack Cardiff, told me in no uncertain terms that it was my problem and I'd better come up with a solution by the time we were ready to start work the next morning.

I was brooding that night at dinner when our production manager, Harry Kaplan, asked me what material I needed to make the eye tabs. "I could use thin transparent rubber," I said.

"Well," said Kaplan, "I've got a condom." Before I had a chance to tell Kaplan what a wonderful idea he had come up with, he began to unroll one. I gaped at it because it was the most enormous condom I'd ever seen in my life. I looked at the short, unimpressively built Kaplan with wonderment and asked if the condom was his. "No," he said glumly, "it's my brother's."

Shirley was just as nervous as I had been about the lack of eye tabs. After all, it was as much her picture as it was her husband's, and she stood to lose a lot of money from any delay. When I told her evasively that I had found a new source of supply, sufficient to keep us in business with satisfactory substitutes until the pipeline to Hollywood opened again, she insisted on knowing just what I intended to use. Finally I was forced to show her the condom. Her laughter turned to wide-eyed amazement as I unrolled the enormous contraceptive. As I began to cut it into small pieces for the eye tabs, she said, "You bastard, that can't be yours." I acted insulted and made it perfectly clear that the super-rubber indeed was custom made to accommodate my extraordinary anatomy. Shirley was impressed.

Later that day, after my improvised eye tabs had undergone several hours of successful filming, I left the set to go to the men's room. As I walked down a long, dark, hardwood corridor, I heard the unmistakable sound of stealthy footsteps behind me. When I stopped, the footsteps stopped. I shrugged and continued to the bathroom and proceeded to a urinal. The footsteps came up directly behind me. I finally turned my head, not at all surprised to see Shirley standing at my shoulder, looking downward.

Then she said, "I *knew* that rubber wasn't yours," turned on her heel, and contemptuously strode away.

After *My Geisha*, I did Shirley's makeup in nearly all her films in the 1960s, the peak decade of her career: *Two for the Seesaw*, *Irma La Douce*, *What a Way to Go*, *Sweet Charity*, and several others. The good pictures usually went smoothly. The less memorable ones brought on the most memorable flaps.

Probably the least memorable film of all was *Two Mules for Sister Sara*, in which Shirley agreed to play a prostitute impersonating a nun after producer Martin Rackin agreed to meet her fee of a million dollars for the picture. Apart from the money, the whole notion intrigued her anyway, since the one thing she had never been accused of was of being holy. I think she felt if she could pull off such an offbeat role, she would be considered a consummate actress. What she didn't count on was her co-star, Clint Eastwood, who was wooden and uncomfortable and gave Shirley little in the way of the reaction she needed to spark a fine performance.

My problem was the location. Most of the filming was done in the rugged mountains of the Mexican interior, where the sun was remorseless and a potential hazard to Shirley, a true redhead with the typical redhead's delicate skin. In order to prevent her from burning to a crisp or, at the very least, sprouting more freckles than she already had, I mixed a sun-blocking ointment directly into her makeup. Such sunray screens now are common in makeup bases because of the skin cancer scare, but at that time only a few were on the market—none of them effective enough for Shirley's exceptionally vulnerable skin—so I had to improvise my own from the basic chemicals.

When director Don Siegel noted my complicated procedures for protecting Shirley from the sun, he went a step further and hired a short middle-aged Mexican gentleman to carry a huge black umbrella at all times and to keep her covered with it whenever she was not directly before the camera. Siegel so impressed the little fellow with the importance of his job that, even when Shirley was seated inside a makeshift lean-to, he was right there in the shade with her, still sheltering her with his umbrella. So zealous was the Umbrella Man, so eager to excel at his assigned task, that several times Siegel—through an interpreter—had to shoo him out of a shot.

Then came one of the key scenes in the picture, in which Shirley is set upon by *bandidos* whose unmistakable intention is to rape her. Eastwood arrives in the nick of time and rescues the pseudo-nun, but not before most of her clothes have been ripped off by the terrorists. Two versions of the scene were to be filmed: one for American audiences, where only her shoulders and part of her back would be in view; the other for the European market, where all of Shirley would be visible.

The double effort called for a hard day's shooting in the Mexican wilderness on a large rock formation. The day was staggeringly hot, already 110 degrees at seven o'clock in the morning. I slathered Shirley's face and hands with the special sun-screen makeup and waited for Siegel to get his camera set up on top of the rock. It was slow work, and the terrible heat and relentless sun began to frazzle the tempers of everyone in the company—everyone, that is, except the Umbrella Man, who happily rushed hither and yon with Shirley, faithfully carrying out his designated function.

Finally Siegel was ready. Shirley clambered aboard one of her two mules, both of which were at best balky and at worst downright unmanageable. This day her animal was altogether recalcitrant. Shirley came down the rock a dozen times or more, the mule kicking and braying and losing its footing on the slippery surface. I watched with growing dismay as I saw the familiar signs of an approaching MacLaine tantrum. Director Siegel was aware of them, too, but he was determined to finish the shot as quickly as possible so we could get the hell out of the sun.

Eastwood, on a beautiful little filly, was having an easier time of it, following along as Shirley and her mule stumbled through one take after another. Finally Shirley had had it. She screamed to Siegel, "I'm not going down this rock one more time on this insane animal!" When Siegel protested, Shirley shouted, "Do it my way, or we don't do the shot at all."

Siegel told her they would do it *his* way, or she could take her million dollars and stuff it. Then he added bitterly, "You don't like the way I work, get off your ass and direct the rest of the picture yourself." Shirley got off her ass, all right. She leaped from the mule and took off down the rock, her nun's habit streaming behind her, running like mad toward a jeep which could take her back to the hotel. She looked like an oversized penguin escaping from a zoo. Most ludicrous of all, tearing after her was the single-minded Umbrella Man, desperately trying to do his job and keep her covered. Her long dancer's legs gave her a decided advantage over the unfortunate short-legged Mexican, whose big black umbrella kept trapping air and twisted him around like a top as he ran.

Then I—as official MacLaine temper specialist—took off after her. Halfway down the rock I launched myself into a flying tackle and brought Shirley down flat on her belly. She fought with every bit of strength she had left, which was considerable. I managed to get a hammerlock around her neck, put her face gently into the dry soil, and said, "Keep this up and your face will become just another part of the history of this rock." I had forgotten the Umbrella Man but I suddenly sensed we were in the shade, and there he was, covering Shirley—and now me—with his black umbrella. Still locked in combat, Shirley and I simultaneously noticed something from our ground-level point of view. A scorpion was scuttling across the sandaled feet of our Umbrella Man, but not even that deadly threat could tax his loyalty and cause him to shift position.

The sight of the scorpion was an instant antidote to Shirley's rage. She stopped struggling and whispered that she would be good. I suggested she put that in writing. She did so that evening, sending Don Siegel a lavish array of flowers and a hand-penned apology.

That's the way Shirley used to be—before she became a philosopher, politician, author, and expert on the People's Republic of China.

18

IT was indirectly because of Shirley MacLaine that I met Gloria. In 1962, Shirley was signed to co-star with Robert Mitchum in *Two for the Seesaw*, and as usual I went along with the package as Shirley's makeup artist. When I reported for work at the Samuel Goldwyn Studios I was told that Shirley was in Mitchum's office, and I went there to check in with her. She and Mitchum were in a meeting, but a beautiful blond girl, one of Mitchum's assistants, greeted me in the anteroom. She had the loveliest brown eyes and the softest-looking pink complexion I'd ever seen.

I stared at her, and for one of the few times in my life I was speechless. Then, to impress her with the fact that I was a suave world traveler newly returned from the exotic *My Geisha* location, I asked her for a cup of coffee in the few words of Japanese I had acquired. To my amazement, she threw her head back and guffawed. I was about to be insulted but she explained that she was laughing only because she had been talked into going to a fortuneteller the night before and the clairvoyant had told her she was "going to meet a dark handsome man who spoke in a foreign tongue." She introduced herself as Gloria Christian. I fell in love with her immediately.

From that moment on, Gloria became the most important part of my life, though we didn't marry until six years later after the longest courtship in the annals of the modern Westmores. Already twice burned, I was, perhaps, unreasonably overcautious. Gloria is a wise and gentle woman, and living with her has calmed my bombastic nature and curbed my sharp tongue. In temperament, Gloria is a lot like Edith, the family diplomat, and she did much to smooth out the constantly erupting differences among the mercurial Westmores. She got along with all of them.

Her particular favorite, strangely enough, was the now-mellowed Perc; she could scarcely believe the stories I told her about his evil-genius days. Not only did she help cement my new friendship for the brother I had once hated for cruelly sentencing me to military schools, but she spent hours with him, listening to his tales of the old days and subtly—with Ola—bolstering his still shattered ego.

Perc called Gloria "little sister." In tandem, "little sister" and "Myola" did quite a job on Perc. He was working, but only sporadically, and between jobs his health deteriorated and the old depressions returned.

Then, with the encouragement of his woman and mine, Perc was on the move again, though it didn't start out auspiciously. In fact, his first step was considered to be a degrading comedown by the industry.

One day in 1964 Perc got a call from a Universal Studios executive named Herb Steinberg. Steinberg had been head of exploitation at Paramount during its most profitable years, and through his association with Wally at his old studio, he had witnessed at first hand the power and prestige the name Westmore implied. Universal now was on the upswing again both in movie and TV production, having been purchased by the huge show-business conglomerate MCA, Inc., and the MCA brass had wooed Steinberg away from Paramount to work his public-relations magic for them. They wanted him to help organize bus tours through their massive 420-acre back lot (an area larger than the Principality of Monaco), the idea being to induce tourists to pay good money not to see movies but to see how movies and television shows are made. The simple concept has since become, along with Disneyland, one of the most profitable must-see attractions in Southern California, but back in July 1964, when Steinberg first met with Al Dorskind, vice-president in charge of real estate development for MCA, they had nothing more tangible than a few buses. In their discussion about possible attractions for the tours, Dorskind idly suggested that they hire Perc Westmore to give lectures on film makeup for visitors. Steinberg's publicity instincts leaped at the idea, but he doubted that the legendary Perc Westmore would agree to do what was basically a demeaning job. Nevertheless, he agreed to find out. To his astonishment, Perc's response was "When do I start?" He didn't even ask what Universal would pay.

On July 15, 1964, in the basement of the newly opened Universal commissary, Perc, resplendent in his trademark clothes of white jacket, white pants, and white shoes, began his twice-a-day lectures and makeup demonstrations. Young Mike Westmore, our nephew and Bud's apprentice, assisted him. Perc was ecstatic. I was despondent. Watching him was like seeing Sir Laurence Olivier as a carnival barker. But to Perc it was like plasma. As Ern had done years before on his New York-based television show, Perc would point to a woman in the audience, have Mike bring her to the platform, and proceed to redo her makeup. As much as he had dreaded this chore in the salon, he loved the exposure, the adulation of the crowd, the joy of being "on." He was an instant success. The newspapers, which had ignored him for so many years—except to report on his suicide attempts and his illnesses—now sent reporters to interview him. Soon his tourist audiences became so large that they overflowed the commissary basement. The entire "Perc Westmore Makeup Show" had to be moved outside to an area called the Visitors' Center. Instead of two lectures a day he now did four. Jane Wyman remembers the afternoon she was on the lot, standing above the crowds, horrified at the spectacle of Perc Westmore delivering his spiel like an open-air pitchman. As she attempted to skulk away, Perc spotted her. Unabashed, he rushed up the hill, grabbed by the hand, brought her down to the audience, and announced to the ladies, "Always remember, if you look like Jane Wyman, don't wear any makeup at all."

None of this sat well with Bud, seemingly safe as the head of Universal's makeup department in the magnificent new $750,000

222

building designed by him. The specter of Perc had risen again to threaten his empire. He was convinced his older brother was out to get his job. He insisted to Steinberg that Perc was sick and unreliable, but the strategy backfired. In deference to his health, Perc was elevated to the position of "consultant" to the tour's makeup show, with nephew Mike and others doing the actual performing. Perc himself was moved to an office in Bud's own new building to function as a specialist on hair and wigs and to lend his expertise to the studio's expanding list of television shows. Bud was livid, but there was nothing he could do about it—then.

One of the first shows assigned to Perc was *The Munsters*, which began on CBS in September 1964. The chief makeup artist for the series was John Chambers (who later won an Oscar for his superb gorilla-chimpanzee-orangutan creations in *The Planet of the Apes* movie for 20th Century-Fox). Chambers, who liked and respected Perc, asked him to assist in applying a complicated human-vampire makeup to an actor named Al Lewis. Perc, not fully recovered from his previous illnesses and terrified at doing his first journeyman makeup artist job in years, could barely handle the elaborate Dracula-like prosthesis Chambers had fabricated for Lewis in the lab. Chambers noticed how Perc's hands were shaking and gently took the rubber facial strips from him, saying, "That's all right, Perc, let me do it." Perc just stood around watching as Chambers glued the strips onto Lewis's face.

Such was the magnitude of the Westmore reputation, however, that when Chambers finished, Lewis turned around in his chair, looked at himself in the mirror, and unerringly rushed over to wring Perc's hand, not Chambers's. "Perc," exulted Lewis, "you've done it again."

That, too, was plasma for Perc. Beginning the next day, his hands stopped shaking and he did apply Lewis's *Munster* makeup for the rest of that season's shows. He also worked efficiently on several other Universal TV series, in addition to carrying out his consultant duties for the tours. But the inevitable finally happened. Bud, watching stars flock to Perc's office instead of his own, couldn't stand it any more. Working behind the scenes, he did just what the old Perc would have done at Warner Brothers twenty years before: He got Perc fired. I still don't know how Bud managed it, but it was obviously a masterpiece of undercover manipulation.

By then it didn't matter any more. Perc, his confidence restored and now totally unashamed to go down to a set, makeup case in hand, went to Gordon Bau at Warner Brothers and said, "Here I am. Forget I once was the head of this department. I'll take any makeup job that's available, at the studio, on location, anywhere." Perc worked steadily thereafter as one of the finest journeyman makeup artists in the business.

The Westmore Dynasty—at least in the grandiose form in which it had flourished from the 1920s through the 1950s—was crumbling. Saddest to Gloria and me were the last days of The House of Westmore. Only Perc and Ola had kept the salon going after the other brothers, though still financial participants, had lost interest in its operations. It was, after all, Perc's self-proclaimed "monument" to himself, but by 1965 even he recognized the old palace of beauty was a ghost of things past—like the departed spirits of the Gables, Lombards, and Laughtons who once had frequented its gold, coral, and white halls.

In its final months, all that was left of The House of Westmore was a pervading sense of shabby elegance. Its Sunset Boulevard neighborhood had deteriorated, with porno bookshops and souvenir stands sprouting where fine boutiques had flourished. Inside the salon, the once-beautiful draperies drooped from lack of proper cleaning; the gilt furniture was flaking. Half the booths were untended, the best beauticians having quit because they couldn't make enough money in the shop. Few important female stars were clients any more, and the general public stopped coming as the Perc Westmore $25 beauty consultation became an anachronism. It was the beginning of the Vietnam war protest period, during which a whole new breed of star—the rock and folk singer—popularized a new look: long straight naturally colored hair and very little makeup. Older women adopted the fad from their children, and there was no longer any great demand for an elaborate Westmore coiffure or a complicated Westmore facial

224

analysis with corrective artistry. Every week there were fewer and fewer names in Ola's appointment book.

On August 10, 1965, thirty years and four months after The House of Westmore attracted worldwide news coverage with its star-studded grand opening, Ola simply tacked up a "closed" sign on the golden doors, wept briefly, and went home. Perc had sold the building to a New York realty firm; Universal Studios had contracted to buy all the movable equipment. Ola didn't want to see the men arrive to begin crating the familiar chairs and hair dryers.

But the old salon died hard. A group of male stars, headed by Milton Berle and Ozzie Nelson, insisted that they be allowed to continue to come to the salon during the packing process, in order to have their hair tended by Bob Matz, The House of Westmore's fine old master barber, who had been with the organization for its full thirty years. Touched, Perc left the rear door open, and for two weeks—until the new owners' carpenters moved in—Berle, Nelson, William Holden, Raymond Burr, Fredric March, Sir Laurence Olivier, and others defiantly trooped down the alley to the back door and sat amid the debris while the white-haired Matz trimmed and shaped their locks. It was a final act of loyalty, as fans gaped once again in The House of Westmore alley, and it impelled Matz to move to a barbershop just down the street. Now in his seventies, Matz still cuts the hair of Holden, Burr, et al., and he refers to his single chair as House of Westmore, East.

The wealthiest and most successful of my brothers, Wally, did not fret much over the demise of the salon. He had earned back his original 1935 investment many times over, and he was disturbed only by the fact that his frugality had caused him to enter too low a bid for The House of Westmore equipment, thus enabling brother Bud to win it for the new Universal Studios makeup building. Actually, Wally had more to worry about than he realized. On the surface, he seemed as secure as anyone could be as he completed his thirty-ninth year as the unchallenged potentate of the famous Paramount makeup department. He still played cards with Ray Milland, went hunting and fishing with

225

Bing Crosby, clipped stock coupons with his banker friends, and kept a hawk's-eye watch over his makeup inventory; but it was a long time since he had worked on an actor's face or cast a face mold in his superb laboratory. Not only was he out of touch with the family, seeing us socially now only on Christmas or an occasional birthday party, but, like Perc fifteen years earlier, he was out of touch with the realities of the industry as well.

I first noticed this in the late 1950s when NBC asked me to help devise the proper makeup for one of television's first full-time, full-color dramatic series, *Bonanza*. No one knew at that point whether the still-unperfected color TV cameras would pick up red lipstick as orange or purple. I did the experimental work at Paramount, where *Bonanza* was to be filmed, and immediately ran into trouble with Wally. He announced in unyielding terms "that no goddam television upstarts, not even my own brother, are going to use *my* makeup building." He made us work in a shack on the *Bonanza* set in a far-off corner of the Paramount lot.

I finished my work, designing a correct makeup color chart for NBC, and after a shaky start, *Bonanza* became a smash hit series which remained on the air for fourteen years. NBC paid an enormous rental for the use of Paramount's facilities, considerably more than the studio was making on many of its feature films, but Wally stubbornly refused to let his department have anything to do with *Bonanza* or with any other television series. To him, the movie industry was the movie industry, and if these outsiders needed makeup for their piddling little productions, let them bring in their own people and use portable trailers.

From 1960 to 1965, when I was doing so many films at Paramount, I begged Wally to open his eyes to the fact that more and more television crews were moving onto the lot and, in fact, TV shows were outnumbering the diminishing total of movies then being made at Paramount. He remained adamant, refusing to let a TV makeup man set foot inside his department. "Believe me," he said, "there's still plenty of film work, and the movies will come back at this studio, stronger than ever." He was right—but he wasn't around to see it.

Just about the time The House of Westmore closed its doors

for good in 1965, Wally was on a ladder, painting the exterior of his palatial house in Toluca Lake, near Bob Hope's estate. Professional house painters cost money, and besides, Wally always liked to do the job himself. A neighbor saw him suddenly stiffen, clasp his head, and fall backward off the ladder. Fortunately, the fall was broken by a clump of shrubbery, but Wally had suffered what was later diagnosed as a stroke. Without even mentioning the accident to his wife or his doctor, he went back to work the next day. It soon became apparent that his memory and thought processes were impaired, and the pro-TV people at the studio felt emboldened to challenge his monolithic authority for the first time. Wally continued the battle, but a definite slippage had occurred in his position and he never regained the lost ground.

The battle raged through 1966 and 1967, with Wally occasionally out of action with other, smaller strokes, for which he now *had* to be hospitalized. His arguments with the Paramount brass became less and less forceful as he'd stop and grope for a thought in the middle of a sentence.

The final blow fell, as it frequently does in movie studios, when Wally was on vacation with Edwina in Hawaii. It was the time of year when the TV producers renting facilities from Paramount were negotiating the "overhead" they were to pay the studio. Included, as usual, was the Paramount makeup department. The TV producers rebelled at the Wally Westmore item. "Why should we pay for his facilities," they said, "when he won't let us use them?" In the overhead, they were charged for all the studio's toilet paper and mimeograph machines (also without using them to the extent they were paying for them), but the toilet paper and mimeograph machines had not been so vocal about it.

Unsuspecting, Wally returned from his Hawaii vacation to be greeted with a notice that his services with Paramount were there and then terminated. For the first time in nearly fifty years, the mighty Wally Westmore was out of a job.

Wally's accumulated wealth being what it was, Gloria and I and the rest of the family didn't anticipate any charity benefits would have to be held for him, but we did worry about what his sudden downfall would do to his mind. Remembering Perc's sui-cidal reactions after his similar dethroning at Warner Brothers in 1950, we dreaded any phone call from Wally's wife, Edwina, al-ways fearing the worst.

For a while Wally was curiously sanguine; he played golf nearly every day with his banker and movie star pals. The blow fell from an entirely different and unexpected direction.

In 1966, Ern had suddenly materialized from nowhere, return-ing in triumph from his self-imposed fifteen-year exile in the East. I had heard from him sporadically during the exile—notably in the course of my ill-fated dispatching of him to Bud's bedside in Atlantic City—and I knew he had been making a fair-to-frugal living as a salesman for various cosmetic firms in New York. But now he was visiting in Hollywood in person, his wife, Betty, with him, looking prosperous in a new pinstripe suit. I hardly recognized him, however. I knew he had been on the wagon for more than ten years and that he had replaced his drinking with an eating compulsion, but I wasn't prepared for what I saw. Ern was enor-mously fat, considerably more than 300 pounds; his girth was double that of Perc. Together, the twins looked like triplets.

But inside the vast bulk was still Ern the Teacher. I remem-ber that one of my nephews was working on a western movie at the time and the director wanted to give the audience a gory glance of a man's fractured leg. Ern, hearing about the problem, said without hesitation, "Here's what you do, kid. You go to the butcher store, see, and you buy the biggest soupbone you can find. Then you strap the bone to the man's shin and you lay plastic skin over everything but the edge of the bone . . ." He went on, and in a matter of about two minutes had solved the entire problem for his wide-eyed young pupil.

But it wasn't teaching or movie work that brought Ern back to the West Coast. With the closing of The House of Westmore the year before, a California promoter had devoted himself to thinking up a new way to capitalize on the still-magical Westmore name in the beauty business, and he hit on a rather ingenious scheme. He got in touch with Ern in New York and offered to make him the nominal head of a company which would merchandise a full line of cosmetics through housewife salespersons, operating out of their homes. He would move Ern and Betty to the company's headquarters city, San Rafael, California, and pay Ern a starting salary of $3,000 a month. As the front man, Ern would travel around the country, extolling the products as if they had been developed under his direction at the famous House of Westmore.

Ern eagerly accepted the job. He bought the new pinstripe suit, made the move to San Rafael (which is near San Francisco), and immediately came to visit us in Hollywood like the successful prodigal returned.

Ern worked harder than he ever had worked before in his life—traveling the country, making his brilliant sales pitches—but the company barely got off the ground because it could not deliver what Ern promised. It is still the subject of complicated litigation. On February 1, 1968, Ern—still hopeful, his attaché case bulging with lists of prospective customers to interview—arrived in New York and stepped up to register at the front desk of the Park Sheraton Hotel. Just as he signed the name Westmore to the registration card, his huge body slumped against the desk and crashed to the floor. The hereditary Westmore bad heart had given out, and he was dead on arrival at the hospital. Of George's seven children, there were now four.

Ern's body was brought back to California to be buried in the same city as my father and mother, Mont, and Dorothy. During the funeral ceremony, I heard Wally mutter, "I wish they'd get this over with so I can get back to practicing my chip shots." He really didn't seem to understand what was happening.

19

I was very upset over Ern's death, though I had had very little contact with him since my teens and early twenties, and when he had his fatal heart attack at the age of sixty-three I was not yet forty-five. I guess I was mourning more for a lost tragic genius than I was for a brother. For weeks after his funeral, the movie studios buzzed with stories of how Ern's remarkable creativity had helped make classics out of films like *Lost Horizon* and *Cimarron*, most of the anecdotes coming from great makeup artists like Emile LaVigne and Alan (Whitey) Snyder, but some were told by younger actors who had never laid an eye on him. Among these was Robert Wagner, for whom I was doing the *It Takes a Thief* television series. That's how legends thrive in Hollywood. Another propagator of the legend was James Stewart, who had become a good friend of mine and had requested me for all his films ever since I did his makeup for *The Man Who Shot Liberty Valance* in 1962. What Jimmy didn't realize was that he was repeating all the Ern Westmore stories I had told *him*.

My brother Bud, like Wally, acted as if he couldn't care less about Ern's death. Edith was genuinely grieved. She had always liked Ern and suffered for him even when he was a wild, hard-drinking youth. Perc, of course, was shattered. Not only was he exactly the same age as Ern and with a similar heart ailment, which reminded him of his own vulnerability, but all the old guilts returned over how he had savaged Ern in the past. But the new

Perc had grown resilient and quickly bounced back, more determined than ever to be considerate of other people's sensitivities— a characteristic totally lacking in his old attitude toward his twin brother.

For example, he came to me a few weeks after Ern's funeral in 1968 and told me he'd been offered the job as chief makeup man on *The Bill Cosby Show*. Cosby was one of the biggest stars of television then, and the series—regarded as a surefire hit—would guarantee Perc a full season's work at $500 a week or more. I was amazed to hear what was troubling my once-arrogant brother. "Since there are so many black people on the show," he asked, "would they be offended if I wore my regular white suit, white shoes, and white tie?"

I burst out laughing. "Of course not," I said, "they'd be offended if you *didn't* go to work in your very own Perc Westmore trademark clothes." So Perc reported to the show in his standard whites and proceeded to do some extraordinary experimental work with new makeup techniques for dark skins—procedures largely ignored before but now in general use with the many black performers in TV and movies. To obtain the proper skin tone for each actor and actress, he blended twenty-five different shades of brown on a slab of white marble. Perc was never happier than he was on *The Bill Cosby Show*. The cast and crew venerated him, and because of his white suit some of them even called him "Doctor."

Ern's death, followed so quickly by Perc's coming to me for advice, brought me to the realization that a strange turnaround had occurred in the structure of the Westmore clan. It had begun when I took charge during Bud's heart attack in Atlantic City, but here I was, the baby brother, now acting more and more as mediator and counselor to the others. Perhaps it was because I had a stronger sense of family, owing to my lack of it as a child; perhaps it was because I was so much younger and had never been caught up in the feuds among contemporaries. But somehow, I found myself increasingly involved in Westmore family matters concerning men who were successful adults before I was born.

In 1969, for instance, I got a call from Wally to come see

him at his house. I walked into the magnificent home and found the former Paramount mogul sitting alone in a corner of the huge living room. He was recovering from another small stroke and looked drawn and gray. Gone was the I-don't-give-a-damn attitude of his golf-playing days in the period after he was deposed. He peered at me pleadingly and said, "Frank, I have all the money I'll ever need, but that's not important. I want to go back to work."

I was dumbfounded at first, then started to say something, but he raised his hand to stop me and continued.

"I know it's been a long time since I've gone down to a movie set with makeup case in hand, but I have to get back in the business or I'll go crazy. You do movies and TV shows all the time. Could I please work with you on one of them?"

I didn't know what to say. Here was the man to whom I had been apprenticed, who had doled out eyebrow pencils to me—and he was begging to go along on one of my jobs as an assistant. I thought quickly. I had finished *Two Mules for Sister Sara* with Shirley MacLaine and my next assignment was to be *The Cheyenne Social Club*, in Sante Fe, New Mexico, with Jimmy Stewart and Henry Fonda. I was going to do Stewart as usual, and Fonda had his own makeup man, so there was no place for Wally on that production. But the fleeting thought of Fonda's name gave me an inspiration. He was then in Indio, California, doing *There Was a Crooked Man* with Kirk Douglas. There were eighteen weeks to go on the picture before Fonda would start *The Cheyenne Social Club*—and the makeup artist on *There Was a Crooked Man* was Perc Westmore.

I said to Wally, "How would you like to work with Perc? He's doing a picture right now in the desert in Indio."

Wally looked startled. "Aw, Perc wouldn't hire me," he grumbled. "We've never worked together before, and you know we don't like one another."

I said, "Forget that crap. You be ready to go to work on Monday. Perc is coming home on the weekend and I'll talk to him." Wally looked grave and doubtful as I left.

That Saturday I confronted Perc with the proposition that

Wally could help out on *There Was a Crooked Man.* Perc said, "Are you crazy? You know that s.o.b. and I never got along."

Suddenly baby brother was playing big brother again. I said, "Perc, you're sixty-five years old and Wally is sixty-three. Ern died last year. How much time do you think you and Wally have left? We're all the same flesh and blood, and in spite of all our problems we all love each other. So why don't you give it a try—before it's too late."

"All right," said Perc. "Have the s.o.b. ready to go down to Indio with me on Sunday night."

Not only did Wally go to Indio but so did Wally's wife, Edwina, and Perc's wife, Ola. They lived together, worked together, and played together for more than four months. Edwina and Ola got to be real friends, and it was the start of a whole new relationship. The film got a lot of publicity because two of the greatest Westmores were working on it—together, really, for the first time in their long careers. They all came back glowing. They had had a ball. For me, on the sidelines, it was the most gratifying thing I had done in my entire life.

A few months later, on September 30, 1970, Ola awakened in the luxurious new apartment she and Perc had rented in a prestigious new building in North Hollywood. Perc's side of the bed was empty, and she took it for granted that he had left for the office, since his comeback had now reached the point where, in addition to his movie work, he had opened a headquarters for a new national chain of Perc Westmore wig boutiques and makeup schools.

Ola dressed and prepared to walk their two dogs. Pausing under the enormous oil portrait of Bette Davis as Mrs. Skeffington, given by Bette to Perc as a memento of the film *Mr. Skeffington*, she noticed with alarm that Perc's attaché case was standing on the floor beneath the painting. He had meticulously packed the case the night before, preparing for the day's work ahead. Also, the chain bolt still was latched on the inside of the front door.

Filled with dread, Ola rushed back through the apartment to their bedroom. The door to Perc's bathroom was closed. She forced the door open and screamed. There was Perc, dead of his final and most massive heart attack. Apparently it had come so fast that he'd scarcely felt it. There was a look of quiet peace on his face.

One of Perc's former enemies cruelly suggested that he had ended up where he belonged: in the toilet. I decked the man for saying that. To this day I believe that Perc, with all his faults, did die in peace, reconciled with Wally, with me, and most of all with himself. That's what I was thinking as we once again made the sad trek to Forest Lawn Cemetery.

Of the seven original Westmore children, now there were three. To be more accurate, there really were only two because Wally kept having strokes and his mind had deteriorated to the point where he was permanently confined to a nursing home. So basically it was just Bud and I. In my own career, I continued successfully on the free-lance path I had deliberately and wisely chosen for myself. I did the movie *Fool's Parade* in West Virginia, with Jimmy Stewart and Anne Baxter, and then a full season of *The Jimmy Stewart Show* in television, not only supervising the makeup but also dabbling a bit in casting, since I was the one who suggested to Jimmy that he choose Julie Adams to play his wife. After that came the two-hour *Kung Fu* movie for television, for which I won the 1971 Emmy—mostly for making twentieth-century actors look like believably authentic bald nineteenth-century Chinese Buddhist monks. In 1972 and 1973, I was the chief makeup artist on the *Kung Fu* TV series which followed, devising Oriental ritual scars and such for David Carradine. This got me another Emmy nomination.

For Bud, the going was no longer easy. Now it was *his* turn to feel the pinch of studio economies, just as Perc and Wally had at Warner Brothers and Paramount. Universal, bustling with TV production and still maintaining a modest list of actors and actresses under contract, was the last of the major studios to determine that it no longer needed a lavish old-time makeup department headed by a high-salaried, all-powerful autocrat, so Bud managed to hang on through the 1960s. He survived by ruthlessly suppressing all challengers to his supremacy, and also by emerging from time to time to do his brilliant lab work for films relying on ingenious disguises, such as *The List of Adrian Messenger* and *Man of a Thousand Faces*.

In 1970, however, Universal went the way of all other studios. There were too many free-lance makeup men like myself on call for contract work on specific shows and films, too many stars who now demanded their own favorite artists to do their makeup. Suddenly Bud was the target not only of a cutback in the Universal makeup department's budget but also of a revolt from below by those assistants he had ground down over the years. He was fired, just a few months short of his twenty-fourth year as head of the department.

Again, Westmore family history repeated itself. Bud went into a decline and became a total recluse all through 1971 and 1972. He told me, "I don't want to come out and hear people say, 'He got what he deserved.'" He still had some good friends at Universal, among them producer Ross Hunter, who called Bud soon after he left Universal to go to Columbia for a musical remake of *Lost Horizon*. Hunter wanted to hire Bud for the picture, but Bud, shaking, said, "I can't. I haven't got the guts. I don't know how to do daily makeup any more." After about two years, Bud's money ran out (he always had had to pay heavy alimony), and when Charlton Heston offered to get him the makeup job on a film called *Soylent Green*, he was so desperate that he accepted. He had to learn the rudiments of makeup all over again, but he got through the picture satisfactorily.

I managed to get him a few jobs after that, mostly on the strength of the Westmore name, but then all Hollywood production closed down during the writers' strike of 1973. Bud went into a panic when he realized there'd be no more work for a while. He offered to sell me a ten-foot skiff, all that was left from the magnificent yacht he once owned. I didn't need the skiff, but I bought it from him for three hundred dollars. He insisted on delivering the small boat himself. I wasn't home when he brought it over, and I felt a strange apprehension when I realized he must have had to wrestle it off the top of his car by himself.

The next day, I called to see if he was all right. His wife,

Jeanne, told me, "Bud is downtown." I phoned again the next day and the day after that, both times getting the same message: "Bud is downtown." Finally I lost my temper, demanding to know where he really was. Jeanne still refused to tell me.

The following Monday, Bud himself phoned at about four thirty in the afternoon. His voice was so weak that I could hardly recognize it. I said, "You sound terrible. I'm coming over to see you."

Bud said, "No, no, I'd rather talk to you at your house." I started to protest but he cut me off, saying "I'm on my way."

I was stunned when he arrived. He bore no resemblance at all to the handsome brother I had known. His face was ashen and covered with a stubble of beard. He was barefoot, and instead of his usually immaculate clothes he wore filthy rumpled jeans. He wouldn't come into the house, saying, "I don't want Gloria to see me like this," so we stayed in the yard and sat under an avocado tree. He apologized for Jeanne's refusal to tell me where he was. He said, "I've been in the hospital again, and I didn't want anybody to know. I got bad heart palpitations after I lifted that skiff I sold to you, and I was worried that if anybody knew I was sick again I wouldn't get any work when the writers' strike is over. I've been doing a lot of practicing with my makeup box, and I'm getting really good at it, like I used to be. I really need the bread, Frank."

I said, "You're my brother and I love you. When the strike ends next week, there'll be a lot of work and we'll help each other. I'll work with you and you'll work with me." He smiled for the first time. Then, remembering that I had a two-day makeup assignment on a Ford commercial that Wednesday and Thursday, I told him, "You take the job. They don't care who does the makeup, just so long as it's a Westmore." Bud mumbled his thanks and left.

Bud did the Ford commercial and performed creditably, finishing up on Thursday night. On Saturday he decided to use the money to buy paint and touch up the front of his house. He went inside late that afternoon and sat down on the couch to watch television. Jeanne served him a bowl of soup and went marketing. About an hour later, their teen-age son, Bobby, came in and settled on the couch to watch *The Mary Tyler Moore Show* with his father. Bobby suddenly became aware that Bud was breathing shallowly and had slumped into a strange position on the couch. The youngster rushed across the street to the home of a neighbor who was a doctor. By the time he and the doctor got back, Bud was dead. It was June 23, 1973, and he was only fifty-five years old.

Wally, the other ex-autocrat of the Westmore Dynasty, died just ten days later. He had been little more than a vegetable in the hospital bed in which he had lain, crippled by strokes, for more than two years. He was sixty-seven.

So of the original seven Westmores, now there was only one. Me.

20

Two deaths in ten days, four deaths in five years—a total wipeout—was almost too much for me to bear. How do you try to console five widows without accentuating your own grief and loneliness? I did it with the only antidote I knew, plunging myself into my work and getting caught up in the daily challenges of a movie set, such as when I had to convert a white man into a plausible-looking black man in the Dean Martin film *Mr. Ricco.* I found that there was a deluge of work for the last remaining Westmore brother; the name was still magic in the industry. I worked on TV movies of the week, the television-series version of *Planet of the Apes,* big important films like *The Towering Inferno* and *Farewell My Lovely.*

At first, in 1973 and 1974, I made the mistake of looking too much to the past. I regarded myself as the end of the fifty-eight-year Westmore Dynasty, which hadn't done too badly, as dynasties go. What I overlooked in my grief was the remarkable accomplishments of the *third* generation of Westmores and the fact that, rather than being the last of a line, I was really a part of its continuing growth. I was like a man staring fixedly at the dead lower branches of a tree, ignoring the new flowering branches above and forgetting there was a trunk connecting the two. I was the trunk, but it took me many months to realize it.

In my preoccupation with the past, I did everything I could to memorialize my dead brothers and even my dead father. I wanted the Hollywood Chamber of Commerce to award them a star in the sidewalk on Hollywood Boulevard, where other sidewalk-embedded stars immortalize the great actors, actresses, producers, and directors of the industry. I started a campaign to have a Makeup Artist Oscar added to the annual Academy Awards presentations. All my brothers deserved them, but only Ern was ever given one—in an extraordinary-accomplishment category presented just sporadically, such as the special Oscar won by John Chambers for *Planet of the Apes*. To this day, there is no regular makeup Oscar, despite the fact that our work can make a picture a success or a disaster. *Elizabeth and Essex*, for example, would have been laughable without Perc's authentic conversion of Bette Davis into the middle-aged queen.

I remember discussing this oversight by the Academy with William Holden and Fred Astaire when I worked with them during *The Towering Inferno*. Holden said, "What sense does it make to give Oscars to set designers and wardrobe designers, and none to the artists who design the face and body that helps us get inside the character we're portraying?" Astaire added, "Just take this picture, *Towering Inferno*, for example. You took my old familiar face and helped me get into the character of a believable con man. Should that type of creativity be so much less important to the Academy than the guy who designed the night club for my big scene? If you can't 'play the makeup,' you're no good, no matter what the director tells you."

The 1974 Academy Awards fed my preoccupation with the past. The afternoon of the Oscar ceremony, I got a phone call from Susan Hayward. She was going to present the Oscar for Best Actress that night, and with 53 million televiewers looking on for her first public appearance in some time, she wanted only a Westmore to make her up.

I said I'd be glad to do so, and I arrived at her house at about 2 P.M. I was distressed at what I saw. Susan had been undergoing radioactive cobalt treatments for a malignant brain tumor, and the damaging rays had destroyed her beautiful red hair, her eyebrows, even her eyelashes. The basic pert and beautiful face was still there, but I had to reconstruct her as she had been thirty

Westmore at work:
(above) I add finishing touches
to the "burn" makeup of
veteran stunt flyer
Frank Tallman;
(right) checking Clint Eastwood's
makeup during the filming of
Beguiled; *(opposite, above) working*
on Fred Astaire on
The Towering Inferno *set;*
(opposite, below) completing a
makeup on Robert Wagner on the
set of Switch.

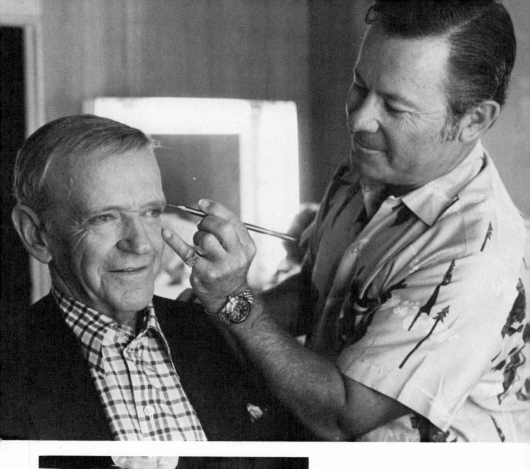

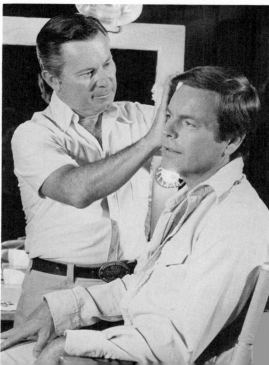

years before. I worked feverishly for four hours, until she had to leave for the Music Center presentation site at 6 P.M. I was never more proud of my craftsmanship than when I saw Susan walk out on that stage, leaning on Charlton Heston's arm, as she announced that the winner was Glenda Jackson. She looked not much different from the Susan Hayward of 1945, and that's how the world will remember her. She died on March 14, 1975.

The Susan Hayward episode was a turning point for me. I decided I had had enough of death and reflections on things past, and I began to look for hope and progress in the present and future. An entirely unrelated event helped extricate me from my melancholia. Gloria told me one day that she had just heard that my niece Lynn—Ern's daughter—was doing extremely well as an artist. We talked about Lynn and dug out some old newspaper clippings about her to refresh our memories about one of the greatest capers ever pulled off in Southern California.

On a Monday morning, November 21, 1966, the population of the Malibu area awoke to find that during the night someone had painted a huge pink nude, sixty feet high, across the surface of a sheer rock cliff above a tunnel on Malibu Canyon Road. The Pink Lady was deliciously voluptuous in her nakedness, and she gamboled free and wild across a heavily traveled commuter route. No one knew the artist, or how he had managed to finish his work in one night and in such a precarious, inaccessible location.

The Pink Lady became an attraction for thousands of tourists and art lovers before the forces of law and order moved in and obliterated her with gallons of gray paint. It took the services of five men, dangling on scaffolding a hundred feet above the road. It wasn't until two years later that the mysterious artist was identified—none other than my niece Lynn, who somehow had scrabbled about on the cliff like a mountain goat and done her enormous work of art in ten nighttime hours. As Gloria and I laughed over the feat some seven years later, I suddenly realized that this was the sort of wildly creative thing Ern would have done.

I then became acutely and healthily aware that the same sort of flow has taken place throughout my family and that, far from being on the edge of extinction, the Westmore Dynasty is alive and well and thriving. There's Mont, Jr., for example, now considered to be at least as good as his father, with the same independent, unflappable thoroughness as his dad. Paul Newman won't do a picture without him if he can get him, and Mont, Jr., has been involved in practically all Newman films of the last decade, up to and including the most recent, *The Drowning Pool* and *The Life of Buffalo Bill*. In the latter, my nephew's blending of the suave Newman into shaggy frontier showman is a genuine makeup masterpiece.

Then there's Marvin Westmore, my brother Mont's second son, cool, intelligent, with a great sense of the comic. He's one of television's most sought-after makeup artists, having done so many ingenious trick comic makeups for Red Skelton and Danny Kaye. Like Ern, he's a master at devising unusual and imaginative clown faces. In movies, just as Paul Newman dislikes doing a picture without Mont, Jr., Rex Harrison doesn't want to work in an American film without Marv Westmore.

Then there's Michael, the youngest of Mont's three sons. He's as handsome as Bud was, strikingly similar to him in appearance, though Michael has inherited his mother's beautiful blue eyes—and he has now surpassed Bud's skill in fabricating the rubber-plastic prosthetic types of makeups in the lab. Ranked second only to John Chambers in this specialized field, it was Michael who was called in by ABC to change actress Jane Alexander into Eleanor Roosevelt for the network's classic four-hour drama, *Franklin and Eleanor*. When the Canadian Broadcasting Company wanted the most horrifying of monster makeups for Bo Svenson in its six-hour version of *Frankenstein*, they sent for Michael, all the way from Toronto.

I am now in healthy competition with my nephews, just as I once was with my brothers. For example, I was doing a TV movie of the week, *Chill Factor*, with Robert Culp, and I had to devise a way of making Culp's face look as if it were coated with a sheet of ice after he had fallen into a tub of water in subzero temperatures. I could have used the old melted paraffin method, as I had with Spencer Tracy in *The Mountain*, but I racked my brain and came up with something new. I cut pieces of ordinary kitchen Saran Wrap and pasted them all over Culp's face with paraffin. The effect was startlingly effective. When Culp opened his mouth to speak, the Saran Wrap fragments cracked apart, just like a crumbling sheet of ice. One of the reasons I did this was to show my nephews there was creativity in the old boy yet.

But there's one area in which I never could hope to compete with Michael and Marvin. They have pioneered a completely new field, medical makeup, which is potentially more important than anything the earlier Westmores ever did. The idea was conceived by Michael, a graduate of the University of California at Santa Barbara with a degree in Art. He and Marvin now own a clinic in which they teach therapeutic makeup techniques to victims of facial burns, skin cancer, chemical abrasions, auto accidents and such. Their patients—both men and women—are referred to them by physicians, mostly plastic surgeons and psychiatrists. The plastic surgeons want interim and postoperative makeup to hide scars and to educate a woman, say, in how to change her makeup to abet a face-lift; the psychiatrists have found great therapeutic value in Michael and Marvin's ability to teach a disturbed patient how to conceal an ugly birthmark or other facial disfigurement. So eminent have my nephews become in this brand-new field that they lecture at universities and medical conventions and spend a good deal of their time writing scientific papers about this unique specialty.

Michael and Marvin operate out of a shop on Wilshire Boulevard in Beverly Hills, the area to which Ola had never been able to convince Perc to move The House of Westmore. In my nephews' establishment—where they also do ordinary hair and makeup treatments—there are haunting reminders of the old House of Westmore; for example, the decor is bright and original: burnt orange, light orange, yellow, with two brown cork walls. But there are two other factors which, to me, at least, prove that we Westmores always manage to come full circle in nearly everything we do. For one thing, the name of the company is The M. G. Westmore Brothers Studios. The "M" stands for Marvin and Michael. The "G" stands for George, my father and their grandfather, who founded the entire dynasty back in 1917. The second factor is most inspiring of all. The office manager of the new M. G. Westmore Brothers Studios is none other than Ola, older but still beautiful, sitting proudly at her desk and running things just as she once did for her Perc and the other original brothers at The House of Westmore.

In April 1975 we had one of our periodic family gatherings, this one at Michael's house. The two matriarchs, Ola and Edith, were there, and even though I was still only fifty-two, I had managed to settle nicely into my new role as elder statesman of the Westmore clan. We all listened proudly as my nephew Mont's daughter, Wendy, told us how her professor in her California History class at UCLA had spotted her as a Westmore and insisted that she do a paper on the family—to read aloud to the entire class.

Then there was a commotion from the rear of the house as eight-year-old Michael, Jr., walked in, almost unrecognizable because he had made himself up as what he called "the Swamp Monster from the Dawn of Time." Here was the *fourth* generation, already with his own makeup box and his own little lab in a corner of his bedroom. As I watched little Michael happily setting about making up his cousin Wendy as Redd Foxx, the thought finally and permanently engraved itself in my mind: There'll always be a Westmore.

INDEX

References to illustrations are in italics.

Academy Awards, 51, 71, 113, 186, 223; for makeup artists, 196, 239; in 1936, 25; in the 1940s, 144; in 1955, 185; in 1974, 239, 242
Adams, Julie, 195, 196, 234
Adler, Polly, quoted, 118
Adorn Cosmetics, 200
Ahn, Philip, 100–101
Aiguille du Midi, 187–88, 191–92
Alexander, Jane, 243
Alland, William, 194
All I Desire, 148
American Broadcasting Corporation (ABC), 15, 243
Anderson, Eddie "Rochester," 112
"Angel's Flight," 43
Arliss, George, 103
Astaire, 15, *241;* quoted, 239
Atlanta, Georgia, 130
Atlantic City, New Jersey, 204–6, 228, 231

Bacall, Lauren, 22
Bad Day at Black Rock, 185
Bailey, Jack, 181
Bara, Theda, 47
Barnett, Vince, 105
Barrymore, John, 15, 20, 65–67, 71, 108, 126, 145; *Spawn of the North* makeup, 95–96
Bau, Gordon, 201
Baxter, Anne, 172, 234
Beery, Wallace, 34, 97
Beguiled, 240

Beni Youssef, Egypt, 153
Bennett, Constance, 110
Bennett, Joan, 110
Benny, Jack, 112
Bergeson, Marion (Mrs. Mont Westmore, Jr.), 197–98
Bergman, Ingrid, 127, 128
Berkeley, Busby, 77, 133
Berle, Milton, 110, 194, 225
Berlin, Germany, 33, 69
Berman, Pandro S., 79, 80
Beverly Hills, California, 31, 32, 35, 47, 91, 116, 200, 244
Beyond the Blue Horizon, 11–13, 133
Big Suzy's French Whorehouse, 16, 47
Bill Cosby Show, The, 231
Bill of Divorcement, A, 68
Biltmore Hotel, Los Angeles, 25, 117
Blasco-Ibáñez, Vicente, 53
Blondell, Joan, 34, 137; and House of Westmore, 104, 105
Blood and Sand, 56, *57, 58*
Blue Angel, The, 69
Blue Veil, The, 179, 180
Blyth, Ann, 138–39; mermaid makeup, 145–47, 195
Boer War, 36–37
Bogart, Humphrey, 22–24, 34
Boles, John, 34
Bonanza, 226
Bond, Ward, 140
Bore, Helen, 113
Borzage, Frank, 27
Bosworth, Hobart, 44

Bougdadli, Abbas, 156, 157, 158; De-Mille granddaughter and, 164, 165, 168, 169
Bow, Clara, 15, 58, 67, 105
Box Office Poll, 93–94
Boy Scouts, 32; DeMille on, 170
Branch, Dr. William, quoted, 130
Brent, George, 82
Brentwood, California, 200
British Army, 36–37, 127
Brown, Joe E., 117
Browning, Ricou, 194–95, 196
Brunton Studio, 91
Buccaneer, The, 88, 200
Buehrlen, Justin, 171–72
Burke, Billie, 43, 45, 46
Burr, Raymond, 225
Busch Gardens, Pasadena, 20
Buster Keaton Story, The, 200

Caesar, Sid, 135
Cagney, James, 34, 113, 144, 186
Cain and Mabel, 76, 77
Cairo, Egypt, Ten Commandments filming and, 150, 152–53, 155, 156, 157, 162, 165, 167
California, 43, 117, 221; film industry's move to, 41–42, 44
California, University of, 244, 245
Camille (Valentino film), 53
Canada, 37
Canadian Broadcasting Company, 243
Canterbury, England, 37
Captain Blood, 82–83
Cardiff, Jack, 209, 211, 212, 214, 216
Carlson, Richard, quoted, 195–96
Carradine, David, 15, 101, 234
Carradine, John, 15
Carroll, Madeleine, 96
Carroll, Ola, see Westmore, Ola Carroll
Carson, Kit, 43
Carter, Kenny, 95, 103
Catalina Island, 55, 56, 61–63
Case, Tom, 194, 196
Chambers, John, 223, 239, 243
Chamonix, France, 184, 185, 186, 188, 192, 193
Champion, Gower, 135
Chaney, Lon, 79
Chaplin, Charles, 41, 44
Cheyenne Social Club, The, 232
Chiang Kai-shek, Mme, 110
Chicago, Illinois, 44, 88, 119
Chicago Cubs, 117
Chill Factor, 243
Christian, Gloria (Mrs. Frank West-

more), 220–21, 224, 227, 236
Churchill, Winston, 36, 37
Cimarron, 71, 230
Cincinnati, Ohio, 183
Citizen Kane, 77
Claire, Ethelyne (Mrs. Ern Westmore), 65, 70–71, 124
Cleveland, Ohio, 37, 40, 41, 42
Cobra, 58
Coburn, Charles, 118
Cohen, Emmanuel, 94
Cohen, Mickey, 122
Cohn, Harry, 112–13
Colbert, Claudette, 68–69, 70, 86, 135; and House of Westmore, 104, 105, 107; takes milk bath, 102–3
College Humor, 93
Collier, Willie, 44, 45
Columbia Broadcasting System, 223
Columbia Pictures, 60, 64, 139, 235
Columbo, Russ, 33
Conflict, 22
Conklin, Chester, 44
Constitution (vessel), 154
Cooper, Gary, 93, 96, 140
Cooper, Jackie, 32, 105
Cosby, Bill, 231
Costello, Dolores, 66
Crawford, Joan, 62, 144
Creature From the Black Lagoon, 194–96
Creature Walks Among Us, 196
Crosby, Bing, 15, 93–95, 102, 226
Crowther, Bosley, quoted, 113
Culver City, California, 30, 46
Cummings, Dorothy, 17
Cummings, Robert, 118, 212, 215
Curtis, Tony, 204

Davies, Marion, 74–77
Davis, Bette, 15, 16, 51, 78, 137, 179, 200, 233; Elizabeth I makeup, 84–86, 87, 239; mouth makeup, 67–68; wedding (1950), 177
Dawn, Jack, 97, 100
Day, Chico, 165, 168, 170
Deadly Mantis, 196
Deane, Shirley, 121
Decker, John, 66
De Havilland, Olivia, 82, 137
Del Rio, Dolores, 110
DeMille, Cecil B., 15, 52, 102, 160, 200; and granddaughter Citsy (Cecilia), 154, 155, 164, 165, 167, 168–69, 170; and Ten Commandments filming, 148–49, 150–52, 154–74, 175, 184; and

Frank Westmore's acting ambitions, 139, 140, 141; and Mont Westmore, 17–18, 58
DeMille, Cecilia (daughter), 154, 164, 167, 168
Dickson, Gloria (Mrs. Perc Westmore), 78, 117, 123
Dietrich, Maria, 105
Dietrich, Marlene, 69–70, 105, 148
Dix, Richard, 71
Dmytryk, Edward, 175, 186–87, 188, 190, 191
Dr. Jekyll and Mr. Hyde, 18–20, *21*
Dolgin, Sol, 182
Donovan, Maggie (Mrs. Perc Westmore), 132, 177–78, 179
Don the Beachcomber (restaurant), 23, 73
Dorskind, Al, 222
Douglas, Kirk, 232
Douglas Aircraft, 135
Dracula, 193
Drowning Pool, The, 243
Durkus, Andy, 153

Eagle, The, 58
Eagle-Lion Studios, 15, 144, 145, 148, 182
Eastwood, Clint, 217, 218, *240*
Egypt, filming in, 148–49, 150–63, 164–69, 184
Elephant Boy, 64, 71, 72, 74, 136
Elizabeth and Essex, 84–86, 87, 239
Emmy Awards, 15, 234
England, 80, 81, 82, 165, 191; Westmore family in, 36, 37, *38*, 78–79, 90, 108–9, 126–27
Ern Westmore Hollywood Glamour Show, 183
Erwin, Stuart, 34
Essanay studio, 41

Factor, Max, 105, 126
Fairbanks, Douglas, Sr., 15, 41, 44, 45, 46, 47, 48–49, 71
Famous Players, 41
Famous Players-Lasky, 53, 54
Farewell My Lovely, 238
Faye, Alice, 138
Fields, Lew, 45
Fields, W. C., 20, 22, 66, 71, 124, 126; banking habits, 108; claustrophobia, 101
First National Pictures, 15, 51, 52, 65, 67, 74, 76
Fisher, Doc, 115

Fitzgerald, Geraldine, 138
Florentine Gardens, Hollywood, 118
Flynn, Errol, 71, 81–84, 85, 126; and House of Westmore, 108
Fonda, Henry, 102, 232
Fontaine, Joan, 127, 128–29
Fool's Parade, 234
Forest Lawn Cemetery, Los Angeles, 27, 66–67, 130, 234
Four Horsemen of the Apocalypse, The, 53
Fowler, Gene, 66
France, filming in, 175, 186, 187–92
Francis, Kay, 34, 74, 135; and House of Westmore, 104, 105, *107*, 109
Frankenstein, 193, 243
Franklin and Eleanor, 243
Frawley, William, *92*
Freeman, Y. Frank, 102
Fulton, John, 166

Gable, Clark, 15, 61–63, 112, 137; and Davies, 76, 77; in *Gone With the Wind*, 127, 129–30
Gable, Ria Langham (Mrs. Clark Gable), 62, 129–30
Garbo, Greta, 75
Garland, Judy, 89
Gaynor, Janet, 137
General Died at Dawn, The, 96–97, 208
Germany, 69, 171
Ghost Breakers, The, 112
Gifford, Gail, 198–99
Gilbert, John, 75
Gilda, 113
Gish, Dorothy, 43, 46
Gish, Lillian, 41, 43, 46
Giza, Egypt, 153
Glass Menagerie, The, 176
Gleason, Jackie, 184
Goddard, Paulette, 140
Godfather, Part II, The, 172
Godkin, Paul, 212, 213–14
Godzilla, 194
Goethe, Johann Wolfgang von, quoted, 172
Goetz, William, 24–25, 145, 193
Going Hollywood, 93
Golden State Military Academy, Puente, 30
Goldwyn, Samuel, 46, 52, 220
Golitzen, Alexander, 196
Gone With the Wind, 114, 127, 128, 129
Goodbye Mr. Chips, 118
Good Earth, The, 97, 100

Grant, Cary, 116, 200
Great Man's Lady, The, 142–44, 190
Griffith, David W., 45
Griggs, Loyal, 153, 154, 157, 158

Hale, Alan, Jr., 89
Haley, Jack, 11, 133–34
Harding, Ann, 74
Harlow, Jean, 116
Harrison, Rex, 243
Harron, Betty (Mrs. Ern Westmore), 133
Hart, William S., 44
Hawthorne Grade School, Beverly Hills, 32
Hayward, Susan, 102, 103, 239, 242
Hayworth, Rita, 112–13
Head, Edith, 197
Hearst, William Randolph, 74, 75–76
Henie, Sonja, 61
Hepburn, Katharine, 16, 68, 86, 110; and Tracy, 185, 190, 192
Heston, Charlton, 235, 242; in *Ten Commandments*, 155–56, 158–59, 165–66, 167, 172, 173–74
Hill, Virginia, 116
Hitchcock, Alfred, 128
Holden, William, 15, 225; quoted, 239
Hollywood Canteen, 136–37
Hollywood Cemetery, 172–73
Hollywood Chamber of Commerce, 239
Hollywood High School, 89, 114, 133
Hollywood Hospital, 130
Hollywood Plaza Hotel, 124, 125
Hollywood Presbyterian Hospital, 180
Hollywood Receiving Hospital, 203
Holm, Eleanor, 33–34
Hope, Bob, 102, 112, 227
Hopper, De Wolf, 45
Hopper, Hedda, 90, 110, 112
Horn, Trader, 11, 13
Hot Spell, 200
Houseboat, 200
House of Rothschild, The, 103
House of Westmore, The, 15, 23, 103, 104–23, 124, 132, 139, 144, 177, 178; cosmetics plant, 109–10, 112 115, 122; decline of, 200, 224–25, 226–27, 228; lobby, *106;* opening, 104–5, *107;* Queens for a Day, 181; and M. G. Westmore Brothers Studio, 244–45; Ern Westmore shares sale, 126, 127; and World War II, 136
Houseparty, 181
Howard, Leslie, 127, 130
Hughes, Howard, quoted, 67

Hull, Shelley, 183, 184
Hunchback of Notre Dame, The, 79, 105
Hunter, Ross, 235
Hutton, Barbara, 110, 116
Hutton, Betty, 78, 139, 140
Hymer, Warren, 34

If I Had a Million, 22
Ince, Thomas, 45, 46
Indio, California, 232, 233
Ingram, Rex, 53
Intermezzo, 127, 128
International Association of Theatrical and Stage Employees (IATSE), 119
In the Sultan's Power, 44
Irma La Douce, 217
Isle of Wight, England, 36, 37, *38*
It, 58
It Happened One Night, 61
It Takes a Thief, 230

Jackson, Glenda, 242
Jacobsen, Max, 162–63, 167
Jaffe, Sam, 126
Jannings, Emil, 69
Japan, 139, 194, 207–17
Jessel, George, 25
Jimmy Stewart Show, The, 234
Johnny Belinda, 144
John's Restaurant, Los Angeles, 44, 45
Joker Is Wild, The, 200
Jolson, Al, 32–33
Judson, Edward, 113
Jungle Princess, 11

Kaplan, Harry, 216
Karloff, Boris, 140, 193
Kaye, Danny, 243
Keeler, Ruby, 32; face mold, *98*
Kellaway, Cecil, 140
Kent, Peggy (Mrs. Ern Westmore), 133
Kent, Sidney, 133
Kevan, Jack, 146, 147, 194
Keyes, Evelyn, 103
Keystone Kops, 43
King of Kings, The, 17, 58, 71
King's Row, 117
Kress, Sam, 44
Kruschen, Jack, 89
Kung Fu, 15, 101, 234
Kyoto, Japan, 214, 215, 216

Lady by Choice, 86
Lake Elsinore Naval and Military School, 35

Lamarr, Hedy, 70, 112, 148
Lamour, Dorothy, 11–13, *14*, 133
Land Unknown, 196
Lane, Rosemary (Mrs. Bud Westmore), 24, 133, 197
Langham, Ria (Mrs. Clark Gable), 62, 129–30
Lasky, Jesse, 18, 19, 20, 71, 91, 102
Las Vegas, Nevada, 24, 116
Laughton, Charles, 61, 62, 127; and House of Westmore, 105; Quasimodo makeup, 79–81
Laurie, Piper, 198–99
LaVigne, Emile, 230
LeConte Junior High School, Hollywood, 35
Leigh, Vivien, 127, 129, 130
Le Roy, Mervyn, 89
Let's Live a Little, 148
Lewis, Al, 223
Liberty magazine, 111
Life of Buffalo Bill, The, 243
Linkletter, Art, 181
List of Adrian Messenger, The, 235
Little Boy Lost, 94
Lloyd, Harold, 15, 90, *92*, 93
Lockridge, Louise, 122
Lombard, Carole, 33, 62, 86, 88, 110, 129; and House of Westmore, 105, 112
London, England, 126
London *Morning Post*, 37
Long Beach Naval Hospital, 135
Look magazine, 95–96
Loren, Sophia, 200
Los Angeles, California, 27; Westmore family's arrival (1917), 42–44
Los Angeles *Mirror-News*, 203
Lost Horizon, 126, 230, 235
Louise, Anita, 105
Love Story, 172
Lowe, Edmund, 34
Loy, Myrna, 105
Luciano, Lucky, 116
Lugosi, Bela, 137, 193
Luxor, Egypt, 168
Lynn, Diana, 148

MCA, Inc., 221–22
McCarrier, Edith, *see* Westmore, Edith McCarrier
McCoy, Frank, 154, 155, 156–57, 158, 165, 172
McDaniel, Hattie, 130
MacDonald, Jeanette, 201

McGeary, Bill, 188
MacLaine, Shirley, 15, 16, 200, 220; in Mexico, 217–19, 232; in Oriental makeup, 207–17
McQueen, Butterfly, 130
Maison Cesare, Los Angeles, 42, 43, 44, 45, 46, 52; Perc Westmore at, 47–48
Makeup Artists Union, 148
Malibu Beach, California, 33–34, 66, 74, 179; Pink Lady of, 242
Mamoulian, Rouben, 18–19
Man of a Thousand Faces, 235
Man Who Shot Liberty Valance, The, 230
March, Fredric, 93, 225; Hyde makeup for, 18–20, *21*
Margo, 126
Marshall, E. G., 184
Martin, Dean, 59, 238
Matchmaker, The, 200
Mathis, June, 53, 55
Mature, Victor, 135, 136, 165
Matz, Bob, 225
Mayer, Louis B., 15, 16, 24, 44, 129; and *Good Earth* casting, 100; and Hearst, 75–76
Maywood, California, 26
Mena House Hotel, Cairo, 153, 162
Menjou, Adolphe, 48–49, 51, 112
Merkel, Una, *107*
Methot, Mayo, 22
Metro Company, 41, 53–54
Metro-Goldwyn-Mayer, 52, 59, 61, 62, 64, 97, 127; Gable loan for *Gone With the Wind;* Hearst and, 74–76; Little Red School House, 89; Spencer Tracy at, 185–86
Mexicali Rose, 60
Mexico, 34, 61, 150, 217–19
Mildred Pierce, 144, 146
Milestone, Lewis, 100
Milland, Ray, 15, 93, 102, 225
Miss America Pageant, 197, 198, 204–5, 206
Mr. Peabody and the Mermaid, 146–47
Mr. Ricco, 59, 238
Mr. Skeffington, 233
Mitchell, Margaret, 130
Mitchum, Robert, 15, 220
Mole People, 196
Monsieur Beaucaire (Valentino film), 58
Montand, Yves, *210*, 212
Mont Blanc, 187
Montrose, Colorado, 186
Moore, Colleen, 86

Motion Picture Academy, Cup (1931), 71; *see also* Academy Awards
Mountain, The, 175, 184, 185, 186–92, 243
Mount Sinai, 156
Muck (chimpanzee), 11–13, *14*, 133, 214
Muhl, Edward, 196
Mummy, The, 193
Muni, Paul, 25, 51, 61; *Good Earth* makeup, 97, 100
Munsters, The, 223
Mutiny on the Bounty, 61, 62, 105, 127
My Friend Irma, 148
My Geisha, 207–17, 220

Naldi, Nita, 47, 56, *57*
National Broadcasting Corporation, 226
Nazimova, Alla, 53
Nelson, Ozzie, 225
Newman, Paul, 243
Newport, Isle of Wight, 37
New York City, 24, 41–42, 116, 144, 183; Ern Westmore in, 200, 205, 228, 229
New York Times, The, 113, 144, 196
Novak, Kim, 88
Novis, Donald, 132
Novis, Julietta (Mrs. Perc Westmore), 132
Nye, Ben, 128

Olivier, Laurence, 110, 127, 222, 225
Olympic Games (1936), 33–34
Once Is Not Enough, 172
Oscar awards, *see* Academy Awards

Paardeberg, Battle of, 36
Pacific Military Academy, Culver City, 30–31
Painters Union, 119
Papas, Irene, 186
Paramount Pictures, 15, 52, 88, 200; merger, 53; *My Geisha* and, 208; Raye and, 24; *Ten Commandments* filming, 148–74, 184; Frank Westmore's first makeup job at, 11–13; Wally Westmore at, 18–20, 23, 68, 71, 73, 89–90, 91, 93–103, 114, 132, 133; 139, 140, 147, 148, 150, 175, 204, 221, 225–26, 227
Paramount Theatre, New York, 144
Paris, France, 94–95, 126, 184
Parker, Sachiko, 207–8
Parker, Steve, 207–8
Parrish, 69

Parsons, Louella, 78, 88, 90; and House of Westmore, 110, 112
Pathé Film Company, 17
Pelanconi House, Los Angeles, 43
Peters, Jean, 89
Pickford, Mary, 16–17, 41, 43, 44, 67
Pierce, Guy, 133
Pincus, Dr. Charles, 19–20
Planet of the Apes, The, 223, 238, 239
Polly of the Circus, 75, 76
Powell, Dick, 34
Powell, William, 146
President Harding (vessel), 126–27
Professor Beware, 90

Queen for a Day, 181

Rackin, Martin, 217
Raft, George, 94, 111
Rainer, Luise, 97
Rains, Claude, 118
Rambova, Natacha, 55
Ramses II, 152
Rancho Notorious, 70, 148
Rand, Sally, 118
Rathbone, Basil, 82
Rat Race, The, 204
Ray, Charles, 44
Ray, Harry, 93, 94, 133–35
Raye, Martha, 24–25, 133
Reagan, Ronald, 117–18
Rebecca, 127, 129
Rector, Johnnie Fay (Mrs. Frank Westmore), 184
Return of the Creature, 196
Reynolds, Debbie, 204
Rhythm Boys, 93
Rhythm on the Range, 24
RKO Studios, 15, 79, 179, 180; Ern Westmore at, 67–70, 71, 78
Roach, Hal, 90
Robards, Jason, 89
Robinson, Edward G., 34, 212, 215
Roemer, Gene, 34
Rogers, Ginger, 70, 148
Roland, Gilbert, 58
Rooney, Mickey, 89, 137, 186
Roosevelt, Eleanor, 243
Rose, Billy, 33
Russell, Rosalind, 110

Sabatini, Rafael, 82
Sabu, 64
Sainted Devil, A, 58
Salty (seal), 95–96
Samson and Delilah, 165

San Antonio, Texas, 26, 27, 37
San Rafael, California, 229
Santa Barbara, California, 244
Santa Fe, New Mexico, 232
Santa Monica, California, 30, 143
Santell, Alfred, 11, 12, 13, 134
Savage, Ada, *see* Westmore, Ada Savage
Scarface, 61
Sea Beast, The, 65
Secrets, 27
Selig, Colonel William N., 44–45
Selig Studio, 44–45, 47, 51
Selznick, David O., 15–16, 114, 127–30, 175
Selznick-International Studio, 114, 122, 127
Sennett, Mack, 43, 45, 93
Shearer, Norma, 76
Sheehan, Winfield, 185
Sheik, The, 53, 54
She Loves Me Not, 94
Shelton, Edwina (Mrs. Wally Westmore), 91, 93, 132, 227, 228, 233
Sheridan, Ann, 34, 78, 86, 112, 118, 135
Sherry, William Grant, 177
Shipway, Margaret, 190–92
Shore, Fran (Mrs. Frank Westmore), 148
Shores, Jeanne (Mrs. Bud Westmore), 197, 205
Siegel, Bugsy, 116
Siegel, Don, 217–19
Sign of the Cross, The, 102–3
Sister, The, 84
Skelton, Red, 243
Smilin' Through, 52
Smith, Alexis, 24
Smith, Sir C. Aubrey, 140
Snyder, Alan (Whitey), 230
Snyder, Venida (Mrs. Ern Westmore), 65, 70–71
Son of the Sheik, 58
Sound of Music, The, 186, 192
South Africa, George Westmore in, 36–37
Soylent Green, 235
Spawn of the North, 95–96
Stanislavsky, Constantin, 18
Stanwyck, Barbara, 60, 70, 148; in centenarian makeup, 142–44, 147, 190
Steinberg, Herb, 221–22, 223
Stevenson, Robert Louis, 18
Stewart, Anita, 41, 47
Stewart, James, 15, 102, 185, 230, 232; in Oriental makeup, 97, *99*, 100; in television show, 234

Storm Warning, 148
Story of Louis Pasteur, The, 25
Stranded, 109
Strauss, Theodore, quoted, 144
Strawberry Blonde, 112–13
Submarine D-1, 117
Svenson, Bo, 243
Swanson, Gloria, 59
Sweden, 128
Sweet Charity, 217
Sylvia (crocodile), 133–34

Tallman, Frank, *240*
Talmadge, Constance, 44, 52
Talmadge, Norma, 27, 44, 46, 52
Tamiroff, Akim, 96–97, 100, 208
Tarantula, 196
Tars and Spars (touring show), 135–36, 139
Taylor, Elizabeth, 15, 89, 93
Taylor, Laurette, 43
Taylor, Robert, 97
Television Academy Awards, 15, 234
Television Station KTLA, Hollywood, 65
Temple, Shirley, 16
Ten Commandments, The, 148–74, 175, 184
Thalberg, Irving, 15, 24; and Hearst, 75, 76
There Was a Crooked Man, 232–33
This Is the Army (touring show), 135
Thomas, Virginia (Mrs. Perc Westmore), 31, 32, 33, 35, 74, 78
Three Musketeers, The, 48–49
Time magazine, 34
Todd, Thelma, 74
To Have and Have Not, 22
Tokyo, Japan, 208, 209, 210, 212, 213, 214
Toluca Lake, California, 227
Tone, Franchot, 61, 62, 97
Too Much Harmony, 93
Toronto, Ontario, 37, 243
Towering Inferno, The, 238, 239
Tracy, Lee, 34
Tracy, Spencer, 15; at MGM, 185–86; and Frank Westmore, 175, 184, 186–92, 243
Trader Horn, 31
Tree, Sir Herbert Beerbohm, 45
Trevor, Claire, 184
Triangle Studio, 45–47, 51–52
Tribute to a Bad Man, 185–86
Turner, Lana, 89, 112
Tuttle, Bill, 62–63

20th Century-Fox, 15, 64, 70, 124, 126; Chambers at, 223; Nye of, 128; Pierce of, 133; Spencer Tracy and, 185; Perc Westmore's resignation from Warner Brothers and, 178
Two for the Seesaw, 217, 220
Two Mules for Sister Sara, 217–19, 232

Unconquered, 139–41, 150, 151
United Artists, 52, 64
United States Air Corps, 135
United States Coast Guard, 135, 139, 142
United States Navy, 135
United States Selective Service System, 136
Universal Pictures, 15, 24, 25, 144; tours, 221–22; Bud Westmore at, 145–47, 148, 180, 193–200, 204, 207, 222–24, 225, 234–35
USO, 136

Valentino, Rudolph, 15, 16, 53–58, 57
Vertigo, 88
Vietnam war, 224
Vitagraph studio, 41
Viva Villa!, 34
Von Sternberg, Josef, 69–70

Wagner, Robert, 184, 188, 189, 190, 230, 241
Warner, H. B., 17, 18
Warner, Harry, 34
Warner, Jack, 22–23, 67, 74, 77, 79, 116; and Flynn, 82, 83, 85; and Hayworth, 112–13; and Perc Westmore's resignation, 176, 177, 178
Warner Brothers, 15, 22, 31, 34, 91, 132, 144, 147, 197, 223; Bau at, 201, 224; Davis at, 78; Flynn and, 81–84, 85; Hearst and, 76; Leroy and, 89; merger, 51, 65, 67, 74; Reagan and, 117; Perc Westmore's contract with, 23, 73, 111–12, 176–79, 228; Perc Westmore's return to (1960s), 224
Way Back Home, 67
Weber, Joe, 45
Weiler, Abe, quoted, 196
Welles, Orson, 113
West, Mae, 59–60
Westmore, Ada (Mrs. George Westmore), 37, 40, 42, 43–44, 50, 90–91, 123; death, 26, 66
Westmore, Anita (Mrs. George Westmore), 27, 29, 30, 132
Westmore, Ann, 91

Westmore, Betty Harron (Mrs. Ern Westmore), 133, 183, 228, 229
Westmore, Bobby, 237
Westmore, Bridget, 133, 197
Westmore, Bud (Hamilton Adolph), 27, 30, 50, 91, 120, 140, 144, 175, 184; and Blyth mermaid makeup, 145–47, 195; Coast Guard service, 136; death, 237; heart attack (1960s), 204–6, 207, 228, 231; and House of Westmore, 114, 225; and Piper Laurie, 198–99; marriages, 24–25, 114, 133, 148, 197; and monster makeups, 193, 194–96; Universal dismissal of, 234–36; and Ern Westmore, 65, 73, 145, 199, 230; and Perc Westmore's dismissals, 199–200, 222–24; and Wyman *Blue Veil* makeup, 180
Westmore, Cora Williams (Mrs. Mont Westmore), 60–61
Westmore, Dorothy, 26, 27, 31–32, 37, 50, 229
Westmore, Edith McCarrier (Mrs. Mont Westmore), 36, 52, 54, 65, 71, 74, 221; divorce, 60, 61; and hairstyling, 58; on Bud Westmore, 193; and Ern Westmore's death, 230; caring for Frank Westmore, 27, 35, 73, 89, 91, 115, 245; and George Westmore's suicide threats, 30; and Michael Westmore's apprenticeship, 197, 198; widowhood, 131, 132
Westmore, Edwina Shelton (Mrs. Wally Westmore), 91, 93, 132, 227, 228, 233
Westmore, Ern (Ernest Henry), 30, 37, 50, 52, 78, 90, 91, 93, 107, 120, 135, 140, 147, 180, 242; Academy Award, 239; alcoholism, 20, 22, 65–67, 70–72, 73, 83, 95, 101, 105, 122, 124, 126, 127, 181; and Colbert, 68–69; death, 229, 230; and Dietrich, 69–70; and *Elephant Boy*, 64, 71, 72, 74, 136; and House of Westmore financing, 108, 109, 123; marriages, 65, 70–71, 124, 132–33, 148; military service, 136; and Sally Rand, 118; sales work, 200, 228–29; "seven basic faces" scheme, 110, 137–39, 182; suicide attempt (1937), 71, 124–25; television shows, 182–83, 184, 222; twin, 26–27 (*see also* Westmore, Perc); Universal Studio offer to, 144–45, 199; and Bud Westmore's heart attack (1960), 204, 205–6; wigmaking apprenticeship, 40–41, 42
Westmore, Ethelyne Claire (Mrs. Ern

Westmore), 65, 70–71, 124

Westmore, Frank, 28, 120, 160, 161, 210–11, 240–41; acting ambitions, 139–41; birth, 26; Coast Guard service, 135–36, 139; education, 27, 30–32, 33, 35; films for Paramount (1950s), 200; first makeup job, 11–13, 133, 214; on location in France, 185, 186–92, 193; on location in Mexico, 217–19; marriages, 148, 184, 220–21; and Oriental makeup for Shirley MacLaine, 207–17; and reconciliation of Perc and Wally, 232–33; television work, 15, 226, 234, 238; on Ten Commandments, 148–74, 175; and Bud Westmore's heart attack (1960), 204–6, 231; and Bud Westmore's unemployment (1970s), 235–36; and Ern Westmore's death, 230

Westmore, Fran Shore (Mrs. Frank Westmore), 148

Westmore, George, 15, 18, 26, 27, 29, 36–50, 39, 50, 54, 58, 90–91, 200; and grandsons' medical makeup studios, 244–45; and greasepaint, 142–43; and Pickford curls, 16–17; relations with twin sons, 40–41, 42, 65, 71–72, 123, 125–26; shop handbill, 38; suicide, 30, 31, 71–72, 73

Westmore, Gina, 35

Westmore, Gloria Christian (Mrs. Frank Westmore), 220–21, 224, 227, 236, 242

Westmore, Gloria Dickson (Mrs. Perc Westmore), 78, 117, 123

Westmore, James, 91

Westmore, Jeanne Shores (Mrs. Bud Westmore), 197, 205, 235–36

Westmore, Johnnie Fay Rector (Mrs. Frank Westmore), 184

Westmore, Julietta Novis (Mrs. Perc Westmore), 132

Westmore, Lynn, 71, 242

Westmore, Maggie Donovan (Mrs. Perc Westmore), 132, 177–78, 179

Westmore, Marion Bergeson (Mrs. Mont Westmore, Jr.), 197–98

Westmore, Marvin, 35, 131, 132, 197, 243; and medical makeup, 244–45

Westmore, Michael, 35, 131, 132, 197–98, 222, 223, 243; and medical makeup, 244–45

Westmore, Michael, Jr., 245

Westmore, Mont (Montague George), 26, 27, 50, 52–53, 65, 90, 120, 145, 243; birth, 37; death, 130–31, 132, 180, 229; and DeMille, 17–18; and House of Westmore, 103, 104, 105, 107, 108, 109, 113, 114, 122; work with Selznick, 127–30, 175; shipwreck (1935), 62–63; and Valentino, 53–58; and Mae West, 59–60; Frank Westmore's life with, 35, 36, 61, 72, 73, 80, 89, 91, 114, 115, 125, 127

Westmore, Mont, Jr., 120, 196, 245; makeup apprenticeship, 197; and Newman films, 243; Frank Westmore's life with, 27, 35, 61, 115, 131, 132

Westmore, Muriel, 65, 71

Westmore, Norma, 31, 32, 33, 34

Westmore, Ola Carroll (Mrs. Perc Westmore): and House of Westmore, 119, 121, 122–23, 132, 200, 201, 224–25, 244, 245; marriage, 179–80, 181, 182, 221; and Perc Westmore's resignation from Warner Brothers, 177–78; and Perc Westmore's suicide attempt (1958), 201–3; widowhood, 233–34

Westmore, Patricia, 27, 29, 30

Westmore, Peggy Kent (Mrs. Ern Westmore), 133

Westmore, Perc (Percival Harry), 37, 50, 90, 91, 98, 120, 135, 147; makeup techniques for blacks, 231; and Bogart, 22–24; breast makeup formula, 86, 88; and Davis's Elizabeth I makeup, 84–86, 239; death, 233–34; in family councils, 73, 93, 140–41; at First National, 52, 74, 76; and Flynn, 81–84; and Forest Lawn, 66–67; and Hearst, 75, 76–78; heart attack (1951), 179–81; and House of Westmore, 103, 105, 107, 108–9, 110, 111, 112–13, 117, 118–19, 122, 123, 126, 127, 132, 178–79, 180, 181, 200, 201, 224–25, 244, 245; and Laughton, 79–81; military service, 136; and Muni, 25, 51; and Reagan, 117–18; relationship with twin brother, 26–27, 52, 64, 65, 125–26, 144–45, 180, 182, 183, 196, 199, 204, 206, 230–31; "seven basic faces" scheme, 137–39; suicide attempt (1952), 181–82, 228; suicide attempt (1958), 201–3; Universal employment (1960s), 221–24; and Bud Westmore's heart attack (1960), 205–6; Frank Westmore's life with, 30, 31–35, 73, 74, 221; and Mont Westmore, Jr's, training, 197; Wally Westmore's reconciliation with, 232–33; wigmaking apprenticeship, 40–41, 42, 47–49

Westmore, Rosemary Lane (Mrs. Bud Westmore), 24, 133, 197
Westmore, Thomas, 109
Westmore, Venida Snyder (Mrs. Ern Westmore), 65, 70–71
Westmore, Virginia (Tommy) Thomas (Mrs. Perc Westmore), 31, 32, 33, 35, 74, 78
Westmore, Wally (Walter James), 27, 37, *50*, 52, 73, 114, *120*, 133, 135, 180, 193; administrative work, 68, 73, 132, 175, 184, 209; and DeMille, 139, 140, 148–49, 150, 151, 152, 169, 174; draft deferral, 136; and House of Westmore, 22, 103, 105, *107*, 108, 109, 122, 225; and Lasky, 18, 20, 71, 91, 102; and prosthetic makeup, 89–90; and Stanwyck centenarian makeup, 142–44, 147, 190; strokes, 227–28, 232, 234, 237; and Tamiroff, 96–97, 100, 208; and Bud Westmore's heart attack, 204–6; and Ern Westmore's death, 229, 230; and Ern Westmore's suicide attempts, 124–25; Perc West-more's reconciliation with, 232–33, 234
Westmore, Wendy, 245
Westmore Brothers (M. G.) Studios, 244–45
West Side Story, 186
What a Way to Go, 217
Wilcoxon, Henry, 162, 170
Williams, Cora (Mrs. Mont Westmore), 60–61
Winchell, Walter, quoted, 198
Windsor, Duchess of (Wallis Simpson), 110
Winged Victory (touring show), 135
Wise, Robert, 186
Wood, Sam, 118
World War I, 67
World War II, 126–27, 135–37, 139
Wyman, Jane, 144, 176–77, 180, 222; quoted, 179

Young, Loretta, 110, 137–38

Zanuck, Darryl, 67
Zukor, Adolph, 97, 150

256